Aubrey Mellor

Theatre Director, Dramaturge and Teacher with expertise in new work and classics — especially Chekhov, Shakespeare and Brecht. Formerly Dean of Performing Arts at Lasalle and Director of the National Institute of Dramatic Art (NIDA), associated with arts training colleges across Australasia, Mellor has directed a range of genres from opera, dance and film. He is well-known as an acting teacher to a generation of acclaimed Australian actors, and renowned for translations and productions of the classics and for development of new work.

Brought up in Variety and Circus, Mellor trained as a dancer, visual artist and musician and graduated from NIDA Production Course. In 1972 he was awarded a Churchill Fellowship, the first Australian to study Asian theatre, from Japan to India.

He was awarded the Order of Australia Medal in 1992 for services to the arts; Australian Writers' Guild's Dorothy Crawford Award for services to Playwriting; and the International Theatre Institute's Uchimura Prize for best production, Tokyo International Festival. He is a visiting professor to theatre schools in Japan, China, Mongolia, India, Indonesia and Vietnam.

Cheryl Robson

Australian-born, Cheryl worked at the BBC in London for several years then developed and produced new writing for theatre before founding Aurora Metro Books. She has edited several collections of world drama.

As a playwright, she won the Croydon Warehouse International Playwriting Competition, was longlisted for the Bruntwood Prize and has had several stage plays produced in London.

Her co-translation of *David's Story* by Stig Dalager was shortlisted for the Marsh Award for Children's Literature in Translation and her co-edited book *Silent Women: Pioneers of Cinema* (Supernova) was voted best book on Silent Film in 2017. As a documentary film director, her film *Rock 'n' Roll Island* won four awards at US film festivals, was nominated at Raindance, London and was broadcast on BBC4 in 2020, named a Sunday Times Critics Choice program.

In 2018, she curated Sight/Unseen, a conference on SE Asian Drama at Goldsmiths College, University of London and Tara Arts. In 2019, she produced a showcase of Indonesian Plays at Oval House Theatre, London and was a finalist in the ITV National Diversity Awards for Lifetime Achievement.

First published in the UK in 2022 by Aurora Metro Publications Ltd.
67 Grove Avenue, Twickenham, TW1 4HX

www.aurorametro.com   info@aurorametro.com

Facebook.com/AuroraMetroBooks T: @aurorametro Inst: @aurora_metro

Printed in the UK by 4edge Limited.

ISBN: (print) 978-1-912430-47-5

(ebook) 978-1-912430-48-2

NEW IRANIAN PLAYS

EDS. AUBREY MELLOR &
CHERYL ROBSON

AURORA METRO BOOKS

Left to right: Maxime Robin (Jimmy) and Sarah Marchand (Shiva) in *A Moment of Silence.* Photo: Bahareh Ahmadi

CONTENTS

INTRODUCTION

Nazanin Sahamizadeh

A Brief History of Theatre in Iran

The Islamic Republic of Iran, also known as Persia, is home to one of the world's oldest civilizations. After Saudi Arabia, it is geographically the second largest country in the Middle East, and one of the first inhabited locations of mankind.

Iran has been always home to diverse ethnicities, languages, and religions and today the official language in Iran is Farsi and the official religion is Shia Islam. It has a population of 80 million and Tehran, with a population of 20 million, is its capital and the main centre of theatre in Iran.

Iran has always been a land of poetry, literature and myth, and its great classical poets such as Hafiz, Saadi, Khayyam, Rumi, Nizami and Ferdowsi, the last often being compared to Shakespeare, have told stories and myths of ancient times. Literature, religious beliefs and traditions have always been an integral part of Iranians' lives. Many think of theatre as a modern phenomenon with European roots but dramatic literature existed in Iran from about the 8th Century BCE, when the first valid kingdom was established in western Iran, and theatre's popularity was not only for the nobility but also amongst commoners.

Before the dominance of Islam, Zoroastrianism was the primary religion and Iran was well-known for theatre as its advent occurred at the same time as the forming of homeland and a sense of nationality.

As in many countries, Iranian theatre was formed initially out of evolutionary changes in religious ceremonies and prayers, the earliest being Zoroastrianism which originated as early as 4,000 years ago, the world's first monotheistic faith, and one of the oldest religions still in existence.

The first signs of literary conversations between two groups in the form of dialogues are from the Avesta songs, performed in ceremonies with a dramatic order. It is not clear how much these conversations could have been the basis of dramatic dialogues.

Religious and Early Drama

The clearest early documented evidence relates to the performance of *The Mourning of Siavash*, a mythical and religious theatre rooted in traditional tales. This story is featured in Ferdowsi's *Book of Kings [Shah-Nameh]* and it is recorded that *The Mourning of Siavash* was performed by minstrels and others in 332 BCE, though the story itself is believed to predate that by three thousand years.

Alexander of Macedonia, during his invasion of Iran in 323 BCE, brought Greek actors to perform in his victory ceremonies. It is said that the cities of Kerman and Hamedan had amphitheatres at that time. Also, during the Seleucid Empire era, when the region had rulers of Greek origins, at least one amphitheatre was constructed between 306–280 BCE.

In the era of the Parthian Empire (247 BCE–224 CE), Greek dramas were performed during ceremonies in the courts of the kings. Stories and tragedies in the Greek language were also written by one of the Parthian kings.

Late in the Sasanian era (224–651 BCE), when Islam entered Iran, storytelling from Ferdowsi's *Book of Kings*, especially the stories of Rostam and Esfandiar, became popular. From that time on, religious content and champions' tales from the *Book of Kings* were the main narratives. The first documentation from Islamic storytelling belongs to the third century. Until then, only men performed in plays and storytelling for the kings.

Based on historical reports, the first Iranian female performer was a musician and storyteller living in the Sasanian Empire era and after Islam, the most important woman performer-storyteller was the wife of Ferdowsi himself.

In the Safavid dynasty (1501–1736), small theatre events were commonly performed in city plazas during people's evening gatherings: these included clown plays and humorous dances and songs of itinerant musicians, called Tamasha [The Spectacle]. This was a beginning for the upcoming more important and humorous plays called *Kachalak Bazi* and *Takht-e-Howzi* or *Siah Bazi*.

In *Kachalak Bazi*, the protagonist of the story was depicted as bald and poor, and the superficial corruptions of commoners were satirized. *Siah Bazi*, which is one of the most important traditional Iranian plays, was commonly combined with dance, songs and music. Its main character is a slave whose face is blackened with soot and he is ridiculed for his appearance and verbosity; though, as a representative of the people, he, in turn, criticized common livelihood issues and mocked the behaviour of the government. As *Siah Bazi* was performed over courtyard ponds, it was also called pool-bed or pond theatre. The performing space was created by placing large boards on the pond in the courtyard, and the actors performed their comedies on those boards. These plays were usually performed at weddings and feasts.

Taghlid [Imitation] and Mazhakeh [Buffoonery] were also humorous theatre forms with dance, singing and clowning. Taghlid consisted of longer stories and their satire came from imitating the accents and characteristics of different cities. Further, Taghlid usually harshly criticized the aristocratic families and tyrant kings.

Mazhakeh consisted of short and humorous stories which were performed as improvisations in public places, at ceremonies and in teahouses to avoid censorship and confrontation with the ruling regime. Since the 4th Century, in the literary texts, puppetry is also mentioned. Its forms included glove puppets, dolls on strings and shadow theatre. After the advent of Islam, ceremonies of *The Mourning for Siavash* were eliminated, since there were similarities between them and the mourning ceremonies for Imam Hossein (the 3rd Shia Imam and grandson of the prophet Muhammad) and performances of Shabih Khani or Ta'zieh [Islamic

Passion Readings] became common. Originally, these were based on the stories of the lives and sufferings of the family of the Prophet Muhammad and especially the stories of the tragic killing of Imam Hossein and his family in the battle of Karbala in the Muharram (the first month of the Islamic calendar) of 680 CE, which gave his followers a distinct religious identity and led to the development of the Shi-ite sect of Islam.

In Ta'zieh, the historic events are reenacted and poetic elegies for the dead are narrated by the characters in the event and include the concept of the act of mourning. Ta'zieh was performed in locations called Takieh or Hosseinieh. For religious reasons, women were not allowed to perform in or even watch Ta'zieh; and the female roles were played by boy actors with treble voices.

There were, however, a very few Ta'zieh ceremonies played by women inside the houses of nobility and the wealthy for an all-women audience; female actors played even the male roles in such performances. At that time, female dancers and actors could also be seen among Tamasha and Mazhakeh groups, although these women were largely regarded with derision and their acting considered as shameful and humiliating. But the inclusion of women in performances changed during various eras. In late Safavid era (1501–1736) when Shia Islam had become the official religion of the country, women were forbidden to act in any groups and, similar to Ta'zieh, men started playing female roles once more.

Western Influences

The first time Iranians encountered Western theatre is mentioned in the travelogues of Naser al-Din Shah Qajar. After travelling to Europe in 1869 and watching a play in an amphitheatre, this Shah ordered construction of the largest amphitheatre in Iran's history, with a capacity of 20,000 people. It was called Takieh Dowlat and was built in Tehran. Translations of Western plays started at that time, and gradually some plays by Moliere, were performed. The first document in Iran's history about international theatre is an article published in *Akhtar Newspaper* in 1887, called "On the playing of the spectacle in the amphitheatre".

INTRODUCTION

Opposing the authoritarian atmosphere in 1905, a movement called Mashrooteh [Persian Constitutional Revolution] was formed to seek justice and to institutionalize political freedom, though it lasted only a few years. During Mashrooteh, following a liberal expansion of political and cultural space, Iranian intellectuals travelled to the West to study, and increasingly brought back into Iran the theatre as it is known today. Constitutionalists and intellectuals started to write plays and established theatrical groups; theatre became a tool to fight for justice and writing dialogues became an instrument to reach democracy. The 1908 publication of the *Theatre Newspaper* by Mirza Reza Khan Tabatabaei Naeeni, a member of parliament, was one of the most important events during Mashrooteh.

Later, in 1909, Mirza Fathali Khan Akhoondzadeh, known as the first Iranian playwright in the Western sense and the founder of literary criticism, published his plays in the Turkish language. After that, Mirza Agha Khan Tabrizi was the first playwright in the Farsi language. He considered himself a student of Akhoondzadeh and his frank tone criticized the tyrannical regime of his time. When the Mashrooteh movement came to an end, the first Iranian theatre group, National Tiatr, was formed, and a performance hall at the Grand Hotel was established for concerts, plays and movies. The Grand Hotel was later renamed as Theatre Nasr and became a place for western-style performances.

The first professional theatre group was established in 1916 by Ali Nasr, a playwright, director and translator, who had studied theatre in Europe. He called his group Iran Comedy as it was inspired by La Comédie Française [French Comedy]. Ali Nasr is known as 'the father of theatre in Iran'. He managed Iran Comedy with a special discipline and held performances twice a month in the Grand Hotel. One of the other important developments in the Mashrooteh period was the inclusion of women in theatre – until then, theatre in Iran was an art only for men.

Molook Hosseini is known as the first Muslim woman who dared to set foot on the stage with an Iran Comedy group. Along with her, the names of two Armenian actors are to be mentioned: Madam Vartoterian and Pari Aghabayoff. They are considered as the first female directors in Iran. Also Sedigheh Dowlat Abadi, Mercedeh Karoubian and Esmat Safavi are included among the first female Iranian playwrights.

But it has never been easy for women, especially Muslim women, to enter the theatre in Iran and many women have lost everything on this path. It is said that Sedigheh Dowlat Abadi was stoned inside her home because of publishing *The Language of Women* newspaper. In 1923, Sari Amani, probably the first Iranian Muslim female director, established the Women's Cultural and Artistic Assembly in the city of Rasht and, with female actors for female audiences, started performances mostly addressing the limitations on women and the violation of their rights. Afterwards, in 1926, a women's group called the Women's Awakening Society was established but, eventually, their slaughtered bodies were found in water canals – a violent male response to the presence of women in the field of theatre. Women active in theatre continued to face such sabotage and hostility until about 1935, following the order of Kashf-e Hijab (banning all Islamic veils) after which, gradually, acting by women was officially recognized. In 1939, the first dramatic school in Iran was established by Ali Nasr called the Acting Art School in which 12 women had the chance to study dramatic arts along with 40 men.

One of the important and influential people in the theatre of Iran was Abdulhossein Nooshin who, as a student, was funded by the government to study literature and dramatic arts in France. After returning to Iran in 1932, Nooshin, working as actor, playwright and director, established Farhang Theatre (The Culture Theatre), using Western criteria. He also started teaching the Stanislavski Method and trained many students who became influential. Nooshin launched the most important theatrical movement in Iran and the impressive legacy of his work can still be observed. With the assistance of his students, he established the Farhang Theatre Hall in Lalehzar street in Tehran. This theatre hall and cinema had a capacity of 500 seats and was inaugurated with a production of *Volpone* by Ben Jonson. Around 1941, Lalehzar Street became the centre of theatrical activities in Tehran and was a gathering place for intellectuals and artists and for performances of plays by Chekhov, Shakespeare, Gogol, Sartre, Ionesco, etc.–works with sharp political and social themes.

Between 1941 and 1953, due to more freedom in the political environment, a golden age of theatre grew, and several new plays were written. After the coup in August of 1953, which led to the overthrow of the democratically elected Prime Minister Mohammad Mosaddegh in favour of strengthening the monarchical rule of the Shah, the new government closed many opposing cultural centres and burned some down. Consequently, theatre groups collapsed, and many artists including Nooshin were imprisoned.

Contemporary Theatre in Iran

A few years later, in 1958, Mahin and Mustafa Oskooei, who were once Nooshin's students (and had studied Stanislavski Method in Russia with Yuri Zavadsky, a student and colleague of Stanislavski), returned to Iran and established Anahita Art School and started to train theatre artists who later became famous. Mahin Oskooei has been one of the iconic female translators and directors in Iran. Another group of graduates from Acting Art School got together and established the National Art Group led by Abbas Javanmard and Ahmad Baratloo, and started to write new Iranian plays. There were outstanding members in this group too, such as Ali Nasirian, Jafar Vali, and Bijan Mofid.

In 1959, Ali Nasirian, one of the most outstanding actors in Iran, wrote the play *Frenzied Nightingale* and it was staged under the direction of Abbas Javanmard. This play was invited to France by the Theatre of Nations, becoming the first Iranian play to be performed in an international festival. Holding dramatic art courses in the literature department of Tehran University and, later on, establishing the Dramatic Art University, led to the flourishing of theatre and playwriting during the 60s and 70s, and important playwrights such as Bahram Beyzai, Akbar Radi, Gholam Hossein Saedi, Ali Nasirian and Mohsen Yelfani created several plays with modern playwriting techniques.

Bahram Beyzai is a significant Iranian playwright, director and researcher. One of the distinguished authors in modern Farsi literature, Beyzai is a unique theatre master of Iranian theatre and his productions have always been praised. *Death of Yazdgerd* is one of his most famous plays.

Another eminent author and famous playwright is Gholam Hossein Saedi. He wrote several well-known social and political plays, his most important being *Choob Bedastan e Varazil*. Akbar Radi is one of the most important playwrights of the Farsi language with most of his work in a realist and critical style. This distinguished and influential playwright was also a pioneer of contemplative theatre with plays such as *Death in the Fall* and *Behind the Glass*.

During the same period, a number of important directors returned to Iran after studying abroad, including Hamid Samandarian, Davoud Rashidi, Ali Rafiei and the only woman, Pari Saberi. Hamid Samandarian, an Iranian director and translator, who studied theatre in Germany, had a serious influence on making theatre more academic and professional through contributions to the establishment of theatre departments at universities in Iran. Having established many acting and directing classes and workshops, Samandarian trained many Iranian actors and directors. During his lifetime, he translated and then staged many famous plays written by foreign playwrights, such as Friedrich Dürrenmatt, Bertolt Brecht, Anton Chekhov, Eugène Ionesco, Arthur Miller, Max Frisch, Tennessee Williams, Jean-Paul Sartre, and Henrik Ibsen.

Ali Rafiei, director and set designer, is the theatre master who returned to Iran with a doctorate in theatre from Sorbonne University and has since staged several magnificent performances of classic plays such as *Blood Wedding* by Federico García Lorca, *Antigone* by Sophocles, and *It Never Snows in Egypt* by Mohamad Charmshir.

In 1965, Sangalaj Theatre Hall was inaugurated to support Iranian plays and, in addition to those playwrights mentioned, works by Abbas Javanmard, Mahmoud Ostad Mohammad, Bijan Mofid and Farideh Farjam were performed at Sangalaj from 1966–1977. Farideh Farjam, author of *Tajmah*, is known as the first Iranian female playwright to use western methods. Her first play collection was published in 1964. There were also other female playwrights active during those years – some of the first were Khojasteh Kia, Mahin Tajadod and the Boroomand sisters.

During the regime of Mohammad Reza Pahlavi, the last Shah, his wife, Farah Diba, paid specific attention to the arts and in 1967 inaugurated Roudaki Hall in Tehran, now named Vahdat Hall and used for ballet, opera and concerts. Vahdat Hall remains one of Iran's most important performance spaces for theatre and concerts.

Shiraz Art Festival was another important artistic event during the regime of the last Shah. From 1967, this festival ran for 11 years with the participation of important international artists, aiming to promote Iranian arts internationally as well as acquainting Iranian people with the world's artists and to be a communication link between the East and the West. Theatre works from all over the world were performed, and important theatre artists such as Peter Brook attended the festival in Shiraz (near the ancient ruins of Persepolis) and many of its young participants later became important theatre artists. Abbas Nalbandian was one of them, becoming quickly known with his brilliant play: *There is no difference between deep and large and new research in the fossils of the twenty-fifth period of geology or the fourteenth or the twentieth or...* and grew into a progressive author and translator.

In 1969, Kargah-e Namayesh [Theatre Workshop] was established by a number of artists such as Arbi Ovanesian, Davoud Rashidi and the female writer Khojasteh Kia, under the management of Abbas Nalbandian, in order to further develop Western-style theatre and to gain new experiences through constant practise. Theatre Workshop played an important role in the development of Iranian theatre, and its artists influenced theatre towards a Western style, producing prominent works and lifting the quality of the artistic community. In 1972, the most modern and most important theatre complex of Tehran was constructed. Named City Theatre, it staged productions by the Theatre Workshop. Molavi Hall, established by the female artist Pari Saberi in Tehran University, was also inaugurated the same year and today is the main venue for university theatre performances.

The Post-revolutionary Era

With the end of the Islamic revolution in 1979, in the midst of political changes across the country, the dramatic arts faced major changes as well. After the revolution, the Theatre Workshop was dissolved and a number of its members, including the manager, Abbas Nalbandian, were summoned by the court. Nalbandian was imprisoned for four months for his views. In that inflamed and turbulent atmosphere, theatre-makers turned to plays with political and social subjects. Several revolutionary plays by Jean-Paul Sartre, Nazim Hikmet, Eugène Ionesco and mostly Bertolt Brecht were performed, all with Islamic, communist, liberal, anti-imperialist, and anti-capitalist themes. Street plays in the south of Tehran with sharp political overtones were initially performed in parks, but these were gradually stopped. Saeed Soltanpour, one of the members of Anahita Art School, playwright and director of the famous documentary play, *Mr. Abbas Worker of Iran National*, performed this play as street theatre in a factory for workers. He was arrested and executed for his political activities.

In one year, from February 1979 to February 1980, 73 plays were staged in Tehran, of which 51 plays were Iranian. However, this productivity didn't last long. With the establishment of the new Islamic regime everything was stopped and faced stagnation, which increased in 1980 with the start of the war between Iran and Iraq. This decline continued until 1982, when the Center of Dramatic Arts started making policies in order to increase theatre productions. But by then, the government had direct supervision over all theatre affairs, applying its own agenda.

At the same time, revolutionary institutions were formed, the Institution of Islamic Thoughts and Arts being the most important one, with the aim of making all theatre and art Islamic. This move towards the values of the Islamic Revolution created a lot of limitations for theatre artists. Gradually, in the City Theatre, conflicts occurred between emerging young Muslims and non-Muslim theatre artists to the extent that a statement was published in a newspaper under the name *'Islamic Advocacy Center'*, threatening non-Muslim artists. A set of conditions, including the war, the Islamic revolution, the following compulsory wearing of Islamic hijab for women, and interdictions opposed by Islamic Organizations, made many artists flee the country or stop working. Abbas Nalbandian was one of several who committed suicide due to restrictions forcing them out of the theatre.

Following the formation of the Center of Dramatic Arts in 1982, in line with the revival of theatre, International Theatre Fajr Festival was established and has remained the most important theatre event in Iran up to now. During the first five years of this festival, which was simultaneous with the Iran-Iraq war, the productions were mostly limited to plays with revolution and war themes and those reflecting the social issues of the day. In 1985, Iran International University Theatre Festival was launched. This annual festival showcases courage and innovation based on education and research and contains a selected number of students' works. In 1989, when the war stopped, theatre prospered again.

In addition to the performances of 68 plays in Tehran, the first Traditional and Ritual Theatre Festival was held, together with the first Puppet Theatre Festival. These featured works from across Iran with the attendance of theatre-makers from a number of countries. At the same time, a number of children and adolescents in the city of Hamedan, performed plays on the subject of war and the bombing of residential areas. These attracted public interest and, in 1991, became the basis for the establishment of the International Theatre Festival of Children and young Adults. Another important event in 1991 was a performance of Ta'zieh [Passion Reading] in the Avignon Festival.

Despite holding different festivals, professional theatre has been very restricted and faced censorship. Yet, new artists with innovative visions, independent from the ruling policies, stepped into the arena and remain some of the most important theatre artists in Iran to date. These include Mohammad Charmshir, who has worked in different and innovative forms throughout his years as a playwright. Also Mohammad Rahmanian, playwright and director, whose work approaches current issues with a focus on history – and exquisite examples of traditional performances like *Takht-e Howzi* and

Ta'zieh can be observed in his plays. Atila Pesyani is another actor and director who started his work in the 80s and is still active.

While all artists were faced with the restrictions and policies of the new regime, women had a diminished presence after the revolution and the war. This continued until 1997 when Khatami became president and, under his reformist government, art and culture evolved. One of the important actions of Khatami's administration was the establishment of the Theatre Forum, which led to the formation of associations for actors, directors, writers, critics and other aspects of the dramatic arts.

The theatre policies of Khatami's government were based on bringing back senior theatre artists to the stage and providing opportunities for youth. In line with that, distinguished young artists entered the field and great Iranian theatre masters stepped onto the stage again after many years of silence. Bahram Beyzai and Hamid Samandarian, two distinctive Iranian directors, had shining performances in the City Theatre after many years of being away from the stage. City Theatre halls were filled with performances of important artists such as Ali Rafiei, Davoud Mirbagheri, Davoud Rashidi, Roknodin Khosravi.

After the expansion of the cultural space, female directors started working again as well, and Pari Saberi and Manijeh Mohamedi produced plays for the stage. Also, because of the annual graduation of many students from theatre colleges, among which a considerable number were women, there was a stronger presence of successful women in different theatre fields. Farindokht Zahedi is one of the distinctive women in academia in Iran. She is an author, researcher and a university professor who plays an important role through her involvement in several festivals and her publications. Many young female directors started working in the 1990s, including Golab Adineh, Rima Raminfar, Parvaneh Mojdeh, Shohre Lorestani and female playwrights emerged including Hengameh Mofid, Azam Boroujerdi, Eliza Varami, Chista Yasrebi and Shabnam Tolooei.

From 1998, Farjr Theatre Festival was held internationally and Roberto Ciulli, director of Theatre an der Ruhr in Germany, the first foreign director who came to Iran after the revolution, has performed plays for several years and produced the first joint Iranian-foreign play which was staged in different countries. He also invited many Iranian theatre groups to the Silk Road Festival in Germany. Other international artists, such as Jean-Claude Carrière and Alain Crombecque from France, also had performances in Iran and these events created another golden time for Iranian theatre. Further important developments were the formation of regional theatre associations which activated theatre in more Iranian cities, and the establishment of Ferdowsi Theatre Hall in front of Roudaki Hall to host puppet operas. During that time many young theatre groups were formed, introducing many brilliant young artists to the theatre profession.

Hamed Mohammad Taher with his production of *The Blacks* by Jean Genet, created a new experience in modern Iranian theatre, basing the work on physicality and de-familiarizing old forms; this became a beginning for Avant-garde formal performances based on dance. There were also others who had experience in impressive performances, such as Asghar Farhadi, Farhad Mohandespour, Hamid Pourazari, Hassan Ma'jouni, Hamid Amjad, Mohammad Aghebati and Asghar Dashti.

Asghar Dashti remains well-known in Iranian theatre because of his experimental performances of a mixture of traditional Shabih Khani with modern plays. Hamid Pourazari is another experimental, innovative director. He focuses on site-specific theatre and usually holds performances in non-theatre spaces. Hassan Ma'jouni also remains influential. He established Leev Theatre Group, one of the most successful groups of that time, focusing on teaching and holding a monologue festival.

There were brilliant young theatre artists starting their work in playwriting as well as performance. Alireza Naderi was one of the first playwrights with a critical view of the war and faced censorship all the time, until 1997, when one of his best plays after the revolution, titled *The Wall*, was produced. Director and playwright, Mohammad Yaghoubi, another theatre icon, has an innovative view towards realism and Iranian playwriting. While frankly addressing important political and social issues, he brings middle class characters to life.

His play, *The Winter of 1987*, about the fear of death in war, is one of the most important plays since the revolution.

A significant and influential woman theatre artist after the revolution is Naghmeh Samini, who started her work in the 90s. She is a playwright, researcher and a university professor. She researches, compiles and publishes on the use of mythology in Iranian dramatic arts and her plays are distinguished by her experimental use of historical content, together with some magical realism. She first became known for her play, *Magic of the Burned Temple* and was soon after acclaimed Iran's most distinguished contemporary female playwright.

At this time, another important young artist emerged: the director and playwright Amir Reza Kouhestani, who is also well-known outside of Iran. With his play, *Dance on the Glasses,* he shows that new forms and patterns can be achieved by breaking the norms of playwriting and directing. Koohestani's theatrical work is often labelled as documentary theatre, includes film footage together with live performance. He has a unique performance language which is simple, yet deep and impressive. His plays have been praised by the critics and performed in several countries and at international festivals like Avignon.

As theatre about social issues soared in the late 90s and early 2000s, successful performance events were made by artists such as Nima Dehghani, Hamidreza Azarang, Hossein Kiani, Nader Borhani Marand, Hamidreza Naeimi and Kourosh Narimani.

The Decline of Theatre

The heyday of Iranian theatre ended with the end of the reformist government. In 2005, when Ahmadi Nejad became president, censorship intensified to the extent that we can say theatre became castrated during the eight years from 2005 – 2013, and social theatre fell from its pinnacle. In 2005, one of Bahram Beyzai's most popular plays titled, *The Passion of Makan and Rokhshid* about the sufferings of university lecturer Navid Makan and his wife, architect Rokhshid Farzin, was suddenly stopped by the authorities.

In 2007, a new section was added to Fajr Theatre Festival called New Experiences. This was for young people, with no critical points of view, so they performed plays based only on form, restricting artists with a critical look at political and social issues. In 2009, objections to the results of the presidential election were suppressed and that led to bitter political and social events. Theatre also faced harsh developments. Several artists were banned or willingly stopped working until the end of the Ahmadi Nejad administration. A number of artists emigrated from the country, and the number who continued working faced constant barriers.

That year, Mohammad Yaghoubi produced *Drought and Lies* which was acclaimed by the public but later performances were stopped due to censorship. Some other large-audience plays were also staged in those years such as those by Hamid Samandarian, Ali Rafiei, Davoud Rashidi and Bahram Beyzai. Beyzai staged his last production in Iran in 2007 and then, faced with obstacles to staging his next play, he emigrated. New theatre artists have more recently entered the field, such as Homayoun Ghanizadeh, Reza Servati, Arvand Dasht Arai. The 2009 inauguration of Iranshahr Theatre Hall which provided two equipped salons located behind the Iranian Artists House, and the opening of Hafez Theatre Hall in 2010, hosting modern performances, were important developments during those years.

In 2013, following the administration of another new government, the artistic environment improved a little and private theatre emerged. The idea of privatizing theatre and creating non-governmental theatre helped to facilitate and accelerate theatre productions with an increasing number of theatre halls. Yet, although this privatization only happened in the establishment of private theatre halls and in privately funded productions, control and censorship remained in the hands of the government. This process led to the current changes in Iranian theatre. Private investors, fearful of risking their capital due to censorship, started self-censoring and this led to the production of commercial theatre with the sole aim of entertainment. As a result, many lavish productions of musical theatre started being performed and, in order to attract more audiences, producers began to cast big stars from cinema and television in their shows. Following such performances, the characteristics of theatre audiences gradually changed and most audiences now seek only to be entertained. On the positive side, due to the establishment of many private halls, no one needed to wait long in line to be able to stage their plays and each evening many different plays are performed, giving audiences much choice. However, there are still a few great theatre artists who are suffering hardship and censorship as they continue to perform social and political plays.

The censorship which increased under the former government is now being applied to other non-theatre organizations outside the government too and, despite obtaining permits, a number of theatre artists are being summoned to the court by extra-judicial organizations after their performances. Some, like Mohammad Rezaei Rad, a brilliant director and playwright, started staging uncensored plays underground for the audience. More recently however, Rezaei Rad has performed successful plays on official stages.

During this time, documentary and biographical theatre were explored and successful examples are still being performed. Since media in Iran is also restricted, this type of theatre acts as an important medium to create awareness, and the public welcomes it. Women also produced important theatre events about women's issues. Some of the successful contemporary female playwrights and directors in documentary theatre are Mahin Sadri, Afsaneh Mahian, Sanaz Bayan and I include myself, Nazanin Sahamizadeh. Their staging of *Acclimatization, Deliberate, Romantic, Murderous* and *An Eye for An Eye*, are examples of successful plays about women's issues. The play *Manus* (included in this collection) is an example of a documentary/verbatim play performed during this period at the Adelaide Festival in Australia too. Other women who had successes in playwriting and directing during this time are Azadeh Shahmiri, Afrouz Forouzand, Leili Aaj and Haleh Moshtaghi Nia.

Today, many women work in various fields of theatre, but the majority of the theatrical community and theatre's governmental authority positions are still occupied by men.

In addition to the religious restrictions imposed on women, since Iran is still a patriarchal society, there is a gender-based perspective on women. It has become harder to believe in women in any position of authority. Compared with men, women writers and directors often face more barriers to securing a performance venue and to attracting investors and producers for their work.

Another innovative playwright and director who stepped into the arena during this period is Mohammad Mosavat. He tries to create new and unique forms with an experimental vision and his plays and productions are considered post-modern. In the 2000s, the Academic Theatre Ring was formed, members of which are many of today's successful newly-graduated theatre students, such as Ashkan Kheil Nejad, Yousof Bapiri, Samaneh Zandi Nejad and Jaber Ramezani. The inclusion of independent performance of Iranian plays in creditable international festivals such as Edinburgh, Adelaide and Avignon was another of the important developments during the 2000s.

In 2019, following the protests on the streets of Iran in November, many people were killed or arrested. In January 2020, Ukraine International Airlines Flight 752 was shot down shortly after take-off from Tehran Imam Khomeini International Airport by the Iranian Islamic Revolutionary Guards Corps (IRGC) and all 176 passengers and crew were killed. These two painful events angered the public and were mourned by the Iranian people and the artists. Consequently, theatre artists boycotted the Fajr Theatre Festival that year. Romeo Castellucci and Eugenio Barba, who were supposed to take part in that festival, withdrew in sympathy with Iran's theatre artists.

Due to the COVID-19 pandemic, theatre in Iran was shut down from February 2019, and it has not been able to reopen fully and become as established as before. Iranian theatre artists and groups are countless and naturally all of them could not be named in this summary, so what is mentioned above, is just briefly the important developments and influential artists in the complexities of Iranian theatre. However, I hope that this overview has provided the reader with insight into the world of Iranian theatre and that, together with the plays published in this collection, they will provide a starting point for further study and performance.

Translators' Note

Home is perhaps the most widely employed of settings in the history of theatre. In fact, there might be few plays that do not make use of home as the place where the events in the drama transpire. Such prominent playwrights as Henrik Ibsen, Eugene O'Neil, Tennessee Williams, Arthur Miller, Harold Pinter, and Sam Shepard have all made extensive use of the home setting. In many plays, home may simply function as a place the walls of which demarcate the interior domestic space from the external world. However, in Naghmeh Samini's works, especially in her *Sleep in an Empty Cup* (2002), *Mimic* (2004), and *Home* (2009), home as the space wherein most of the events and conflicts happen, figures so prominently that she has constructed her penultimate play entirely on it. In this play, home becomes a space wherein personal histories frequently intersect and intertwine with one another. However, the image that ultimately emerges out of this complex nexus of personal narratives is one that many readers find contrary to their expectations.

Samini's play could be quite deceptive both in its diction as well as in its portrayal of the characters. It is at once a highly symbolic play, the unique symbolism of which does not preclude the reader from appreciating the narrative. Moreover, the sharp contrast between the very familiar, though at times exaggerated characters, and the surreal condition of the house further reinforce the anxiety and the suspense that pervades the play. The concept of home occupies a very significant place in the collective cultural unconscious of Iranians and the fact that in Samini's play this sacred space is constantly threatened, violated, and is literally crumbling down could imply important social changes in a country characterized as much by tradition as it is by modernity.

– Hossein Nazari, University of Tehran

nazarih@ut.ac.ir

HOME

Nagmeh Samini

translated by Hossein Nazari & Ghazal Ghaziani

Characters

AZAD – Roya's husband
ROYA – Azad's wife
MAHAN – their son
PARNIYAN – their daughter
HAMOUN – Azad's son by a previous marriage
MAHSA – Mahan's girlfriend
PARNIYAN'S BOYFRIEND
WOMAN'S VOICE
THE WOMAN
THE MAN
MAN'S VOICE
THE VOICEOVER

In the darkness we hear voices.

AZAD/ROYA/MAHAN/PARNIYAN *(calling)* Hamoun!
...Are you there, Hamoun? ...Hamoun!

Lights up. A roofed maquette of a house with all its detail lies on the floor. Roya, Azad, Parniyan, and Mahan have gathered around it. They are calling Hamoun and trying to look inside the house through its small windows. From afar, Hamoun, with an abnormally pale face and an unusually thin body, sits watching them search. They cannot see him there, sitting outside the house.

AZAD/ROYA/MAHAN/PARNIYA *(calling)* Hamoun!
...Where are you? ...Hamoun!

HAMOUN   This is our home. Or should I say, this was our home, before it got this tiny. We used to live here, under its low ceiling, between its bulging walls, behind its sooty windows... Now, they're standing over the house, calling me. None of them wants to see that the house has shrunk. They do see it, but don't want to think about it. They don't want to talk about it. It's not easy to admit it, of course. Maybe later when they calm down a bit, they'll come to believe it. But not now... now they're just busy looking for me.

AZAD/ROYA/MAHAN/PARNIYAN *(calling)* Hamoun!
...Can you hear us? Are you still there? Hamoun!

Tired, they quit calling.

PARNIYAN   It's useless. We're just wasting our time.

ROYA *(worriedly)* I wonder what's happened to him?

MAHAN   I don't have a clue!

ROYA   What do you think?

AZAD   I have no idea!

PARNIYAN   That's it! He isn't here.

ROYA   What do you mean? We can't just leave him like this. We must find him. Come on! Let's search again.

PARNIYAN   There's nowhere we haven't searched already.

Parniyan/Mahan/Roya go back toward the maquette.

ROYA   Let's call him all together.

ROYA/PARNIYAN/MAHAN *(call out in unison)* Hamoun!

Silence for a few moments.

PARNIYAN   What if we turn the house upside down? He'd fall out from wherever he is.

ROYA   Turn it upside down?! It will break all of the poor boy's bones.

AZAD   Listen! I say let's look for him in a different way. Does anybody remember Hamoun leaving the house since last night?

They all think for a moment and shake their heads.

AZAD   So he must still be here. Do you remember where you saw him last?

They begin to contemplate.

PARNIYAN   I didn't see him but I heard him, about 3:30 in the morning. He was talking to someone loudly.

ROYA   Who was he talking to at that time of the night?!

Parniyan shrugs her shoulders.

AZAD *(remembering something)* Maybe! I last heard his footsteps about the same time... about 2:30. He was going down the stairs to the basement, or maybe he was coming up...

ROYA *(remembers)* Oh, yeah! Around three o'clock... As if something fell from his hands and got smashed. I heard the sound from the kitchen. I remember it well.

MAHAN   May I say something, too? I know, of course, it's not normal, but what is normal about us anyway? I'm sure I saw him when I was on the rooftop. I saw his shadow... a hand span of shadow... falling in the yard... precisely a hand span ...This much!

All of them remember the last time they saw a trace of Hamoun. Meanwhile, Hamoun is still sitting in his circle of light and is watching the family.

HAMOUN (*aside*) In all these years, the keys to this house have been the most important thing the five of us have had in common; the keys with identical grooves on them stored in our pockets that made us come back here, to home, by the end of the night wherever we were. But now those keys have got a rival. They are standing over the home and, without wanting to think that the door of the house has got smaller than its keys, are looking for me all together. They are going over their memories to remember the last time they saw me... but... honestly, I feel sorry for them when I see them struggling... because I know they'll never find me.

Lights go out suddenly.

ROOM ONE –THE BEDROOM

A double bed is placed opposite the window. There is a clock beside the bed and a suitcase, open and empty, lies on top of the bed. Standing by the window, Azad is throwing out sheets of paper one by one. Throwing out the last sheet of paper, he turns toward the suitcase. He then picks up his pillow, smells it, and puts it in the suitcase. He looks around. There is nothing else to take. He only picks up the clock and puts it in the suitcase. He closes the suitcase and takes a look around the room... the last look to say farewell forever. He walks toward the door, but suddenly a sound stops him. Someone seems to be throwing pebbles at the window. Surprised, he looks down from the window and opens it.

AZAD   Who's there?

Nothing can be heard. Pause. Azad closes the window and is about to leave, but right at that moment, he hears the sound of pebbles being thrown again. He opens the window once more and looks down.

WOMAN'S VOICE Good evening!

AZAD (*surprised*) Good evening!

WOMAN'S VOICE Did I interrupt you?!

AZAD   Who are you looking for?

WOMAN'S VOICE You!

Azad is taken aback. We do not know whether it is because of the woman's voice or what she has just said.

AZAD   Me?!

WOMAN'S VOICE Is that odd?!

AZAD   How can I help you?

WOMAN'S VOICE How did you know?

AZAD   Know what?!

WOMAN'S VOICE That I need you to help me.

AZAD   I just said it...

WOMAN'S VOICE I would appreciate it if you helped me get up there.

AZAD   Get up where?!

WOMAN'S VOICE There.

AZAD   I don't know what you mean.

WOMAN'S VOICE It's so obvious! I want to get up there!

AZAD   I understand that! I just don't understand why. Anything wrong?! Has anyone hurt you?!

WOMAN'S VOICE Who could possibly hurt me?!

AZAD   I can call 911 if you want.

WOMAN'S VOICE Oh, No! No!

AZAD   What can I do for you then?

WOMAN'S VOICE I told you already! Help me get up there.

AZAD   Why should I help you come up here when I don't even know you.

WOMAN'S VOICE There's nothing odd about this! All people are strangers at first. Then they get to know each other.

AZAD   Do you know what time it is?!

WOMAN'S VOICE I know... It's midnight.

AZAD   Isn't it a bit too late to get to know someone?

WOMAN'S VOICE It's not my fault that it's too late. I had no reason to come earlier.

AZAD Do you have a good reason now?

WOMAN'S VOICE I'll explain when I come up.

AZAD Don't I know you, really?

WOMAN'S VOICE I don't know.

AZAD Do I have to know you?

The woman says nothing.

AZAD I said, "Do I have to know you?"

WOMAN'S VOICE What do you think?

AZAD What about you? Do you know me?

WOMAN'S VOICE No! I don't know anybody.

AZAD If you could just move into the light a little...

WOMAN'S VOICE You can see my face well enough if I come up there.

AZAD I think this is a kind of disturbance.

WOMAN'S VOICE If so, you are harassing me more than I am harassing you.

AZAD Me?! I am harassing you?

WOMAN'S VOICE Well, yes! Because I am trying to come up there and you aren't helpful at all.

AZAD Well, is it normal to throw pebbles at someone's window and ask to be pulled up at this time of the night?

WOMAN'S VOICE Is it normal that no one helps someone, at this time of the night, who is asking for help to be pulled up there?

AZAD Yes, that is normal!

WOMAN'S VOICE That's what I'm trying to say; it's normal!

AZAD No! I didn't mean it that way. I mean this is normal.

WOMAN'S VOICE Which one?

AZAD   That nobody helps someone who wants to normally get up here... *(Suddenly, as if realizing something.)* Oh, OK! So that's how it is these days?

WOMAN'S VOICE How?

AZAD *(gives a signal)* Like this...

WOMAN'S VOICE I don't have a clue what you are talking about! All I want is to get up there!

Azad is hesitant. He decides to stretch his hand out for a moment, but then changes his mind.

AZAD   No! It's not gonna happen! *(Points to the window.)* You threw pebbles at the wrong window. Have a good night.

He moves to close the window.

WOMAN'S VOICE OK! Go ahead! Close the window! But that is the last way people choose to take revenge on themselves or on others.

Taken aback, Azad stands still.

AZAD   What did you just say?

WOMAN'S VOICE Nothing.

AZAD   How do you know that I... How did you know?

WOMAN'S VOICE That you what?

AZAD   That... The revenge...

WOMAN'S VOICE I didn't mean anything.

AZAD   Why from among so many windows did you choose this one?

WOMAN'S VOICE The only room that was lit... and, well, those papers.

AZAD   What about the papers?

WOMAN'S VOICE No one throws away all the files of a lifetime's honest work just for the sake of it.

AZAD   Did you read them?

WOMAN'S VOICE They've all got your signature.

AZAD How do you know my signature?

WOMAN'S VOICE I didn't say your signature! I just said signature.

AZAD You said your signature.

WOMAN'S VOICE I just said signature.

AZAD I'm sure you said your signature.

WOMAN'S VOICE I can't remember, even if I said that!

AZAD Where do we know each other from?

WOMAN'S VOICE From nowhere!

AZAD I'm sure we do. I can't be wrong. No, you can't be a friend of Roya... Who are you?

WOMAN'S VOICE I could be anybody! Depends on who you want to see right now.

AZAD Stay there! I'll come down now.

WOMAN'S VOICE I'll leave if you do.

AZAD Why's that?

WOMAN'S VOICE Because I just want to get up there.

Hesitant, Azad decides for a moment.

AZAD OK! Come. Just quickly and quietly.

WOMAN'S VOICE Are you sure?

AZAD It's what you wanted, isn't it?

WOMAN'S VOICE Yeah... But...

AZAD But what?

WOMAN'S VOICE Don't you want to go to bed?

AZAD No! Come up.

WOMAN'S VOICE What happened then? Why did you change your mind?

AZAD I haven't changed my mind. I just changed the form of my decision.

A moment of silence. Azad makes the bed up quickly, places the suitcase in a corner, and locks the door. But the woman does not appear.

AZAD What happened?

WOMAN'S VOICE I can't.

AZAD Look! Just put your foot on the edge of the wall and grab the edge of the window.

WOMAN'S VOICE I can't.

AZAD Look! Put your right foot up and throw your weight on it, grab the edge of the window with one hand, and give me your other hand.

WOMAN'S VOICE I can't.

AZAD OK, listen. Put your left foot up first.

WOMAN'S VOICE It doesn't make any difference.

AZAD Put your left foot... it does make a difference. Then grab the edge of the window with your right hand. Throw your weight on your foot, then give me your left hand.

WOMAN'S VOICE Can't be done!

AZAD Can you find anything around that you can stand on? ... Aha! What's that?

WOMAN'S VOICE An oil tin.

AZAD Perfect! Put it under the window, then put your right foot on it, put your left foot up on the edge of the window, give me your right hand—

WOMAN'S VOICE My left foot on your hand, my left hand on this...

AZAD No! Your right foot on the tin... left foot on the edge of the wall...

WOMAN'S VOICE Right foot on your left foot, then my left foot on the tin...

AZAD No! Listen...

WOMAN'S VOICE You listen! I can't do it this way.

AZAD You grab my hand and I'll pull you up.

Azad bends out over the window sill and struggles to reach her.

AZAD Aha! Just a little bit higher and you can grab my hand.

WOMAN'S VOICE I told you I can't.

AZAD　　　　　　You can. Just pull yourself up a little.

WOMAN'S VOICE It's not going to happen.

AZAD　　　　　　Just try it once. Come on! Grab my hand... Grab my hand. Stand on your tiptoes... Hold it... Come on! Pish!

Out of breath, Azad draws back desperately. A few moments of silence.

WOMAN'S VOICE What happened?

AZAD　　　　　　...

WOMAN'S VOICE Are you all right?

AZAD　　　　　　...

WOMAN'S VOICE Are you still there?

AZAD　　　　　　Didn't you think through how you wanted to get up here when you were throwing pebbles at the window?

WOMAN'S VOICE I thought I could... but now... it seems I can't.

AZAD　　　　　　You're just wasting your time then.

WOMAN'S VOICE *(quietly)* The thing that's being wasted is not my time.

AZAD　　　　　　What?

WOMAN'S VOICE I said my time isn't being wasted.

AZAD　　　　　　When you can't even come in...

WOMAN'S VOICE You make it sound like it's The Gate of China and I can't get through!

AZAD　　　　　　Stay there then, and I'll come down right away.

WOMAN'S VOICE I told you not to. You are not coming here. Hear me? You aren't. If you do, I'll leave.

AZAD　　　　　　Look! I don't even know who you are. So, it doesn't matter if you leave or not...

WOMAN'S VOICE It doesn't? Even if every cell in your body is curious to see me? Even if all your close and distant memories spin around in your head like a whirlwind and kick up dust, it still doesn't matter? Even if something deep down at the very bottom of your heart, where no surgeon or executioner can reach, tugs at your heartstrings?!

AZAD (*confused*) How do you know that?

WOMAN'S VOICE I don't know anything.

AZAD   You can see me though.

WOMAN'S VOICE You are standing in the light. It's me who is in the darkness.

AZAD   Who are you, really?

WOMAN'S VOICE Help me again to get up there.

Azad looks around the room. He takes a sheet off the bed and rolls it up. He throws it down to the woman.

WOMAN'S VOICE Where did you go?

AZAD   I'm coming! OK, hold this.

WOMAN'S VOICE What should I do with this?

AZAD   Hold on to it.

WOMAN'S VOICE Did I say I was cold?

AZAD   Grab this and I'll pull you up.

WOMAN'S VOICE It smells like...

AZAD   You don't want to get up here because of the smell. Come on!

WOMAN'S VOICE The smell of egg shampoo, of baby powder, of tooth paste. Nice smells... lovely smells... familiar smells...

AZAD   Did you catch it?

WOMAN'S VOICE It slipped out of my hand.

AZAD   Hold on tight.

WOMAN'S VOICE I know it can't be done.

AZAD   Just once. Let's try just once. Ready?

WOMAN'S VOICE Yeah!

Azad pulls up the sheet. Nothing happens. Sad and desperate, he lights a cigarette and stands silently by the window.

WOMAN'S VOICE How nice, you smoke!

AZAD   What?

WOMAN'S VOICE The way you smoke is like taking revenge.

AZAD   ...

WOMAN'S VOICE Are you sleepy? I mean if you want to go to bed ...

AZAD   It's not a good game you are playing. Why right now? Tonight?... With all you've just said... with the sound that still rings in my ears... *(Distressed)* I'm sure I know that voice!

WOMAN'S VOICE Who does it sound like?

AZAD   Forget it.

WOMAN'S VOICE I hate it when people leave their sentences unfinished. When it ignites every cell in your body with curiosity and then you say: "Forget it"!

For a moment it seems like Azad has moved to another time. He repeats the last part of the woman's sentence.

WOMAN'S VOICE/AZAD *(together)* I hate this "Forget it!" part. I hate the part that springs back and hits you hard in the face like a rubber band.

Silence. Azad is surprised. He has just become aware of the situation.

AZAD   Why did you say that?

WOMAN'S VOICE I didn't say anything.

AZAD   Those words...

WOMAN'S VOICE What about them?

AZAD   How do you know all that? Those were her words.

WOMAN'S VOICE Whose?

AZAD   Maybe I'm asleep. Maybe this is just a hallucination. Maybe you're a hallucination, too. But why tonight? Why after thirty-four years?! *(Suddenly)* I'd better close this window and you'd better find another window.

WOMAN'S VOICE Close it to do what?

AZAD   To go back to what I was doing.

WOMAN'S VOICE You mean you want to leave home for good? Leave with a pillow and a clock to destroy yourself? To finish yourself off?

Azad, baffled and surprised, looks out.

AZAD How do you know all this?

WOMAN'S VOICE I don't know anything!

AZAD No one could have told you, because nobody knows. I haven't talked to any of them for ages. Routine chatter, maybe, but no real conversation. It's ridiculous. The people who are so close to me know nothing about me. They don't even see me. But a stranger! It's totally ridiculous!

WOMAN'S VOICE Typical moaning man!

AZAD It's not moaning at all!

WOMAN'S VOICE Of course it is! All men in the world think they haven't been noticed enough or not noticed at all.

AZAD Well, I'm different. I'm really invisible in this place and I get more invisible every day. I didn't used to notice, or maybe didn't want to notice. But one day... Ah! Why am I telling you all this?

WOMAN'S VOICE No, please! Go on.

AZAD What good is it to you?

WOMAN'S VOICE Let's just say it's killing time.

AZAD Yeah! It's good for killing time.

WOMAN'S VOICE So...?

AZAD What?

WOMAN'S VOICE You were saying that one day...

AZAD Well, one day about two or three years ago, I was watching the TV and suddenly I heard my daughter, Parniyan, let out a loud scream from the bathroom. I knew it was a cockroach again, one of those winged ones. So I grabbed a slipper, as usual, and just sat waiting. She rushed out shaking and pale, but it was the first time she didn't ask me to kill the cockroach. She asked Mahan first, then Hamoun. None of them budged. I was still waiting with the slipper in my hand. I was dying for her to call me, waiting to see in her eyes, just for that second, when the monster wiggles its ugly legs under my slipper and gets crushed and squashed, that I still exist... to see that I was still there for her. But she didn't call me. She didn't see me waiting. Not even a single glance. She killed it herself at last. That was when I knew it was all over.

WOMAN'S VOICE So are you sorry for the cockroach or for yourself?

AZAD I don't think there is much difference between us. We both got squished the same way, at the same time.

WOMAN'S VOICE You are too hard on yourself.

AZAD Yeah! I told you how ridiculous everything is. Why should I matter when there are so many invisible people in this world? The Tibetans are invisible to the Chinese, the Iraqis to the Americans, the Bosnians to the Serbs. The TV is full of invisible people. Aren't you yourself invisible to so many others?

WOMAN'S VOICE I'm invisible to everyone!

Silence.

WOMAN'S VOICE *(poignantly)* Is your wife home?!

AZAD Do you know her, too?

WOMAN'S VOICE Is she home?

AZAD In the kitchen.

WOMAN'S VOICE What's she doing there at this time of the night?

AZAD Scrubbing something.

WOMAN'S VOICE Scrubbing?!

AZAD A grease stain on the stove top. I'm jealous of it with every single cell in my body.

WOMAN'S VOICE Of your wife?!

AZAD Of the stain! Roya is crazy about it. If only she stared at me once the way she stares at that stain! One day I decided to make her happy, I mean Roya. She wasn't home. I went after the stain and scrubbed it off hard and it did really fade. I mean it almost vanished. But what do you think she did when she came home?

WOMAN'S VOICE (*mysteriously*) She acted like you didn't exist and you hadn't done her a favour. She poured a little oil on the stove top at once and started scrubbing again. It was then that you seriously thought about taking revenge on her... on them... from that moment till tonight.

AZAD　　　　You may know a lot of things, but this is nonsense. I've never thought of revenge.

Azad turns to the audience for a moment as if he sees us. Right at this moment, Hamoun appears from a corner with his pale face and slim body. Azad does not see him.

AZAD (*to the audience*) I lied! I've thought of revenge so many times. Time and time again! To take revenge on Parniyan, Hamoun, Mahan... all of them, but more than anyone else, on myself. But tonight is the night I'm going to decide. I'll sleep alone here... in this bedroom... like all other nights. I'll lie down and close my eyes. Then I'll stare at the straight line behind me that has no twists and turns, not a back alley, not a No Entry, nor a red light. A lifetime without being fined even once. Every day at eight o'clock, behind the desk, signing. Eight o'clock, behind the desk, signing. Thirty-five years of paying a mortgage. This morning I finally paid the last instalment and realized that I have no reason to live any longer. No reason left for them to want me. Now I'm even more invisible. These bricks are made with my flesh and bones and cartilage. This very home with its dirty white façade has devoured my entire life, all my happiness, everything I've ever had ...I need to do something to at least prove to myself that I still exist. Something like leaving this home, picking someone up on a quiet street, turning off the road towards the valley... when I made this decision an hour ago, I didn't understand it, but tonight, when I think about it, I know that right from the moment that I decided to leave this place forever, the house has somehow fallen apart.

The sound of something crumbling, like the walls of an old house. Hamoun exits.

WOMAN'S VOICE Are you in pain?

AZAD　　　　　What?

WOMAN'S VOICE You were moaning.

AZAD　　　　　No, I wasn't.

WOMAN'S VOICE Yes, you were. Right now. I heard it with my own ears.

AZAD　　　　　I'm fine, darling... *(Baffled)* I... I haven't called anybody that for ages...

WOMAN'S VOICE Don't call me that again. I shouldn't get close to you.

AZAD　　　　　Get close to me?!

WOMAN'S VOICE ...

AZAD　　　　　Are you crying?

WOMAN'S VOICE No!

Silence. Azad seems to be gradually drifting off to sleep.

AZAD　　　　　I'd like to see you.

WOMAN'S VOICE Instead, imagine my face the way you'd like me to be.

AZAD　　　　　You think I can't?! I actually live two lives! One in a fantasy world, one in reality. In my fantasy, I'm with her, in an enormous house with a yard full of coleus, honeysuckle and ivy growing over a shady pergola. There's some nice pottery too in the garden.

WOMAN'S VOICE And sometimes you make those pots, you shape the clay with your own hands.

AZAD　　　　　Sometimes I put them in the oven and glaze them. Something I haven't done in reality for more than thirty years...

WOMAN'S VOICE *(cautiously)* She... the one in that enormous house... Isn't she the one who's got the same ring to her voice as mine?!

AZAD   ...

WOMAN'S VOICE At least tell me what she looks like.

AZAD   Thin, olive-skinned, with brown eyes, pouty lips and rosy cheeks. Just like Parniyan.

WOMAN'S VOICE Your daughter?

AZAD   The whole time that Roya was pregnant with Parniyan, I was wondering if she instead were to deliver the baby...

WOMAN'S VOICE Poor Roya!

AZAD   Yeah... Poor Roya! Or maybe not so poor! Roya doesn't care about these things. She is happy with her grease stains.

WOMAN'S VOICE If she were in your wife's shoes, who could guarantee that you wouldn't end up here? She's obsessed with grease stains, you with an imaginary romance.

Azad begins to yawn. He drifts further into sleep now.

WOMAN'S VOICE Are you sleepy?

AZAD   It's strange! Very much!

WOMAN'S VOICE That's good!

AZAD   I have to go before I fall asleep.

WOMAN'S VOICE You can go tomorrow night... or the night after... Go but only when you are sure from the bottom of your heart.

AZAD   I'm sure from the bottom of my heart right now.

WOMAN'S VOICE No, you're not. If you were, you wouldn't be standing here by the window, talking to a stranger to kill time so as to delay your departure just for a few more minutes.

AZAD *(sleepily)* But I really want to go. I have to go... tonight. I'll prove to them that I'm alive... that I still exist... that I can still do crazy things ... that I hate this house.

It seems that Azad is too drained of energy. He falls asleep while talking. He cannot even stand up and lies down. From now on whatever he does he is half- asleep.

WOMAN'S VOICE Are you asleep?!

AZAD *(sleepily, as if he is in another time)* You won the bet again! It's me who fell asleep again. You are the one who's going to stay awake and watch me in my sleep.

The sound of footsteps is heard. Someone is either going up or coming down the stairs.

WOMAN'S VOICE It's Hamoun's footsteps.

AZAD   What?!

WOMAN'S VOICE Is he OK?

AZAD *(sleepily)* OK?!... I don't know... I don't see him... I don't want to see him.

WOMAN'S VOICE Why?

AZAD *(sleepily)* I'm too far from him.

WOMAN'S VOICE Poor Hamoun!

AZAD   Poor Hamoun... Poor Roya... Poor all of us...

Silence.

WOMAN'S VOICE Are you still awake?

AZAD *(half-asleep)* You put your hair up tight in a bun... with red earrings, a red scarf and red gloves. It's snowing... heavy and calm...

He drifts off.

WOMAN'S VOICE *(as if telling a story)* We walk together through the snow. You hope I slip so I have to grab your hand. I slip on purpose, but you're too shy to grab hold of my hand.

It seems as if Azad has quietly fallen asleep.

WOMAN'S VOICE Are you asleep?

AZAD   ...

The Woman enters quietly and without any difficulty. She looks as Azad has described, but there is a big scar on her face, the trace of a bullet that has cut into her right temple. Her face is covered in clotted blood. Half-asleep, Azad opens his eyes.

AZAD   How did you get in?!

THE WOMAN   Not much distance between the ground and the window... Not anymore!

The Woman smiles sadly. She watches him in his sleep and gently pats his hair.

THE WOMAN *(quietly)* For the last thirty odd years I've been coming every Friday night to watch you from a distance, as you stand alone on the balcony, taking a drag on your cigarette like you are taking the revenge of a lifetime out on it... But tonight was different. I noticed that something was happening to the house. I knew there was something wrong. They let me get a little bit closer. I couldn't do anything more than that to stop you from acting rashly, from suddenly jerking the wheel... to stop you finishing yourself off, my darling...

The Woman squats near the bed and her eyes slowly close. Hamoun enters with a limp. He is carrying a closed box in his hand. At first he opens the suitcase, takes the pillow out and places it under Azad's head. His eyes are drawn to the clock in the suitcase. He takes it out and wipes the dust away. Then he takes a look at the woman, a look that is kind, nostalgic, and curious at the same time. Hamoun pulls the white sheet over her, as if covering a dead body.

HAMOUN *(to the tape recorder)* Mommy dies... the same night that I was born. A stray bullet, from among a thousand stray bullets... No one knows where in all that commotion it came from or which gun fired it. Mommy is sitting in the car and the bullet hits her straight in the head. When Daddy comes back with two ice-creams in his hands, he finds Mommy bleeding to death. It is a year or two before the Revolution. The streets are chaotic. Daddy has just made the first mortgage repayment and is excited. He has taken Mommy out to celebrate. Mommy is in her last month of pregnancy with me. Neither of them knows that their time together is going to be this short. Before that they always remind each other that their happiness isn't going to last forever. That's why they buy this clock and hang it up here across from the bed... to remind them every night and every day how quickly time flies and that in the blink of an eye you realize you've reached the end of the line. This clock is the first thing they bought for this house... And the only trace of Mom that Dad hasn't burnt... I'm the only one who knows about this... nobody else. The only reason Dad has doubts about leaving this home is because of me. He's ashamed to see me. He thinks he has to explain to me why after Mom's death he set fire to all her clothes, her photos, and every last trace of her. He thinks he has to tell me before he leaves, that grief and sorrow have driven him mad. The good thing is that tonight, at last, I get to see Mom... for the first time.

It seems that Hamoun prays for the woman under the sheet. As if in pain, her face contorts for a moment.

HAMOUN   I shouldn't have brought this up. I didn't mean to upset you. After all, I've never told you before... Just forget it. Do you know what I found in the basement? A house!

He opens the box as he is talking and brings out a Lego house. The house is a replica of the maquette that we have seen earlier, only smaller in size.

HAMOUN   I was afraid that I wouldn't find it. I wish you were here to see it... Never mind these things. Have you heard this story before? The one where the tortoise and the hare have a race. This time the hare is really careful... he doesn't fall asleep anywhere, doesn't go after carrots, doesn't eye up lady hares or flirt with them, doesn't fall in and out of love with carrots... nothing! He just runs without any distractions. But when he gets to the finish line, he is amazed that the tortoise has reached the finish line again before him. You know how? Well! This time it has had nothing to do with the poor hare. The tortoise had doped himself up and run like crazy. Well... this is my life story. I'm running, but it's the world that has doped itself up and keeps overtaking me... *(He turns off the recorder, then turns to talk to the audience.)*

I was worried it would get too late... for bringing the house up here. But I finally did it. This was the last useful thing I did... to walk down to the basement and bring this back up... The more I think about it, the more certain I am that it's impossible for them to have forgotten what day today is. No! I'm sure they remember.

Hamoun stands up, but it seems that his knees are weak. Limping, he hangs the clock back on the wall exactly where it used to be.

The lights go out suddenly. The sound of stones grinding... The sound of walls crumbling down... A thunderous sound...

ROOM TWO- THE KITCHEN

Roya is working hard alone in the kitchen. She is surrounded by dishes, pots and pans, lentils and split peas. She sits at a table and is cleaning the split peas quickly, peeling the onions, and chopping the meat. Suddenly, the alarm clock goes off. Panicking, Roya first turns the alarm off very quickly. Then she peers outside and locks the kitchen door. She takes lipstick from her pocket and applies it carelessly to her lips. She rubs a little bit of it on her cheeks, too, arranges her hair and takes her apron off. Then she turns on the small TV, which is placed in front of her, at the other side of the table on a cabinet. She sits in front of the TV with a peculiar eagerness, while cutting the meat and peeling the onions. Music is heard. A black screen and the voiceover.

THE VOICEOVER Home Series. The final episode.

It seems that Roya suddenly falls apart. The previous cheerfulness is gone. Astounded, she stares at the TV.

The image of a man in a cloak with unkempt hair, standing in an eerie, wooded place appears on the TV screen. His face is incredibly calm and attractive. Roya stares at the TV intensely and wipes away a single teardrop with her sleeve. Suddenly, the man turns to her. Roya is not shocked. She was expecting that. But we do not know whether the man is talking to Roya or to someone else in the film.

THE MAN   All the way here I was thinking to myself what if she doesn't come this week, what if I don't get to see her...

ROYA   ...

THE MAN	Is something wrong?
ROYA	...
THE MAN	Are you crying?
ROYA	...
THE MAN	I'm talking to you.

Upset, Roya stands up.

THE MAN	Where are you going?
ROYA	Please go.
THE MAN	Go?!
ROYA	This isn't right. The whole thing isn't right at all.
THE MAN	What isn't right?
ROYA	It shouldn't have ended up here. I don't know why we ended up like this.
THE MAN	Like what?
ROYA	I don't know! Just go... We shouldn't see each other anymore.
THE MAN	What are you talking about?

Roya becomes upset. She suddenly changes the channel. Now there is a rerun of an important soccer match. Roya tries to keep herself busy with something else. She starts peeling the onions quickly. Her eyes begin to stream. She grows impatient again and changes the channel back again. The man is still there, sitting alone, waiting...

THE MAN	Why did you do that?
ROYA	I didn't do anything.
THE MAN	Really, what's wrong with you?
ROYA	If you don't go, I will.
THE MAN	Wait!
ROYA	Why me, of all people?! Go find someone else.
THE MAN	You think I can?!
ROYA	Of course you can.

THE MAN   No, I can't.

ROYA   Yes, you can.

THE MAN   No, I can't, because if it weren't for you, I wouldn't care if I exist or not anymore.

Moved and disconcerted, Roya stretches her hand out to turn the TV off.

THE MAN   No! Wait! Please. Let's talk.

ROYA   What do we have to talk about?

THE MAN   You can't be serious! We really don't?

ROYA   I've got work to do. Friday lunch... unwashed dishes... this stain on the stove top that seems to never go away.

THE MAN   I count every second until our weekly rendezvous. I even count my steps on the way here. I know you do the same.

ROYA   Not at all.

THE MAN   I'm sure you do. It's always been like that. All the weeks before...

ROYA *(evasively)* Well... This time it's different.

Ill at ease, Roya keeps working quickly, but she is clearly paying full attention to the man.

THE MAN   Look at me. Please, look at me...

ROYA   Hush! Do you want to wake them all up?

THE MAN   What's wrong? Has anyone found out about us?!

ROYA   It's not about that...

THE MAN   Let me see. *(He watches carefully.)* How bizarre!

ROYA   There's nothing bizarre here! Everything is the same as usual.

THE MAN   No! It's strange! It seems like this place is choking. As if someone is squeezing its throat tightly.

ROYA   I'm the one who is choking... I'm the one whose throat is being squeezed... not this house.

Hamoun, leaning on a cane looks in through the kitchen door for a moment. Roya sits down and turns to us.

ROYA *(to us)* I'm lying. Something is really going on here. It seems that this house is not like it used to be. Just an hour ago when I came into the kitchen, everything was in its place. I'm sitting here... if you can call it sitting but my heart is like a battlefield... I tell myself, "Roya! What are you waiting for? What else is going to change?! Azad has made the last mortgage payment on the house today. It's over. You are going to stay here forever." I look back... Since I was twenty-three or -four... the babies that were born one after another – that I'm ready to die for, the fridge that kept filling and emptying, the oil that was burned, the stains that were made on the stove, the kettles that got burnt, the dishes that were sometimes clean, sometimes dirty... and the hungry birds that perched outside the window waiting for me to feed them the leftover rice from lunch... *(Pause)* The first time he called me, I suddenly felt as if I was a woman. Something rose up inside my body. I felt hot. In his eyes, I became Roya again. *(The sound of walls falling down.)* ... I didn't understand this an hour ago, but tomorrow, when I think about it, I'll realize that right from the moment that I decided to escape from here, the kitchen began to crumble, just like a balloon that's losing its air.

Hamoun leaves quietly.

THE MAN	Are you in pain?
ROYA	What?
THE MAN	You were moaning.
ROYA	Moaning?
THE MAN	If you just spoke a few decent words to me...
ROYA	I don't have anything to say. Just go... please.
THE MAN	You really want me to go?
ROYA	Yes!
THE MAN	If you really want me to...

The screen goes snowy for a few moments. Roya hits the top of the TV set in a moment of panic and changes the channels. She turns the TV on and off. Still, she only gets a snowy screen. But the voice of the man is heard from somewhere off-stage.

MAN'S VOICE   I'm here...

ROYA *(excitedly)* Where are you?!

MAN'S VOICE   Here!

ROYA   It's just snow.

MAN'S VOICE   I wish to stay here under this snow until I turn into a snowman.

ROYA   Stop being stubborn. Come on!

MAN'S VOICE   I'm not being stubborn.

ROYA   Why are you doing this then?

MAN'S VOICE   Because I know how much you like snowmen. I know how you melt them in your arms.

ROYA   How do you know?

MAN'S VOICE   I know everything.

ROYA   No, seriously, because I really did this once. When I was a kid I made a small snowman. Then I fell in love with it and brought it in to my bed. But it melted by the morning. I got a good spanking from my father. He thought I had wet my bed. I cried my eyes out... not because of the spanking, but for the snowman who had disappeared.

The image of the man appears. He is frozen, with snowflakes sitting on his head and his body.

ROYA   Oh, poor thing! You've turned into an icicle!

THE MAN   I'm cold...

ROYA   Poor thing! Of course this one thin layer is not going to keep you warm. You could catch pneumonia.

Roya covers the TV with a towel, a handkerchief, and anything else she finds.

ROYA   You'll be warm now. I wish I could make you a soup... with turnips and coriander and nettles. That would work miracles.

THE MAN   I just want you to tell me what has happened.

ROYA *(changing the subject)* The roof is leaking again!

THE MAN   You tell me what to do.

ROYA   All the pipes in this house are rusty...

THE MAN   I don't know how to prove to you how much I love you.

Roya is thrilled at what the man tells her. Embarrassed, she lowers her head.

ROYA *(under her breath)* Don't talk to me like that.

THE MAN   Why not?!

ROYA   I don't want to get any closer than this.

THE MAN   What's bad about getting close to someone?

ROYA   Getting close to someone isn't bad, but this whole thing isn't right.

THE MAN   Why not? We can't help being here, right now... and we can't help falling in love either.

ROYA   Oh, Please! Don't talk like that! God will punish us!

THE MAN   Talk like what?!

ROYA *(changes the subject)* Thank God, you're not pale anymore. You can't imagine how worried I was when I saw you like that!

THE MAN *(interrupting Roya)* It's called love. Whether you like it or not, if you fear it... or run away from it... or hide in a forest... it won't change what it's called. It is what it is. It might never have happened. For some people, it never happens at all. But for us... it has happened. It exists and that's what it's called.

A sound is heard from off-stage. Like the sound of something collapsing. Panic-stricken, Roya mutes the TV. The man is just mouthing words. Roya sticks her ear to the door and listens, but she cannot hear anything.

ROYA *(worriedly to The Man)* I think it was Hamoun. He sleeps very lightly these days. The sound of a fly buzzing will wake him up. I don't know what's wrong with him and I can't even ask him.

I don't talk to him much. It's been years. Why are you looking at me like that? It has nothing to do with him not being my own child. I don't know how it happened. I just know everything started from that night! *(She finds it hard to go on.)* That night when there were air raids... down in the basement of this house. Parniyan hadn't been born yet. Hamoun was seven and Mahan was four. As soon as they heard the air-raid siren, they hugged each other and began to cry. I was crying, too. The sound of anti-aircraft missiles and rockets firing all over the place... All of a sudden, Azad grabbed hold of my hand. I was going crazy. I pushed him back and yelled, "Why did you bring another child into the world when you knew the war was going on?! Why did you make me do that? Wasn't this poor child enough? Did you have to make another child become a human shield against the Iraqis? Come on! Finish them off before they die of fear. I hate you. I hate the three of you." *(Pause)*

From that moment something shattered between me and Azad and Mahan and Hamoun. By the time they heard the all-clear siren, they had become different people. Since then I haven't been able to look Hamoun in the eye. I try not to see him at all. Just sometimes when I catch a glimpse of Mahan, I shake my head and think, "What a huge mistake I made, what a huge mistake." Do you think I have any other choice? You think I'm out of my mind, don't you?

The man is still mouthing. Roya realizes that the TV is still mute and she quickly turns up the volume. The man is scowling and sad.

ROYA　　　　　　Oh, I'm really sorry about that. I got distracted. I don't know why I told you all this stuff. I haven't told anybody about that before.

THE MAN　　　　　...

ROYA　　　　　　I'll shut up now, OK? Look, I won't say anything else. I don't know why but when I see you, I start rambling on about things. Come on, I'll be quiet now and let you talk.

THE MAN   I'm just thinking that you care about everybody and everything else, except me, the one who loves you more than anyone in this world...

ROYA   You think I don't care about you? So who am I cooking this Gheymeh[1] stew for? Parniyan keeps asking why we have Gheymeh for lunch every Friday? I can't tell her that you like the smell of it.

THE MAN   Do you know how much I'd like to...?

ROYA *(as if she knows what the man wants)* No!

THE MAN   Why not?!

ROYA   No!

THE MAN   Please!

Roya places her hand on the TV screen where the man's hand is. We can see the man's pleasure at touching Roya's hand from behind the screen. Right at this moment a TV commercial comes on. Upset, Roya pulls her hand back from the screen.

We see a short commercial for a miraculous washing up liquid which removes all stains. The image of the man appears. He is clothed differently and looks agitated and restless.

ROYA   When did you put those on?

THE MAN   I worked it all out for myself.

ROYA   Worked what out?

THE MAN   I didn't get a wink of sleep for three days... until this morning when I finally figured out what was going on ...

ROYA *(nervously)* Three days?! What do you mean – three days?! It's hardly been half an hour. Shameless bastards! They're cutting corners! Those bastards are really cutting corners!

THE MAN   You should've told me ... the moment you found out...

ROYA   But how? I was so overcome with grief! I still am...

THE MAN   Now I think maybe I should never have seen you that day... there, beside the window! The moonlight was shining on your face... on your fair hair... You were feeding the birds... The most beautiful picture I'd ever seen in my whole life. When you sighed, it took my breath away. Then I called you...

ROYA *(a moment in the past)* Yes, darling!

THE MAN   That word... that word drove me crazy.

ROYA   I couldn't help it, could I? You did something that made me visible again. No one has noticed me for an entire lifetime. The more electric appliances we got, the more invisible I became. Electric pasta-maker... electric sandwich-maker... electric tea-maker... electric husband-sitter... electric baby-sitter... the only thing that hasn't been invented yet is an electric stain-scrubber. But don't worry! One day I came home and saw Azad was giving the stain a good scrubbing... he was scrubbing away the last thing I had left... the only reason for me being in this house! I told myself, "Now they may as well dump you in the basement and replace you with an electric doll." All I could do was pour some oil on the stove and start scrubbing again.

THE MAN   I wish you'd made up your mind sooner. I think I'm done! I've come to the end. The end of everything.

ROYA *(choked up)* You're right! This is the last episode and there won't be any reruns.

Silence. The man looks at Roya in distress and shock.

ROYA   I hate it when a series comes to an end. All the endings are fake. Just like food that isn't completely cooked! And no one cares to ask what people have done to deserve this? Why do you play with their emotions like this?

THE MAN *(agitated)* Are you sure about today?

ROYA   Any moment now... and there's not going to be a rerun. This is the very end.

THE MAN   ...

ROYA *(consoles herself and The Man)* Well, all stories are bound to come to an end one day, after all. That's what we learned when we were kids. In those days the stories ended when we fell asleep, but when you're a grown-up, the stories end while you're still awake ...

THE MAN   I know they are on their way to take you away with them. I've been expecting that moment. I knew the time would come sooner or later... But not this soon... Not today... I can't let it finish like this. We must finish our story by ourselves. The way we want it to end.

ROYA   You think we can?

THE MAN   Yes! But on the condition that... you were supposed to give me an answer.

ROYA   I didn't think it would be this soon. I didn't think it would end so soon.

THE MAN   Now you have to. We both have to.

ROYA   I ... I've made up my mind...

THE MAN   So...?

ROYA   I've made up my mind to come with you.

The Man jumps up excitedly.

THE MAN   What did you say?

ROYA *(shyly)*   Yes, you heard it right!

THE MAN   Really?!

ROYA   Yes!

THE MAN   Wow! I can't believe it! After six months of coming and going every week... to hear this from you. Let's go right now! We'll run away... to somewhere none of them could ever find us. They'll look for you for a while, then they'll give up and go their own way. Let's go right now...

Roya is silent. It seems as if she has believed it all but she is suddenly anxious.

ROYA   Just...

THE MAN   Just what?!

ROYA   What will happen to this house if I come with you?

THE MAN   What is supposed to happen? Everything will carry on the same as usual.

ROYA   No! To be honest, I didn't expect it to be this soon. I thought it would be at least another two or three weeks, so I could sort out all my stuff. Put a little bit of food in the freezer... at least vacuum the floors... sew a button on the sleeve of Azad's jacket... change Parniyan's bed sheets... put the clothes on the line... make donations to the Emamzade Saleh shrine[2]...

THE MAN   All that could be done without you.

ROYA   Well, you can see what a mess the kitchen is. Everything is such a mess... Everything needs sorting out. The doors to these cabinets all stick... the fridge door hits the wall... the oven door bangs into the washing machine door...

THE MAN   You are making excuses.

ROYA   Why? What excuses?! *(She catches sight of the clock.)* Oh my God! It's three-thirty. Just three minutes left.

THE MAN   Look! Happiness is not waiting for you there. They're exploiting you, treating you like a slave. That man doesn't love you. It's such a shame... How much longer do any of us have in this world after all? Who knows how much time we have? Isn't it a pity to waste it... being sad and lonely?! Do you want to do that?

ROYA   What are you talking about? I told you I'd come with you.

THE MAN   If you really want to come, we have to go right now.

ROYA   Let me at least finish cooking the stew.

THE MAN   There's no time for that.

ROYA   How can I leave them all here like this? If it was any old kitchen, I would. I wouldn't even think about it. I'd just close my eyes and leave. But how would they manage, when even I can't find where anything is, let alone them. I don't want them to go hungry today... They'll figure out what to do later on. They'll find their way around...

Roya is back to cooking, cutting meat, and peeling the onions quickly.

THE MAN   Look! It's their shadows approaching from far away.

ROYA   The split peas! It's really important that the split peas be well cooked for Qeymeh! Split peas are really awkward things and they take forever to cook.

THE MAN   They're getting close. I can hear their footsteps now.

ROYA *(helplessly)* What should I do?!

THE MAN *(cheerfully)* Just decide. Close your eyes, decide, and hold my hand.

The Man stretches his hand out toward Roya. Roya is uncertain. She closes her eyes for a moment and stretches her hand toward the screen but pulls it back quickly and opens her eyes.

THE MAN   What happened?

ROYA   Where would I go with you anyway?

THE MAN   What difference does it make? Wherever we can be together.

ROYA   You mean we become wanderers? Like homeless people?

THE MAN   A home is where you belong to the people you are with – otherwise, it's no different from a hotel or a prison. I am your home...

ROYA   OK, then. If you let me, I'll just finish this. This is the last thing I can do for them. *(Murmuring)* Where is the tomato paste? There used to be so much space in here. Now it's no bigger than the palm of my hand...

THE MAN   They've passed over the hill now.

ROYA   It's almost done. I wonder where the salt and pepper are?

THE MAN   They've passed the lake now...

ROYA   If I put some onion juice in the stew, it'll make it taste better. Now if I could only find the grater. Oh God! What a mess!

THE MAN   We may never see each other again.

ROYA   Just a quick sauté... Sautéing is very important. If you don't sauté well, the food tastes raw and not properly done, even if you cook it a thousand times. If only this pan wasn't stuck in there...

THE MAN   It's no use. You don't really want to come with me... They're already here... But just remember that whatever story I get into... wherever I will be... I'll think about you... and I will always love you... Goodbye!

Music. The man throws himself down from a high place as if over a cliff. Roya watches in shock.

ROYA   Goodbye!

Now she has only enough energy to go out of the kitchen. The red siren sign appears on the screen and then the siren is heard: "Attention! Attention! The siren that you are hearing..."

Hamoun enters. He is walking with a limp. He leans on a stick to keep his balance. He is carrying his box under his arm. He turns off the TV and turns on the recorder.

HAMOUN ...the kitchen shrinking is just an excuse. Roya won't ever leave this house. She won't leave us, because she feels guilty about that night, that she has to apologize to me, to us ... because of what she said about Mahan and me... She still dreams of that night and no one knows about it but me. Honestly, I have the same nightmare too... just like Roya. I still wake up suddenly at the swish of the rockets in the air. Then I think I have no right to sleep... no right to run away, because I was lucky enough that one of those rockets didn't land right on my head. Some kind of borrowed life that you think you should settle for before it's taken away from you. Maybe this madness we both have about running away is from all those nights... from those fears that have got right into our DNA. There's something else too that only I can tell you. On the nights of the air raids, when I saw how worried Roya got seeing us terrified, I thought to myself I shouldn't be scared anymore. I was only seven years old, but even at that time I thought I shouldn't let Roya know how frightened I really was. That's when I began to run away from things. I ran away to hide my fears.

A moment of silence. Hamoun tries to keep his emotions in check.

HAMOUN *(to the recorder)* Anyway, never mind these things. Let me tell you something interesting. I've recently realized that me and Rodin, Rodin the sculptor, must be distant relatives. It was Rodin, wasn't it, who once broke the hands of his sculpture so that the rest of it wouldn't be overshadowed by the beauty of the hands?! I should get rid of these hands before I get lost under their shadow. To tell the truth, I'm happy. I'm happy that soon I'll be rid of my hands, too. Please don't get all sad if you find this recorder and hear these things. I just want you to know that I'm fine. I wish you were here and could see my hands are having a really good time. I really mean it. I left it for them to decide what they want to do before their battery goes dead. They chose this... to do the Lego house...

He opens the box. The house is crushed. He smashes the remaining walls down.

HAMOUN I smashed them down. On purpose. I'm afraid I might've woken them up. My biggest wish from childhood was to be able to play with these pieces... to make anything I wanted with them... a man, an airplane, an astronaut. But one Friday before I could even touch them, Daddy and Roya made a house with them and then they'd never let me touch them again. It became a decoration piece on the top of the cupboard and gathered dust up there. Roya cleaned it endlessly and nagged about it non-stop... and it gathered dust again and again. Then it ended up in the basement. I'd forgotten about it for a long time ... till last night when I remembered it again. I figured my hands had the right to fulfil their last wish. But now they have no idea what they want to make with all the pieces. *(He turns the recorder off and stands still for a moment.)* I say if they remembered what day April 27th is, they wouldn't be sleeping tonight. Maybe they've forgotten. Maybe not! Or maybe they haven't, but... No! I think they've forgotten.

Lights go out suddenly. The sound of stones rumbling... The sound of walls crumbling down... A thunderous sound...

ROOM THREE – THE BATHROOM

A glass bathtub that is smaller than the regular size. So much smaller that a person can hardly lie or even sit in it. The water tap runs and the bathtub is gradually filling up. Leaning against the bathtub is Parniyan in a white wedding gown. In front of her on the ground is an alarm clock. There is also a small MP3 Player and some pills. She has a small laptop on her lap and is chatting with somebody. The text of their chat, which is in Finglish (Farsi/Persian written with English alphabet) should be projected on a screen when acting out the play.

. What happened?

P. Still Nothing.

. How many r left?

P. Just 1.

. What if it doesn't work?

P. U sure about the expiry date?

. No idea.

P. Dumbass!

. I'm worried about u.

P. Shut up! Did u look up "baignoire" in Eng.?

. Means bathtub.

P. It says "Après avoir ressenti une douleur, allongez-vous dans une baignoire remplie d'eau chaude. Si vous ne le faites pas, vous éprouveriez éventuellement des effets indésirables."

. Means "After feeling the pain, lie down in a bathtub full of warm water. If not, u may face unusual side effects."

P. I knew that myself.

. Lie down then.

P. Well... There is a problem.

. ?

P. Nothing. Go sleep. When u wake up tomorrow, u'll not be a dad anymore. If this works, of course.

. What a downer u r!

P. Geez! U were scared more than me.

. Now it's a downer... Tell him I'll miss him.

P. Go to hell! He's just the size of a pea.

. U tell him anyway.

P. Cut it out!

PARNIYAN (*to her belly*) He says he'll miss you, but don't believe him. He got scared to death when he found out; like the police were after him! He ran away to Dubai to stay with his uncle. I asked him to read the news about a thirteen-year-old English dad to give him some hope, but he wouldn't listen. I told him "If you were his age when you became a daddy, your child would be six by now!" He was really scared to death! You won't die! Don't be scared! You're not supposed to die! I'm talking about you, not him. You'll slip into the water like a fish. So don't be scared.

. Did u tell him?

P. Yep.

. What did he say?

P. He said "My dad is a chicken."

. What does that mean?!

P. Means they export the dimwits to Dubai!

. Stop taunting! When u get better, I'll bring u here, too.

P. I'm fine right now...

. R u in pain?

P. A little.

. Just 1 every 3 hours. Not more than that.

P. I know. Hushhhh! Let me see.

She suddenly hears something. She hears Hamoun talking loudly in another room. She sticks her ear to the door.

. What's up?

P. I got scared to death. Heard something and thought it was my mom.

. Who was it then?

P. No one. I think it was my brother. He's a little bit dumb! A bit of a kook.

. R u OK now?

P. Yep! Go sleep.

. Buzz me if anything happens. I'll b online.

P. OK.

. Look...

P. ?

. LOVE!

P. Me too.

. Good night!

P. Nite.

PARNIYAN *(to her belly)* Listen to me! Don't be so stubborn or you'll regret it. You think I'm doing this for myself? Not at all! I'm going through this hell just for you. You think you'll be born with a silver spoon? There is nothing here. Nothing! There is! Obviously there is! It's also your fault that you have come to this world now that there is no other fun. Roya says, I mean my mom, your grandma... she says: "In those days having a boyfriend or a girlfriend meant something else. It took three years for a boy to hold his girlfriend's hand. And that if it was snowing... and the girl happened to slip... if the boy had the guts to hold her hand... if the girl didn't pull her hand back out of shyness" Geez! How patient they were! So what now? At the end of the day they would get to where we get to now in just two days. Well, it's the age of speed. Everything is speedy. Speedy cooking... speedy Internet... speedy love. After all you belong to this age, don't you? Speedy Baby! Ouch! I'm sick of Mom's stupid advice. "Don't accept anyone's phone number. Don't look at men. All men are wolves and hyenas. They're AIDS!" Yuck! I just want to throw up. But I can't. That's the problem.

She reads the instructions on the pill package.

This is the third hour of the three hours. They say it works in the first three hours, but it hasn't. Don't know why? Nothing. No cramps, no vomiting, nothing. The foul smell of this sewage would make any normal person throw up, but me... nothing! Forget about the sewage! If I ate one small unhealthy piroshki on the way to school, it would give me away. For a week I'd be going back and forth between the bedroom and the bathroom! ...up and down! That's how the world is. *(To her belly)* Are you listening? I'm talking to you! Look! I said there's something wrong with this world! I'm telling you these things so you don't feel too sad that you are not going to live here. I just want you to know how funny this world is. I mean whatever is delicious has either got bugs or makes you fat, or causes cancer or all three together. Instead everything that stinks and tastes like shit is so good for you! *(She feels something, which makes her smile.)* What? Are you laughing? Is it really funny? There you go laughing again! You fool! I'm telling you! I don't know why I feel like eating in the middle of this mess! No idea! Maybe it's because my belly is vibrating. You don't know what being hungry is like, because you just know one food: blood. It's bullshit that when humans come to this world, they're innocent and pure as the driven snow. We're all vampires when we're born. Seriously! Vampires! And Daddy still gets mad when he sees on the TV that this something-Ovich, who had massacred the Bosnians, has got a huge double chin. Or why that fat Israeli guy, who's murdered thousands of Palestinians doesn't just drop dead? Or why the Chinese don't just leave the Tibetans alone? Well, that's the way it is!

The alarm clock goes off and Parniyan turns it off.

PARNIYAN   It's time again.

She takes another pill.

PARNIYAN   Look Monsieur Prostel RU-486! I'll kill you if you don't work this time! Ah, is it going to hurt a lot?

She puts the pill under her tongue. A moment of silence. She cannot talk properly because of the pill.

PARNIYAN *(to her belly)* Don't be scared, OK? I mean... Listen! This way you'll go straight to Heaven! No, you won't! If you live for forty years, you won't go to Heaven; you'll definitely go to Hell! Look at me! I'm one of those who, like our theology teacher says, will have my *Book of Deeds* in my left hand in the afterlife, get a kick in the butt... and straight into the middle of hellfire... I'm not sure if you can even hear me or not. I wish I could chat with you. You know what chatting is?

A buzzing sound is heard from her laptop.

. Dropped?

P. U think it's an apple waiting to drop from a tree?

. It's the size of an apple?

P. What the hell are u talking about?

. What r u talking about?

P. I told u I'll let u know.

. Look! I think u should tell ur mom.

P. R u nuts?! Because I'm not.

. No, seriously. Wake her up and tell her. I'm afraid something bad might happen to you. It shouldn't have lasted this long.

P. Wouldn't be caught dead telling my mom.

. Why? My mom was a witness. You can say everything was done legitimately.

Parniyan suddenly turns to us. Right at this moment Hamoun enters. He is sitting on a wheelchair and can hardly move his hands.

PARNIYAN *(to us)* He's telling the truth. His mom did the temporary marriage contract for us just for the sake of it. She's not religious at all but then she insists on doing the temporary marriage contract for all her son's girlfriends! No! It just doesn't add up. Nothing in this family adds up. If Mahan sees them, he would give them a lengthy lecture about the conflict between tradition and modernism... He's crazy! I don't mean Mahan. I mean him! What am I supposed to tell my mom and dad?! I should stay quiet till I die? I'll never do that! Not that I'm scared or anything like that. I just can't put up with their dirty looks. Like they've given birth to something they're stuck with now. Because I'm one of those unwanted children. Daddy wanted to have Mahan, but Mommy didn't. But for me... it was the other way round. Mommy wanted to have me, but Daddy didn't. Then Mommy says she doesn't want me either but decides to keep me just to piss Daddy off and Daddy is like "To hell with it!" And then I'm born! I sometimes want to spit in the face of Mahan's and Mom's stupid friends who say, "We don't know how it happened! We didn't want the baby! It just dropped down from the sky! It was just God's will!" Bullshit artists!

Suddenly everyone has become an unwanted baby. The only one who is not unwanted in our house is Hamoun. Both his mom and dad wanted him. That's why he can write so well. I'm telling you, it has something to do with it. He wrote all my essays at school. I used to cry my eyes out when I read them in the class. Especially the one that said write something about yourself. It was like he knew me better than myself. He had even written about that cockroach. I'd never told him about it. I don't know how he found out. I mean the cockroach story. It was about unwanted babies. Whenever Daddy killed a cockroach, *(She starts to feel the pain gradually)* I felt sick. For me it was like he kept thinking to himself, "If I'd crushed Parniyan with a slipper while she was this size, I wouldn't be stuck with her now." That's why I decided to kill the cockroaches myself. *(She wants to get into the bathtub but she hesitates for a moment.)* It wasn't this size, or was it?! It was. It was exactly my size. Well, you don't grow to this size in one week, do you? I don't know. Don't laugh at me but as soon as I took the first pill, I heard something. Then I felt the walls were falling in on themselves. This bathtub got smaller, too. As if everything shrank.

Hamoun exits. A buzz is heard from the laptop. This time Parniyan is not typing and the text on the screen is being automatically typed. It seems everything that she is thinking about gets typed.

. R u moaning?

P. Not yet. How come?

. Just thought u were moaning. What's up?

P. Something is happening.

. How does it feel?

P. It's painful.

. Keep it if u can. Whatever the size, keep it.

P. Idiot! Go on the Internet instead and see what happens if I don't lie in the bathtub.

. Don't u have a bathtub?!

P. Just go… and let me know…

Parniyan looks at the bathtub. The pain intensifies. It comes and goes.

PARNIYAN   Ouch! What the hell is wrong with you?! Did you prefer that I went to one of those filthy houses and give you to one of those old witches? Like in those shitty soap operas? Or should I have secretly sold my mom's jewelry and gone to one of those high-class doctor's offices, with those tattoo-covered secretaries who don't have a part in their bodies left without implants; one of those who call you "Darling!" Yuck! I hate those who call you "Darling!" or "My Darling!" It's so phony that it makes me sick.

. Dropped?

PARNIYAN *(in pain)* Oh, shut up for God's sake! You think it's just me? Fifteen each day! Fifteen foetuses in Tehran's gutters, each day!

A short buzz is heard from the laptop.

. Listen! It says it's dangerous if you don't lie in the water. Says something strange will happen but doesn't explain much.

PARNIYAN ...

. U OK?

PARNIYAN ...

. Parniyan?!!!!!!!!

. Love you, love you, love you, love you...

PARNIYAN *(in pain)* Shut up! Shut up! Shut up! Shut up!

Parniyan is writhing in pain. Anxious, she gets up. The pain intensifies and she begins writhing again. She wants to sit in the bathtub. She bites down on a piece of cloth out of excruciating pain. Suddenly she lets out a cry. A few goldfish slip into the bathtub and on the ground. Parniyan passes out in the water. A strange beep, like that of children's wind-up dolls is heard from the laptop. And then words in a strange red font appear on the screen.

I DON'T WANT TO DIE MOMMY!

Hamoun enters. He is sitting on a wheelchair and moves with difficulty. He is still holding on to the Lego box in his hand. He struggles to pick up a few goldfish from the floor and throws them into the bathtub. He tries to help Parniyan out but he cannot. Parniyan is unconscious and Hamoun has no energy left. The recorder is on. He talks in an abnormally loud voice.

HAMOUN　　　　Everyone seems to have lost something... I've lost you; Daddy has lost mommy; Roya has lost Daddy and Parniyan has lost her baby's father. Yes! She's lost him. These messages aren't real. At least Parniyan thinks that. These could be from anyone. Who knows who is sitting behind that computer miles away? Parniyan is scared deep down that perhaps the one she's chatting with is somebody else... a stranger... someone other than her baby's father. That's why when he asks her to move to Dubai, she's scared... deep down. But she hasn't told anyone about her fears. I'm the only one who knows about this and no one else. You know, after all she's so fragile... just like our relationship was... *(He gets lost in a distant memory.)* Niloufar! Do you remember?! Right on the day that Parniyan was born, I found you for the first time. Imagine it's spring time and a girl with beautiful lush, fair hair peeking out of her scarf, is sitting on a bench on college campus reading *Adieu Gary Cooper*... How am I not supposed to fall in love with her suddenly? What happened? How did I lose you? Everything was so good at the beginning, wasn't it? The laughs we shared... Together we laughed at everything... everything! Even the day when the Police stopped us in the park and asked how we were related, we laughed. A whole lot of questions about you from me...! A whole lot about me from you... and all the answers were wrong! You said my aunt's name was Homa... and I don't even have an aunt to begin with! And I said your uncle was fat and had a thick moustache... and your uncle was only twelve at that time! They held us for a night, remember? I got beaten up a little bit, too! You know, he asked me about my job and I told him that I'm a story writer and he thought I was making fun of him... he slapped me in the face. And then those hard times of driving a taxi ... going to the university in the mornings, and driving my friend's rickety old Perykan cab at nights. Wasn't it somewhere in the middle of all that cab driving that I lost you? All of a sudden I opened my eyes and realized that you were gone, that I no longer had you... I'd left you behind somewhere... but don't exactly know where.

Hamoun becomes choked up with tears. He busies himself with his Lego. Lego pieces fall from his hands. He gets himself under control again.

HAMOUN   Don't worry, I'm fine. It's getting late and I still haven't told you the main thing I wanted to. I've been avoiding it on purpose because it's not easy to talk about it. I want to tell you about my illness. You're entitled to know about it. Maybe I'm telling you this so I can believe it myself, too. My illness isn't contagious. I'm telling you this so you don't have to worry about touching this recorder. I mean it won't be transferred through germs or anything like that. This is not rabies or MS or Cellular-Muscular cancer. This is Acute Lymphocytic Leukaemia. It means destroying the body in order to rebuild the mind. Simply put, it's kind of contracting of the body in favour of expanding the mind. A kind of physical deterioration and an insane expansion of thought. We can call it mind cancer... a very rare kind of brain cancer. An unknown illness that only one in every ten-billion, seven-hundred-million, nine-hundred and thirty-five-thousand people have. There is no known cure for it but its progress can be slowed down. I mean they drill a hole on your back and insert a tube into your body parallel to the spinal cord. It settles on the nerves and reduces their sensitivity. It's painful, so painful that more than feeling the pain, the patient gets shocked from the intensity of it. I was really stunned at how much pain the body could endure. *(He laughs.)*

The first time I realized I had this disease was when I felt that I had shrunk to the size of a molecule and crawled into the minds of my family. You wouldn't believe it, but I was really inside their minds. I couldn't help it but I heard things that I shouldn't have. Since that time three years ago, I noticed that all my life has become their voices. Dad's loneliness... Mom's sorrows... Parniyan's fears... Mahan's tiredness... and I mean their voices, not their words. I heard their voices and felt my mind was exploding under the pressure. I would go into convulsions and bite my tongue... But I'm fine now... quite fine... *(He turns off the recorder with difficulty and turns to us.)* Doctors have told me that every one of my cells will get smaller and smaller until one night when the illness will deal its final blow. Then everything will be over. The body will be over but the monstrous energy of your mind will spread everywhere. You'll turn into a fluid voice and then you'll be everywhere. Tonight is the night. April 27th! They don't know what my disease exactly is... but is it possible that they have forgotten that today is my birthday?

Lights go out suddenly. The sound of the stones grinding... The sound of walls falling down... A thunderous sound...

ROOM FOUR – THE ROOF

On the roof. Midnight. The roof is unusually small. The evaporative air cooler, the satellite dish, and the TV antenna are all entangled.

A sheet is hanging from the clothesline. There is just enough space for one person to stand and that space is occupied by Mahan. There are many white balloons filled with gas and tied to the clothesline. Mahan is still busy blowing the balloons up with gas. A small sports bag lies beside him. His cellphone rings. He looks around to find his cellphone.

MAHAN Hello... Hello... Me? Right here... on the roof. Yep, I'm all ready. Where are you?... *(He glances around.)* No, I can't see you... where are you?... Where? ...which direction? I'm looking that way... No, I can't see you. Hang on! Geographically, you must be in the west... or, to be more precise, north-west. Hello?... Let me see... No, I can't really see you. I'm looking in the same direction... near that skyscraper... *(Suddenly)* Aha! I see you! Got you! Do you see me, too? Wave if you see me. Yeah, that's me. *(He waves.)* What are those things beside you?... You don't really want to carry three suitcases with you, do you? What's inside them?... Are you crazy? You can find all that stuff over there... Why do you want to bring extra luggage?... Me? *(He points at his bag.)* Just this... I said just this one. There is nothing in it. Just a bunch of clothes, a dictionary, an electric toothbrush and... that's all. Light as a feather... No, of course it's not enough. You should blow up more balloons! We've still got some time. *(He takes a look at his watch.)* Ten minutes and thirty seconds ... Because only then we'll be all set.

It's really simple... an equation between air current, our weight, and the gravity. There's only one moment at the sunrise when the atmospheric pressure reaches a degree which makes it possible for take-off. It means the gravity index multiplied by the Theodor number plus the weight divided by the atmospheric pressure... and then fraction of the result divided by the wind velocity. Theoretically, it's perfect! It's a simple solution for a complex problem. And basically when a problem is complicated, it's better not to make it more complicated with a complicated solution. Otherwise the problem will resonate and their synthesis will become hyper-complicated. You see what I mean?... It's really amazing that you understand what I mean, because Dad,

Mum and Parniyan never understand me at all. The only one who sometimes understands me is Hamoun but the problem is that I don't understand him... because of his poetic prose.

Listen, Mahsa! This proves that you have no reason to be mixed-up about whether you're finally in love with me or that hook-nosed pseudo-Wittgensteinian idiot Ramtin Tirbayati. I mean, holographically, when your mental orbit is in accordance with my mental orbit, this makes it clear that you're in love with that crazy Ramtin Tirbayati! Because, from a female psychology perspective, love means the unknown. That is, as soon as women don't know something, they either clean forget it or fall in love with it. In your case, the latter has happened. Because apparently you know me very well. Therefore, we come to the conclusion that you must be in love with that Tirbayati, not me ...What? Well, you're coming with me because he can't even imagine that this might be the way to cross the border. This is my theory... my discovery... my genius! Now maybe physiologically, you'll fall in love with me at a height of four hundred feet. Because at that height the blood pressure will change and basically there is a direct relationship between love and blood pressure... Well, not sure enough!... If you tell me what your blood pressure is now... I'm talking about the love theory. What do you mean? ...Oh, OK! The project. Well, we're just testing it out to make sure. I mean if we can get to the lake in the first phase, we sure can cross the border too... Well, experimentally we can't be sure about anything. But logically, yes! I'm sure. I mean I'm sure but not so sure. Well, to be honest, some factors have changed. See, if my distance from the ground was three metres and I weighed forty-nine kilos, then everything would be feasible. But now my distance from the ground is just one metre! ... I don't know how this has happened. Anyway, we have to give it a shot... You keep blowing up the balloons.

He puts his cellphone aside and continues to blow the balloons up with gas. His cellphone rings and he answers it.

MAHAN   Yes dear?... What's up Mahsa?... Scared?... Of what?!... Listen! You should separate natural fear from impressionable fear ... Yes darling? Me? Well, I just have some natural fear but I'm not susceptible to other kinds ... No! No! I'm not making fun of you!... Yes dear?... Afraid of getting homesick? No, not at all. I mean from a familial perspective, I'm the middle child... and the middle child means the excess one. Basically, I don't have a file in their minds, and naturally they don't have any in my mind, either. The middle child means the fileless file! It means invisible. For example, Parniyan has at least got a file, but it's virus-infected. Hamoun's file is blank... nothing. Clear as crystal! However, I'm doing them a great favour. I'm making room for them. Because there has never been a place for me in that house... and I can read that in Mom's eyes when she looks at me and mutters under her breath "What a mistake! What a mistake!" ... Mom, of course, is substantively a peculiar creature. She is the mistress of discovering soap operas that are total nonsense. Seriously, what's good about this stupid series?! A man falls in love with a woman who feeds the birds outside the window, but in the end, he can't be united with her and kills himself. It's a catastrophe from a dramatic and aesthetic point of view ...Well, no! This series isn't my main reason for sure. I'm not sure what my reasons exactly are and how logical they are. Maybe I'm deluded about my reasons and I don't actually have any reason for leaving at all...

Hamoun cranes his neck. His face is pale and he is unusually thin and weak, sitting on a wheelchair. Mahan turns to us exactly at the same time.

MAHAN *(aside)* Sure I do! I have a good reason, but I can't say what it is. Mahsa asks if my reasons for leaving are good enough and I know that they are. From the moment that I decided not to make do with a grade of fifteen anymore[3], this moment began to take shape. From the first year in elementary school till I was fifteen, I only got fifteens in a row. My report cards were all fifteen, in the line at school I was the fifteenth, my birthday was the fifteenth of some month. When I was fifteen, all of a sudden I began to hate fifteen, to hate being this ordinary... being so mediocre... then I hammered away at my studies. I started reading and reading and reading... so much so that I went from one who only got fifteen to ranking fourteenth in the university entrance exam. But something strange had happened. Nobody wanted me anymore.

When I was a professional fifteener everybody liked me. I looked harmless and safe to them! But after that, they all began to ignore me. I became a stranger among other fifteeners. Nobody wanted to talk to me. They would either make fun of me or bully me. I was going mad. All of a sudden I began to realize how lonely I was and how many fifteeners were out there and what a strong sense of unity they all had. A kind of overt Freemasonry, where an outsider is condemned to either death or invisibility. When I opened my eyes, I found myself on the rooftop with fifteen balloons. I don't quite get it right now. It will only be tomorrow that I'll begin to see what has happened. When I blew up the first balloon, it was like the house started to crumble somehow.

Hamoun exits. Mahan becomes emotional for a moment. Then he composes himself and takes a look at his watch. He stops blowing up the balloons.

MAHAN   Hello? Mahsa! Are you still there?... No, I'm fine! ...moaning? No, I'm really fine. ... Look, it's almost time! We only have four minutes. Fasten the balloons to yourself. First the suitcases... then yourself... Keep the last one until the right time.

Mahan fastens a balloon to his sports bag. The bag goes up in the sky. He looks at it excitedly. He slowly fastens the rest of the balloons to himself. He keeps the last balloon fastened to the clothesline. Then he dials a number.

MAHAN   Dear Mom and Dad. When I'm leaving this message, you'll be fast asleep and when you hear this message I'll be high in the sky flying with the balloons left over from my childhood. I know that you'll be upset that I didn't stay and put up with things, that from an epic perspective, you were so much like Castro and Spartacus and we, the spoiled, sissy rap kids of this generation, aren't like you used to be. But actually we are!

At least I'm similar to you. You know when I decided to leave here, Dad? One day when you were sleeping, I watched your face carefully and saw that we were very similar. Suddenly, I got scared by how similar our faces looked. You never know! Maybe our destinies would be similar, too. Maybe the sperm that made me has given me more than your face... what if it has given me your future, too? What if my whole life is spent paying a mortgage? No, dear Mom and Dad! I don't want to repeat everything you've said... If I had gone, if I had said, if I hadn't backed down, if I had backed down. I've heard enough. I hate this "if" as damn much as I hate the number fifteen. Exactly as much as I hate fifteen. I just wanted to say goodbye. This is Mahan... the middle son ...Goodbye!

Mahan seems to be drained of energy. He chokes with tears and turns the cellphone off. A moment of silence. He takes a look at his watch and springs up.

MAHAN It's time! It's time!... *(He rapidly dials a number.)* Mahsa, it's time! Tie the balloons... to your hand. You must tie them to your hand and your coat buttons ... then come to the edge of the roof... Yes, you should close your eyes and lean over as if you're flinging yourself down. Well, your centre of gravity should form a Sine axis with the balloons' centre of gravity at a three hundred seventy two degree angle. You got that? Three hundred seventy-two... And the distance between your feet must be twenty-nine centimetres. I can't put too much pressure on this roof because I'm afraid it will collapse... but you push down as hard as you can to go up higher... That's good...

Mahan fastens the last balloon to himself.

MAHAN *(to his cell phone)* Three, two, one, go!

Mahan goes on the edge of the roof. He is about to fling himself down. But nothing happens. He pulls back just in time in order not to fall down. He tries several times but it is no use. He looks at his watch disappointedly and heaves a sigh of regret. Something in the sky catches his attention. It seems like a trace moving away in the sky. He does not talk on the phone anymore. He talks to that invisible trace in the sky.

MAHAN   Mahsa! Are you gone?... Me?... No, my calculations were wrong. I told you, remember? That the distance between the roof and the ground has shrunk... No, you go! Go, Mahsa! Because, schizophrenically, you may only be a hallucination ... Yes, I can see you, dear. But optically this whole thing could be an illusion. It could all have come out of my insane desire to fly away to a faraway place. Maybe you're now sitting with that asshole Ramtin Tirbayati laughing at a crazy boy with his balloons on the roof. And if we look at it from the point of view of regretting, maybe you actually are flying away right now, from a masculine psychological projection perspective, I'm visualizing you at that hook-nosed, fifteener Ramtin Tirbayati's place... *(He waves to the sky.)* I don't know which one would make me happier – you being in the sky or with Ramtin Tirbayati ...To tell you the truth, neither of them. In either case, I've lost you. I've lost you, Mahsa, and everything is over.

Upset, Mahan stands up, goes to the edge of the roof and jumps off. Hamoun enters at the same time. He is sitting in the wheelchair, not able to move or talk much. He can hardly speak. He is even weaker than before. He is still holding his box and his recorder in his hands.

With the last remnants of his energy, Hamoun stretches his hand out and unties the balloon strings fastened to Mahan's bag. He knocks off the Lego box, which falls down and spreads out on the ground. The bag lands in Hamoun's hands. He struggles to unzip the bag with his crippled hands. There is only one item inside the bag: an old family photo album.

HAMOUN *(to the recorder)* You know what's in the bag?! A family photo album. It had been lost. Nobody knew Mahan had it. This is the heaviest luggage any passenger can take... Don't worry. He's fine. He did jump off but nothing bad really happened. Because the distance between the roof and the ground is less than one metre now. From the early evening, he knew that the house was getting smaller and smaller. He could have gone on another roof and jumped off from there. But in the deepest reaches of his heart he wanted to have a trap door... an escape hatch... he is now sitting in the yard thinking about all the frustrations that have been eating him these last few days. That it makes no difference whether he stays or leaves. If he stays, this damn if, this "if I had gone" would drive him crazy. And if he does go abroad, there would always be a gaping wound in his heart, which would pain him whenever somebody as much as mentions here. The kind of pain that no one knows how to deal with. Mahan will forget Mahsa within two weeks and fall in love for the twenty-fifth time, but he can never get rid of the chronic loneliness of someone who is no longer a professional fifteener...

A moment of silence.

HAMOUN   Never mind all this stuff. These are the last moments, Niloufar! I don't know what will happen to me until dawn. I don't know how I will get so small that my body disappears. But in any case, I am already missing you so much... missing you and the walls of this house. Have I told you that me and this house are alter egos? I was conceived here on the first day that my mom, who I've never seen, and my dad, set foot in this house. The mortgage for this house has finally come to an end today. The house has also come to an end. I've come to an end, too. Didn't I tell you we were alter egos?... Don't worry, I'm fine. I get lighter as time goes by. This is compensation for all the pain. As if I'm everywhere now. My voice is everywhere. It's been several years since I've lost you. I know there is no way this recording will ever get to you. I have no address for you. But I still love you... as much as the first day. *(To us.)* There is one more thing that I should say. There are some things that I should rescue before they get smashed under the weight of the walls... Now I'm sure they've forgotten that tonight, April 27th, is my birthday. *(He takes a Lego piece.)* I kiss this one for Mom and Dad. *(He takes another Lego.)* I kiss this one for Parniyan and this one for Mahan. I didn't get to say goodbye to them.

Light goes out suddenly. The sound of stones grinding... The sound of walls tumbling down... A thunderous sound...

THE FINAL ROOM

Similar to the fist scene. Roya/Azad/Parniyan/Mahan are standing over the maquette of a house. Only this time the maquette is smashed and they are taking out Hamoun's Lego pieces one by one. All of them are excited. Quite a few Lego pieces are piled up on the ground. The place where Hamoun was sitting before is now empty. Instead of him an invisible hand places a fish bowl, a clock, an old TV and a family photo album on the ground one by one. We can hear Hamoun muttering an old song under his breath.

AZAD　　　　There is another one over there.

MAHAN　　　　Yep! I see it.

ROYA　　　　No! Don't take it out, Mahan! Parniyan's hand is smaller. She can reach it.

PARNIYAN　　　　Here! I got it.

AZAD　　　　Aha! This is one of those handy four-cornered ones?

MAHAN　　　　Look! There are a few more over there.

PARNIYAN　　　　Shall I get them?

MAHAN　　　　I'll take care of it.

ROYA　　　　Be careful not to get your hand stuck in there.

PARNIYAN　　　　Wow, how many pieces are there?

MAHAN　　　　Exactly five.

PARNIYAN　　　　I meant the whole thing.

ROYA　　　　No idea! We haven't counted them all yet.

AZAD　　　　There should be around two or three hundred.

MAHAN　　　　From an enumeration perspective, there are exactly two-hundred and thirty-two pieces.

PARNIYAN　　　　Wow! That's a lot.

MAHAN　　　　There should be at least one more piece.

ROYA　　　　How do you know?

MAHAN　　　　Lego pieces are always an odd number.

AZAD　　　　Here! I've got it.

MAHAN	This is it!
ROYA	You mean that's all?
AZAD	I can't see anything else.
PARNIYAN	Me too! This smell!
MAHAN	What smell?! *(He sniffs the Lego.)*
PARNIYAN	Ah! It smells like Hamoun... *(They all smell the Lego parts in their hands.)*

Parniyan and Mahan play jauntily with the Lego pieces like children. Roya and Azad still stand beside the smashed maquette.

ROYA	How bizarre! His toys are here, but he himself isn't.
AZAD	Maybe he's somehow sneaked out.
ROYA	Maybe.

ROYA/AZAD *(together)* He set my mind at ease anyway.

They both laugh and gently pull each other's hair.[4]

ROYA	You go first.
AZAD	No, you first.
ROYA	Well, if he's found his childhood toys in the basement and brought them up here, it means he's fine. Maybe he's been playing.
AZAD	I just want to say the same thing. If he was playing he couldn't have been feeling too bad. And he's not the kind of boy who feels bad anyway.
ROYA	Knock on wood! He's always happy, always doing something.
AZAD	Exactly! I'm sure he's doing something now, too...
ROYA	Thank God! I was so worried about him.
PARNIYAN *(to Mahan)*	No, Not there! Not there. Put it here.
MAHAN	OK, give it to me.
AZAD	What are you doing?
PARNIYAN	Building a house.

MAHAN   Logically, it'd be foolish to build a house in this situation, but from a foolish point of view, it's totally logical.

ROYA *(laughs)* Well, do whatever you want to do, just hurry up, because it may rain any minute now.

Roya and Azad join in the play with a childlike enthusiasm.

MAHAN *(joyfully)* Then let's build the roof first.

ROYA   Azad?

AZAD   Yes, darling?

ROYA *(taken aback)* What did you say, dear?

AZAD *(taken aback too)* What did you say?!

ROYA   No, what did you say?

AZAD   I said, "Yes, darling".

ROYA   I said do you know how to build a tin roof? The kind of roof that you can hear the rain on.

PARNIYAN   Can anyone really live in here?

ROYA   Let's not talk about it right now. Instead, let's see what we can do for a tin roof.

MAHAN   From a structural assessment perspective, it's not impossible of course but I need a calculator.

AZAD   No need for a calculator. Here you go! I'll build it in a minute. Piece of cake.

ROYA   Really?

AZAD   You think I can't?

ROYA   I think it'll definitely be great.

PARNIYAN   Now that it's got a tin roof, think about the windows too. I mean those huge windows which are the size of a human.

ROYA   Right on! If you find thirty, forty pieces this size, I'll build it myself.

AZAD *(building the roof)* And I'm telling you, it's going to be south-facing.

MAHAN   You mean because of the yard?

AZAD   Because of the pergola that I'm going to build in its yard.

ROYA   Can it have a TV-room, too?

AZAD   Why not?

PARNIYAN   A pond! A pond! A pond is the most important thing. We can have some goldfish in it.

AZAD   You build that yourself.

MAHAN   Not blue, green, OK?

PARNIYAN   A green pond? It might look like a vomit bowl!

AZAD/ROYA *(together)* Parniyan!

PARNIYAN   OK, OK! I said "might"!

MAHAN   Can we build an attic for me to put my telescope and other stuff in there?

ROYA   Only if you promise you wouldn't spend your whole day in there.

MAHAN   Well, no! Because from the bladder point of view, it's not possible.

ROYA   I meant from the point of view of seeing you, you twat!

MAHAN *(incredulously)* Is that a new name?!

ROYA   Not too new.

PARNIYAN   Dad! I want it to be a first-class house.

ROYA *(philosophically)* First-class house has nothing to do with these things. It has to do with the people living in it; otherwise, no matter how fancy and flashy, it won't be any different from a hotel or a prison for that matter.

PARNIYAN   Wow! My philosopher mom!

AZAD   How is the roof now?

ROYA   Perfect!

AZAD   So, stop talking and get down to business. Back to work before it starts raining.

They all get back to work cheerfully. Spotlight is on the objects that Hamoun has salvaged from the smashed house: the TV, the clock, the family album, and the fish bowl.

HAMOUN'S VOICE   They still don't know what they want to make this time. Maybe another house. A place where the dead come back to life... where foetuses can grow up... a place where you can fly up to the sky from the roof and see the stars; where you can talk to your imagination through its walls... That's how homes are, after all! Like humans... they sulk, they make up, they get ugly... get beautiful... they catch acute hepkolamphadia! That's what homes are! The best places in the world...

Lights down.

The End

Nagmeh Samini

Naghmeh Samini was born in 1973 in Iran. She received her BA in Drama and her MA in Cinema, both from the University of Tehran. She holds a PhD in Drama and Mythology. More than twenty of Samini's plays have been staged in Iran, France, and India. An award-winning playwright, she has also written several screenplays.

Samini has been working as a Professor of Drama at the Faculty of Dramatic Arts at the University of Tehran since 2005 and has also run several workshops in Iran and abroad. As a researcher, she has published books on *One Thousand and One Nights* as well as drama and mythology in Iran.

Some of Samini's awards and achievements include: Best Book of the Year in Iran for Myth's Theatre, *An Archetypical Approach to Iranian Dramatic Literature*, 2009; Winner of the Best Playwright in the Second Playwrights' Forum Festival, 2008; Winner of the Best Screenwriter in the International Fajr Film Festival, 2007; Winner of the Best Playwright in the City of Tehran, 2005; Winner of the Best Playwright in the International Fajr Theatre Festival in the years 2001, 2002, 2003, and 2004; One of the selected playwrights by the "Center of Dialogue between Civilizations", 2003; Best Woman Film Critic and the Best Playwright in "Kwosar" Cinema Festival, 1997.

About the Play
Mohammad Yaghoubi

The revolution that toppled the Shah's monarchy in 1979 resulted in the creation of the Islamic Republic of Iran with Ayatollah Khomeini at its helm. The spring of freedom was soon followed by the reign of terror and the Iran-Iraq war. By 1982, wearing the veil was mandatory for all women, the governmental, educational and cultural institutions had been cleansed of all anti-revolutionary elements, and the prisons were filled with members of opposition groups.

After the eight-year war with Iraq ended in 1988, Rafsanjani became president and facilitated a number of social and economic reforms. In 1998, Khatami became president during which time individual and social freedoms gained increased legitimacy as well as freedom of expression and freedom of the press.

During Rafsanjani's presidency, a group of writers, publishers and newspaper people were harassed, threatened and killed by unidentified individuals. This became known as the Chain-killings. During Khatami's second term in office, it became clear that the Chain-killings had been instigated by individuals within the Ministry of Information and Security.

A Moment of Silence has been hailed as the best play to emerge from Iran since the 1979 Revolution. Among its many awards are Toronto Fringe Festival's 2015 New Play contest and the Playwrights' Society of Iran's Best Play prize. It has been translated into English, French, Czech, Turkish and Kurdish.

"An unexpected contemporary play from a culture we do not meet every day, A Moment of Silence... charts the recent history of the country of which we hear plenty on the news but about which we do not know that much." – Michaela Příkopová, Prague.

A MOMENT OF SILENCE

Mohammad Yaghoubi

translated by Torange Yeghiazarian & Mohammad Yaghoubi

To my dearest, my love, Aida

The English premiere was presented by Nowadays Theatre Company at SummerWorks Performance Festival at Factory Theatre, Mainspace, Toronto, Canada, August 6th to 14th, 2016 with the generous support of the Toronto Arts Council.
The cast was as follows:

SHIVA	Sarah Marchand
JIMMY	Maxime Robin
SHIRIN	Parmida Kakavand
SHEIDA	Melanie Pyne
HASTI	Lara Arabian
SOHRAB	Paul Van Dyck
MEN'S VOICES	Art Babayants
WOMEN'S VOICES	Jada Rifkin
ANNOUNCER'S VOICE	

Director – Mohammad Yaghoubi

Stage Designer – Saeed Hasanlou

Lighting Designer – David DeGrow

Live Music – Pedran Khavarzamini

Costume Designer – Setareh Delzendeh

Stage Manager – Steve Vargo

Assistant Directors – Art Babayants, Marjan Moosavi, Mona Ketabian

Photographer – Bahareh Ahmadi

Characters

SHIVA – female, 24

JIMMY (JAMSHID) – male, 25, Shirin's husband

SHIRIN – female, 26, Shiva's older sister

SHEIDA – female, 29, Shiva's eldest sister

HASTI – female, 30, playwright

SOHRAB – male, 35, Hasti's husband

VOICES on the phone **KAYVAN, RAMIN**

MEN'S VOICES

WOMEN'S VOICES

ANNOUNCER'S VOICE

A VOICE

Time
Twenty year period from 1980 – 2000

Setting
Shirin's three-bedroom apartment.
Sohrab and Hasti's two-bedroom apartment.
Both are situated in Tehran, Iran.

1.SHIVA

The door of a bedroom opens slowly. Shiva cautiously enters. She looks frightened. She doesn't know where she is.

SHIVA *(at the doorway)* Anybody there?

Shiva rushes toward the phone, dials a number.

WOMAN'S VOICE Hello?

SHIVA　　　　　I'd like to speak with Mr. Arshia, please!

WOMAN'S VOICE You've dialled the wrong number.

Shiva hangs up and dials the number again.

WOMAN'S VOICE Hello?

SHIVA　　　　　Is this *Iran Daily*?

WOMAN'S VOICE Yes, how can I help you?

SHIVA　　　　　I'd like to speak with Mr. Arshia, please.

WOMAN'S VOICE Which department, ma'am?

SHIVA　　　　　The editorial.

WOMAN'S VOICE This is the editorial, but there is no Mr. Arshia.

SHIVA　　　　　Mr. Arshia is the editor of the paper.

WOMAN'S VOICE Mr. Arshia is not the editor and we have no Mr. Arshia in this department.

SHIVA　　　　　Put me through to the editor's office, please.

WOMAN'S VOICE Excuse me, who do you want to talk to? Mr. Arshia or the editor?

SHIVA　　　　　Mr. Kayvan Arshia, the editor.

WOMAN'S VOICE Mr. Arshia is not the editor of this newspaper, ma'am.

SHIVA　　　　　It's urgent. Put me through to the editor, please.

WOMAN'S VOICE He's not available now, but you can leave a message for him.

SHIVA　　　　　Put me through right away! I'm his wife.

WOMAN'S VOICE *(laughing)* Is this a joke? I'd recognize his wife's voice.

SHIVA *(angrily)* Who is this speaking?

WOMAN'S VOICE Why do you ask?

SHIVA   Put me through to Mrs. Gooran.

WOMAN'S VOICE Who is Mrs. Gooran supposed to be?

SHIVA   The editor's secretary.

WOMAN'S VOICE *(laughing)* I am the editor's secretary.

SHIVA   How long have you been there?

WOMAN'S VOICE I don't have time to go back and forth with you like this.

SHIVA   Put the damn phone through to my husband, I need help.

WOMAN'S VOICE Listen, ma'am. You're just keeping the line busy for no good reason. I am the editor's secretary and I'm telling you that Mr. Arshia, your husband, is not the editor of this newspaper.

SHIVA   Since when?

WOMAN'S VOICE How the hell should I know?

The Woman hangs up. Shiva hangs up the phone desperately then dials another number.

WOMAN'S VOICE Hello?

SHIVA   Sorry, I must have dialled the wrong number.

Hangs up and dials again

WOMAN'S VOICE Hello?

SHIVA   Excuse me, is this Mr. Arami's home?

WOMAN'S VOICE No, ma'am, you've dialled the wrong number.

SHIVA   Oh, I'm sorry.

Hangs up and dials again. The same woman answers as before.

WOMAN'S VOICE Hello?

SHIVA   Sorry, I dialled 651440, but it seems to connect incorrectly.

WOMAN'S VOICE This is the right number, who do you want to talk to?

SHIVA My brother. This is his phone number.

WOMAN'S VOICE Who's this speaking?

SHIVA This is Shiva.

WOMAN'S VOICE What's your brother name?

SHIVA Shahram.

WOMAN'S VOICE They must have given you the wrong number.

SHIVA *(repeats hesitantly)* 651440?

WOMAN'S VOICE Yes, maybe your brother used to live here before us, I don't know.

SHIVA How long have you been living there?

WOMAN'S VOICE About seven or eight months.

SHIVA Something must be wrong, I dialled 651440.

WOMAN'S VOICE You dialled the right number, this is 651440, but this is not your brother's home. Listen, I'm sorry but I don't feel too good and my nerves are shot, please don't call here again.

SHIVA I'm really sorry. I don't mean to bother you, but I'm sure this is my brother's phone number.

WOMAN'S VOICE How many times do I need to tell you? 651440 is not your brother's number. It is the number to my home!

SHIVA I'm sorry.

The Woman hangs up. Shiva hangs up, desperate and confused. She looks frightened. She examines the money on the table looking surprised. Shiva then notices the newspaper on the table and looks through it and dials another number.

MAN'S VOICE Hello?

SHIVA Excuse me, sir. What year is this?

MAN'S VOICE What do you mean?

SHIVA Would you please tell me what year it is?

MAN'S VOICE Hey Niloo, you little fox!

SHIVA   No. I just dialled randomly, can't even remember the number I dialled... just want to know what year it is.

MAN'S VOICE What year do you want it to be, baby?

SHIVA   I beg you, please tell me what year it is.

MAN   It's 1980.

SHIVA   Really?

MAN   Stop pulling my leg, baby. OK, I give up. Who the hell are you?

Sound of a key turning in the keyhole. Shiva hangs up the phone. Jimmy enters.

JIMMY   Well, well. Hello, Shiva.

SHIVA   Who are you? Don't come near me!

JIMMY   My name is Jamshid but they call me Jimmy.

Jimmy approaches her.

SHIVA   Don't come near me. *(Jimmy continues to approach her.)* I warn you, stop!

2. MOSQUITOES

The sound of a TV program is heard in the darkness. Lights up, slowly. Shirin is watching TV. Jimmy is reading a book.

JIMMY *(very loudly)* I'm an attractive man.

SHIRIN   Shut up Jimmy, you scared me.

JIMMY   It's written here. Flies only bite attractive people. *(Reads from the book.)* David Butler, an insect expert from the University of Florida claims that mosquitoes never bite indiscriminately. In fact, they choose their target.

Shirin continues to watch TV, Jimmy reads louder facing away from Shirin.

JIMMY   Mosquitoes distinguish between attractive and unattractive people through their body odour and then choose the most delicious ones—

SHIRIN   That's enough, Jimmy, I'm watching TV.

JIMMY   OK, listen to me as you're watching.

SHIRIN   How can I do both at the same time?

JIMMY   Why not? It's like me saying I can't shift the gear or talk to my passengers because I'm holding the wheel.

SHIRIN   Will you let me watch this movie, Jimmy? I already know you're an attractive man, darling.

Jimmy picks up the receiver and dials, a man answers.

MAN'S VOICE Hello?

JIMMY   Up yours!

Jimmy dials again, another man answers.

MAN'S VOICE Hello?

JIMMY   Shit-head!

Dials again. A woman answers.

WOMAN'S VOICE Hello?

JIMMY   Hello, Good afternoon!

WOMAN'S VOICE Good afternoon!

JIMMY   How're you doing?

WOMAN'S VOICE Fine, thanks, who is this?

JIMMY   This is Jamshid but they call me Jimmy.

WOMAN'C VOICE Who do you want to talk to?

JIMMY   Excuse me, I just wanted to ask you a question.

WOMAN'S VOICE Yes?

JIMMY   Thanks. I wonder, do mosquitoes bite you, ma'am?

WOMAN'S VOICE How dare you!

JIMMY   Seriously. *(Shirin approaches him.)* I'm reading a book right now called *About Insects* by David Butler. On page five, it says that mosquitoes only bite attractive people. My question for you is, do they bite you too?

WOMAN'S VOICE Yes, they bite me a lot. You too—?

Shirin grabs the receiver and listens for a second before hanging up.

SHIRIN   Who the hell was that?

JIMMY   How should I know?

SHIRIN   Don't lie to me, Jimmy.

JIMMY   Why should I lie? I'm not afraid of you.

SHIRIN   Don't do this again, Jimmy. I don't like it.

JIMMY   And I don't like it that you prefer the TV to me; that you never listen to what I say.

SHIRIN   Fine! Read it to me.

JIMMY *(reads from the book)* "David Butler, an insect expert from University of Florida—

SHIRIN   You already read that part.

JIMMY   ...claims mosquitoes never bite indiscriminately. In fact, they choose their target. Mosquitoes distinguish between attractive and unattractive people through their body odour and then choose the most delicious ones. They prefer targets rich in cholesterol and Vitamin B, meaning me. They can distinguish the scent of an attractive man," meaning me, "from four miles away. During exhalation, carbon dioxide and other fragrant body odours dissipate in the air. This appetizing odour", meaning me, "alerts mosquitoes of a delicious target nearby."

Mumbles through the last few sentences quickly.

SHIRIN   Is it over, darling?

JIMMY   Not yet, but it looks like you prefer watching TV.

SHIRIN   I missed this movie anyway, so keep reading. But you have to promise to take me to the movies tonight.

JIMMY   You got it!

SHIRIN   Go ahead.

JIMMY *(reads from the book)* "Only the female insects bite. During their pregnancy, they bite to suck the blood out of human veins." Are you listening? It says that only the female ones bite. I was sure the males wouldn't do something like that. The male species is honest, loyal...

SHIRIN What do they do then?

JIMMY They fuck.

A quick light shift indicates passage of time.

JIMMY *(reads from the newspaper)* "Steel Formation?"

SHIRIN Which theatres?

JIMMY Rivoli.

SHIRIN What else?

JIMMY *"The White Buffalo"*, starring Charles Bronson, Astara Theatre.

SHIRIN Something else?

JIMMY Let's see a comedy. *Six Naughty Officers* starring Louis de Funés *(Reads from the newspaper)* "Full of laughter and clean family fun! You will enjoy watching it again and again!" Pars Theatre.

SHIRIN *(overlapping with Jimmy reading)* Not that one! What else is showing? Something else.

JIMMY *The Tough One* starring Franco Nero, "TISFOON" Theatre.

SHIRIN No.

JIMMY *Night over Chile?*

SHIRIN Where is it showing?

JIMMY *The Brute and the Tramp* starring Jean-Paul—

SHIRIN Which theatre is showing *Night over Chile*?

JIMMY Diana.

SHIRIN Let's see that one.

JIMMY I don't feel like watching a political movie. It just isn't my kind of a film.

SHIRIN Please …

JIMMY OK, if you insist.

Lighting shifts to the other space.

SHIVA No. I just dialled randomly, can't even remember the number I dialled... just want to know what year it is.

MAN What year do you want it to be, baby?

SHIVA I beg you – please tell me what year it is.

MAN It's 1980.

SHIVA Really?

MAN Stop pulling my leg, baby. OK, I give up. Who the hell are you?

Sound of a key turning in the keyhole. Shiva hangs up the phone. Jimmy enters.

JIMMY Well, well. Hello, Shiva.

SHIVA Who are you? Don't come near me!

JIMMY My name is Jamshid but they call me Jimmy.

Jimmy approaches her.

SHIVA Don't come near me. *(Jimmy continues approaching her.)* I warn you, stop!

Shirin and Sheida anxiously appear at the doorway.

SHIRIN *(joyfully)* Shiva!

SHEIDA Shiva, sweetheart!

3. HASTI

Hasti puts some books on the table. Then she puts a handheld video camera on the books, pushes the record button and sits on the sofa in front of the camera.

HASTI Sohrab!

SOHRAB *(offstage)* Yeah?

HASTI Hurry up! The camera is ready.

SOHRAB *(off)* Just go ahead without me.

HASTI Oh, come on. I want to introduce you.

SOHRAB OK. I'm coming.

Hasti pushes the record button of the video camera and sits in front of it.

HASTI Hi, Mom! I read your letter. So happy to read that you are getting used to your new surroundings. I'll be sending you videotape messages from time to time to let you know about my life. I'm glad I don't have to write letters anymore!

Sohrab comes in.

HASTI This is much better than writing boring letters, right? Let me quickly end the suspense and introduce you to this distinguished gentleman next to me. This is Sohrab, my husband. Yes, I've got married again, last week. Now, I'll let Sohrab speak to you directly.

SOHRAB Hello there! Well, I–I don't know what I should say. Anyway, we are married. I would love to meet you —

HASTI Tell her about your work. He's a director, Mom.

Telephone rings.

SOHRAB I should answer the phone.

HASTI Talk to my mom!

SOHRAB Hope to see you here soon.

Sohrab moves to the phone.

HASTI Mom, please don't worry about me anymore.

SOHRAB Hello? Hello? Hello?

HASTI I promise you I'm happy, really happy. Do not worry at all! OK, I'm sure you would like to see our house, I'll pick up the camera and show it to you later, all the rooms and everything. Mom, I miss you so much! Come back please. *(Shows a photo)* Mom, this sweet doll is Sohrab's daughter from his first wife. She mainly lives with Sohrab's mother. Unfortunately, his wife became ill and passed away two years ago. Look how sweet she is! This way I don't need to give birth to a child. You know how much I fear being pregnant. Fortunately, Sohrab doesn't want to have another kid. Well, it's now time to show you the house. I've prepared a special piece of music to play while you are looking at our home. Listen to it while you're watching. It's a special song for you.

4. WHAT DO YOU REMEMBER?

Sohrab lies on the sofa, reading a book. Hasti enters and sits beside him, strokes his hair.

HASTI   What comes to mind when you first think of the year 1980? I myself remember street riots and clashes, bombs, and executions. What do you remember? When someone says "1980," what do you think of?

SOHRAB   Hijab. Just imagine, before 1980 most women used to go out without a headscarf. I remember the first time my mother came home from work wearing one. I really couldn't recognize her at first. I thought she was a stranger! For a long time, I couldn't understand why all women accepted to wear that thing.

HASTI   As if they had a choice.

SOHRAB   I'll never forget the first time our literature teacher came to the classroom wearing a chador.

HASTI   The one you fell in love with?

SOHRAB   Yeah. She used to only wear miniskirts, nothing else would do. Until one day, she came to school fully covered. It was unbelievable! The same women we used to see without head scarves, in short dresses, were covered up just two months later.

Telephone rings.

SOHRAB   Hello? Hello? *(Hangs up the phone.)*

HASTI   What else do you remember from 1980?

SOHRAB   A series of names and words.

HASTI   Like what?

SOHRAB   The oppressed.

HASTI   What else?

SOHRAB   Dictatorship.

HASTI   Would you write down what you remember from 1980 for me?

SOHRAB   Are you writing a new play?

HASTI	Yeah.
SOHRAB	What is the title?
HASTI	Goodbye until I don't know when.

Lighting shifts.

SOHRAB   Hello? Hello? Um, I can hear you're breathing. Say something, please ... Nothing? OK. Bye bye! *(Hangs up the phone.)* Maybe somebody doesn't like my voice.

HASTI   Keep going.

SOHRAB   Imperialism, world domination. Cultural purification. Executions. Personal vendettas. I remember one of our neighbours, he was an army officer, in those chaotic days when everybody could carry a gun, someone knocked on his door, he opened the door and bang! The guy simply shot him. You remember how being a revolutionary was fashionable back then. Everybody used to talk politics. I remember my brother's room used to be full of photos of pop stars but after the revolution, he tore down everything and put up pictures of martyrs and revolutionaries. Looking at those bloody faces and torn up bodies used to make me feel sick.

HASTI   Yeah. In those days, the city was full of pictures like that: in the streets, on the walls, on the school billboards.

SOHRAB   Sadegh Khalkhali, armed robberies. Changing the names of streets and schools, changing the currency, the nationalization of banks, long lines for gas, revolutionary movies, *Ayandegan* newspaper, and those slogans written on the walls ...

HASTI   What slogans?

SOHRAB   "Bread, Shelter, Freedom. Cover your head or we'll smack your head." I just remembered something written on the wall in capital letters: Read Mardom Newspaper. And someone has added under it: "We read it, what nonsense!" And I remember some songs: *(Sings)* "Iran, Iran, Iran, machine-guns running on..."

HASTI *(overlapping)* "machine-guns running on..."

Telephone rings.

HASTI   Hello?

A MAN   Is this Hasti Yekta?

HASTI   Yes, how may I help you?

THE MAN   Write down your Will, you dirty intellectual! We're going to take care of you one of these days.

Hasti hangs up.

SOHRAB   Who was it?

HASTI   Some arsehole.

5. WHILE YOU WERE SLEEPING

Shiva is sitting between her sister Shirin and Jimmy, Sheida is standing a little far away from Shiva. They are talking simultaneously.

JIMMY   Shah is gone...

SHIVA   Where's dad? I called Shahram's —

JIMMY   We don't have a royal family any more. We are a Republic now, no more Shah. The head of the government is a religious guy.

SHEIDA *(immediately after Shiva's question, overlapping Jimmy)* Shahram and his family left for America, they took father with them. Hey, Jimmy, will you be quiet and let me talk?

SHIRIN   Dad wanted to take you with him but you didn't wake up in time to apply for a passport.

SHEIDA   We'll call them tonight and tell them you've woken up.

SHIVA   Where's Kayvan?

SHIRIN   He'll be here in an hour or two.

SHIVA   You've changed so much.

SHEIDA   Sweetheart, it's been three years since the last time you saw us.

JIMMY *(overlapping from: "Where's Kayvan?")* I wish you were here to see what happened. The people flooded in to the streets shouting: "Down with the Shah!" *(Laughing)* Shah burst into tears!

SHIRIN   Queen Farah also cried.

JIMMY   But it was the Shah who took a fist full of Iran's soil not the Queen.

SHIVA   Oh, my God! What does it mean that I've slept for three years?

JIMMY   Well, maybe you needed it. You were tired.

SHEIDA   Did you ever dream during these three years?

SHIVA   I don't remember anything.

SHIRIN   I've been waiting so long for this day, to take you out. I am dying to see your expression when you look at everything. Jimmy, let's take her out right now. I really want to see her stunned. Look, darling; don't be surprised when you see all the women are wearing headscarves.

SHIVA   Why are they all wearing headscarves?

SHIRIN   There's an Islamic government now, honey. No woman is allowed to go out without hijab. Ebi, who you adored so much, left for America. You'd be amazed when we go out now. Jimmy, would you take us for a ride?

JIMMY *(overlapping)* The revolution happened! They closed all the bars. All the singers left. Everyone who left took a fistful of the homeland's soil, even Ebi, the singer. The homeland almost ran out of soil!

SHIVA   Whose house is this?

SHIRIN   This is ours. Real estate prices fell, we could afford to buy our own place.

JIMMY *(overlapping)* The previous owner of this house took a fistful of homeland's soil too!

SHIVA *(to Sheida)* What's wrong with you?

SHEIDA   I'm just happy that you're awake.

JIMMY   Shiva?

Shiva turns toward him but Jimmy stares at her without saying a word.

SHIVA   Yeah?

JIMMY   Just keep looking at me like that so I can figure out which animal you look like.

SHIRIN   Jimmy, come on! This is not the time.

JIMMY   Behind every human face, there is an animal which you can't recognize. But because I am an animal expert, I can immediately figure it out *(Stares at Shiva).*

SHIRIN   At least tell her the whole story. Jimmy used to study Zoology, but they closed all the universities after the Cultural Revolution.

JIMMY   And now I'm a taxi driver. What's wrong with that?

SHIRIN   No one said anything.

JIMMY   You keep looking at me.

SHIRIN   Why don't you first tell us which animal you are, Jimmy.

JIMMY   Donkey, and sometimes, dog. I'm alternating between the two.

6. SHEIDA

Sheida is alone at home, feels desperate. Then she picks up the phone and dials a number.

KAYVAN *(voice only)* Hello?

SHEIDA   Hi.

KAYVAN   Hi!

SHEIDA   Can I ask you a favor, Kayvan?

KAYVAN   Sure honey, anything.

SHEIDA   Will you go and live with your sister for a while?

KAYVAN   Why?

SHEIDA   I would rather we didn't see each other for a while.

KAYVAN   For how long?

SHEIDA   I don't know, a month or two.

KAYVAN   Are you feeling OK?

SHEIDA   Don't make fun of me. If you don't want to do it, just say so.

KAYVAN   What did I say? I just —

SHEIDA   Say no if you don't want to. Just be honest.

KAYVAN   Fine, I'll go. I'll leave you alone.

SHEIDA   Thanks, bye.

Sheida hangs up, paces the room. Then she picks up the receiver and dials a number.

KAYVAN   Hello?

SHEIDA   Hello, Kayvan.

KAYVAN   Hi.

SHEIDA   What's new?

KAYVAN   Nothing.

SHEIDA   Can I ask you a favour, sweetheart?

KAYVAN   Go on.

SHEIDA   Will you live with your sister for a while?

KAYVAN   There is something wrong with you.

SHEIDA   Don't talk to me like that.

KAYVAN   What is wrong with you?

SHEIDA   I just want to be alone for a while.

KAYVAN   We already had this conversation. You asked me to go to my sister's and I said OK.

SHEIDA   When?

KAYVAN   Just a minute ago.

SHEIDA   Oh.

KAYVAN What do you mean "Oh"? You really don't remember calling me?

SHEIDA I thought I imagined it. I didn't think I actually spoke with you.

KAYVAN You asked me to go to my sister's, and I said OK.

SHEIDA Thanks. I love you.

KAYVAN You're behaving very strangely. I don't even recognize you.

SHEIDA Sometimes this happens to me. I do something then I'm not sure if I actually did it or just imagined doing it. I say something then I'm not sure whether I said it or just imagined saying it. Or, I say nothing but imagine I did.

KAYVAN This is the first time I've seen you like this. You never mentioned this problem before.

SHEIDA It hasn't happened in a while, just when I'm anxious.

KAYVAN Why are you anxious now?

SHEIDA I can't tell you.

KAYVAN But I have to know.

SHEIDA I don't want you to know.

KAYVAN See? It really bothers me when you use this tone of voice. When you say you don't want me to know, it makes me even more curious to know.

SHEIDA I don't want to... I —

KAYVAN Why?

SHEIDA I can't tell you the reason.

KAYVAN But I need to know.

SHEIDA You really irritate the hell out of me when you keep pushing me like this. It's as if you know exactly which buttons to push, and you keep pushing them. Then you wonder why I get upset. When I tell you that I can't tell you the reason— that I don't want to, I really need you to just understand.

KAYVAN   Why are you so upset, Sheida? Tell me and get it over with.

SHEIDA   Shiva woke up.

7. HIDDEN ORDER

Shirin is shocked by what Sheida has told her. Shirin doesn't know what to say. Sheida acts as if she did nothing wrong and it makes Shirin angry with Sheida.

SHIRIN   You say it just happened, as if you weren't two adults, as if you're talking about two animals during mating season who can't control themselves, as if you were not two thinking adults aware of your relationship.

SHEIDA   I think we behaved like any two normal adults. A normal man and woman who live together in one house, well, we started to care for each other. In circumstances like these, it is only natural for something to happen between two normal people. In the beginning, I tended to Kayvan like a good sister-in-law but then gradually I developed some feelings for him... I fell in love with him, and then I wondered maybe there was a reason behind Shiva's long sleep. Do you believe in the Hidden Order theory?

SHIRIN   Don't bullshit me.

SHEIDA   It's not bullshit. This is how I see it. I believe that the world is governed by some kind of a hidden order; I have often felt it in my own life. While Shiva was asleep, Kayvan and I had the chance to get to know each other, to realize that we really understand each other. I felt that it should have been me who married Kayvan, not Shiva.

SHIRIN   You should be ashamed of yourself for talking like this.

SHEIDA   Why? Kayvan and I love each other.

SHIRIN   You're trying to justify yourself in the most disgusting way. I hate you right now. I'm thinking if I fell asleep for a long time, you would probably go right ahead and snatch up Jimmy!

SHEIDA Not in a hundred years!

SHIRIN Hey!

SHEIDA Oh, I'm sorry!

SHIRIN Whatever happened between you and Kayvan has to end. Tell him to come home, Shiva is worried about him.

SHEIDA Kayvan and I are married.

SHIRIN That's bullshit!

SHEIDA We married two months ago.

SHIRIN That's impossible. It's even illegal. No man is allowed to marry two sisters at – did Kayvan divorce Shiva?

SHEIDA Yes, and he married me.

Light shift indicates the passing of time.

SHIRIN I don't care about you or that stupid Kayvan right now. My only concern is Shiva. I put myself in her shoes; if I had gone to sleep for a couple of years and I woke up to see Jimmy had married someone else, and who? My sister! It would drive me nuts! You must divorce Kayvan!

SHEIDA I can't.

SHIRIN What do you mean? You have to leave that stupid ass!

SHEIDA I told you, I can't.

SHIRIN Why?

SHEIDA Because I'm pregnant.

SHIRIN What? Run that by me again!

SHEIDA I'm carrying Kayvan's baby.

SHIRIN God, you make me sick!

SHEIDA Look —

SHIRIN Shut up!

SHEIDA Shirin, you —

SHIRIN Shut up! I'm really sick of you.

SHEIDA   Don't talk to me like that. Any kind of stress could harm my baby!

SHIRIN   He'd better not show up here ever again, or I'll really give it to him!

SHEIDA   It's not his fault. I asked him to marry me.

SHIRIN   And he couldn't refuse!

Lighting shifts to indicate passage of time.

SHEIDA   I really wanted to have a baby. I am approaching thirty, I wanted to have a child before I turn thirty. A child that I gave birth to, of my own body, my own blood. To raise a child who carries my mark, is a part of my soul, a continuation of my life. And of course, one that is born of a loving relationship. I wanted to have a child before I'm over thirty. But no one of any real potential had ever proposed to me.

SHIRIN   Because you are ridiculously picky!

SHEIDA   Well, I was never too excited about marriage. I did it in order to have a child. If I could have a child without getting married, a child who would enjoy all legal and social rights like any other children, I would not have married. How could I have had an illegitimate child who would be granted the most basic social rights in this country? No birth certificate, no inheritance, an illegal human being. When I realized that I was pregnant, from a man I love, I proposed to him and he accepted. Once I deliver my baby and Kayvan's name is recorded on the birth certificate as the father, Kayvan can divorce me if he wants to and marry Shiva again. I just want my baby to have the same rights as any other child. Just let him stay my husband until I deliver my baby, then if he chooses to marry Shiva again, it's up to him.

Lighting shifts to indicate passage of time.

SHEIDA   We had given up on Shiva ever waking up again.

SHIRIN   You wish that she hadn't, don't you?

SHEIDA   No.

SHIRIN   Sure you do. You would rather she kept on sleeping. I wouldn't even be surprised if you wished her dead. I wouldn't put anything past you.

SHEIDA   Shirin, you're accusing me of the worst sins.

SHIRIN   Oh, and you are so innocent? Give me a break! You haven't done anything wrong at all. I'm the one who is wrong, backwards. It's pretty common to steal your sister's husband and brainwash him into divorcing your sister and marrying you. It happens every day, not immoral at all. I have no idea how to explain all this to Jimmy.

SHEIDA   It's none of Jimmy's business.

SHIRIN   What do you mean? It's a matter of family honour. I want to be able to hold my head up high in front of my husband. As soon as Jimmy and his family find out, they will lose all respect for me.

SHEIDA   So what? What do you expect me to do?

SHIRIN   You're asking me?

SHEIDA   If I didn't need your help, I wouldn't have told you all this. Obviously, I need help!

SHIRIN   I can do nothing for you. You're the only one who can clean up the mess you made!

SHEIDA   Fine. I'll tell her myself. I've done nothing wrong.

8. A PIECE OF MUSIC FOR HER

Sheida is listening to a calm and peaceful piece of music with headphones on. We hear the music. Jimmy is talking to Shiva. We do not hear Jimmy and Shiva's dialogue. Shirin is painting her nails. Then she stands up and picks up the phone and speaks to someone, we cannot hear her voice; she hesitantly looks at Sheida and Shiva. Sheida takes off her headphones.

SHEIDA   Is it for me?

SHIRIN   It's Kayvan.

Shiva stands up and takes the receiver.

SHIVA   Hi! Where are you? It's been two days. When will you come over? Can't you come sooner? What's wrong with you? You sound strange. What is it? *(Lightly)* Aren't you happy that I woke up? Maybe I should go back to sleep! OK, OK. I'll be waiting for you.

Shiva hangs up the phone, feels the weight of the others' stare, goes to her own room. Sheida puts the headphones back on. We hear the music again. Jimmy and Shirin whisper to each other.

9. FEMALE PRAYING MANTIS

This scene is the same as the previous scene, but this time the audience can hear Jimmy and Shiva's dialogue. Shirin is painting her nails and Sheida is listening to the music with headphones on. This time we do not hear the music.

JIMMY   I read something in a book today and I thanked God a thousand times that I'm not an insect! Female bugs are really something. They are much stronger than the males and eat them up! There's a type of spider called Epirus —

SHIRIN   Will you give it a rest, Jimmy?

JIMMY   She can speak for herself.

SHIRIN   She is too polite.

SHIVA   No, Shirin. I want to hear it.

JIMMY   Thank you. So, it's called Epirus. Whenever the male Epirus is, as they say, in the mood for love, he first clears a getaway path then very carefully – and lustfully – approaches Mrs. Epirus. Sometimes Mrs. Epirus is in such a hurry that she gobbles the poor bastard up before he has had a chance to do anything. But if she too is in the mood for love, then she gets all coy and starts flirting and leading the guy on and the stupid guy of course who is blinded by desire follows her around and begs until at last Mrs. Epirus submits herself. Then they gently rub their antennas and exchange love poems and what not. But as soon as it's over, the stronger Mrs. Epirus jumps on the poor bastard and lovingly eats him right up. Of course, if the guy is smart, he beats the Mrs. to it and runs as fast as he can through the getaway path he prepared before. Only to repeat the same old story a couple of days later when he feels the urge again. Female mantises are way hornier; they can have sex with seven males one after the other and eat them all. Sometimes while the male mantis is still busy having sex, the female has already started eating part of his body. Male insects are pitiful! Thank God a million times that I'm not an insect!

The telephone rings. Shirin answers.

SHIRIN   Hello? Oh, hi. Who's speaking? No, just a minute.

Looks hesitantly at Sheida and Shiva.

SHEIDA *(takes off the headphones)* Is it for me?

SHIRIN   It's Kayvan.

Shiva stands up and takes the receiver.

SHIVA   Hi! Where are you? It's been two days. When will you come over? Can't you come sooner? What's wrong with you? You sound strange. What is it? *(Lightly)* Aren't you happy that I woke up? Maybe I should go back to sleep! OK, OK. I'll be waiting for you.

Shiva hangs up the phone, feels the weight of the others' stare and goes to her own room. Sheida puts the headphones back on. Jimmy and Shirin whisper to each other and this time we can hear them.

JIMMY   Will you tell her or should I do it myself?

SHIRIN   Ah! It's none of your business!

JIMMY   What do you mean? Poor thing.

SHIRIN   It's not up to you. Don't get in the middle of it.

JIMMY   How come this one has become so interested in music these days? She wasn't into it before.

SHIRIN   For her child.

JIMMY   What do you mean for her child?!

SHIRIN   Her doctor told her that a foetus can feel everything from a few months on. She listens to peaceful music to train the baby right.

Jimmy laughs quietly.

SHIRIN   Don't laugh, Jimmy.

10. OURASHIMA

Sheida and Shiva are alone at home. Sheida is sitting on the sofa, Shiva on the floor looking at her.

SHEIDA   On a moonlit night, Ourashima was out fishing as usual. The mermaid saw him and fell in love with him. Taking his hand, she pulled him into the sea. When they reached the bottom, Ourashima begged her: "Let me go to the land. I'm married with two children. They're waiting for me." The mermaid answered: "I'll give you as many pearls as you wish. Just stay with me." Ourashima said, "Shiva, I have something to tell you. Kayvan has married me. He waited for you for a long time but then divorced you and the mermaid insisted but it was all in vain." At last she said: "I beg you to stay with me just this one night." Ourashima accepted. The next day, when Ourashima woke up to head back towards the land, the mermaid gave him a box made of seashells as a present. "Listen to me, Shiva, I have something to tell you. Kayvan and I are married. He waited for you for so long but then we both realized that when he went back to his house, he found it covered with seaweed. He knocked and knocked but no one answered. When he pushed the door, it fell off. No one was there. Everything was so strange, just like the time you woke up.

Astonished and desperate, he asked a man passing by whether he knew what had happened to the family who used to live there. The man replied: "This house belonged to a fisherman called Ourashima who drowned at sea a hundred years ago." Desperate Ourashima asked: "What happened to his wife? His children?" The man answered: "They all died – his wife, his children, and even his grandchildren." When the stranger saw his eyes fill with tears, he asked him whether he was a relative of the family. Ourashima replied: "I am Ourashima." The man stared at him, stunned, just the way we stare at mad men, then he went away. Ourashima, I have something to tell you. It's so hard for me to say it, I just beg you to please try to understand. The gravedigger in the graveyard guided him to his family's graves. Ourashima cried out: "Oh, my Lord! Help me, I'm so alone." Shiva, sweetheart! I have something to tell you. It's so hard for me to say it, I just beg you to please try to understand me, my dear. Kayvan and I are married.

SHIVA　　　　I already know. I just wanted to hear it from your own mouth. I wanted to see how you would tell me, how you would find the words.

SHEIDA　　　　However you insult me, whatever you do, it's understandable.

SHIVA　　　　Why Kayvan?

SHEIDA　　　　What can I say? It just happened. A long time passed and you didn't wake up. We had given up on you waking up at all.

SHIVA　　　　Maybe you even wished for my death?

SHEIDA　　　　Shiva, sweetheart, please don't say that. Kayvan and I will separate if you want. But for God's sake, please let's wait till after I have my baby.

SHIVA　　　　Oh, my God! You're carrying his child?

SHEIDA　　　　He ran towards the sea and cursed the mermaid. He opened the box made of seashells and threw it away. A white smoke came out of the box, and suddenly all Ourashima's hair turned white. His skin began to wrinkle and his body folded upon itself. His knees gave way and Ourashima fell on the sand slowly and passed away.

Sheida begins to cry.

SHIVA　　　　Sheida, my dear!

SHEIDA   What if you kept sleeping and didn't wake up until we were all old or even dead. What would you do then?

SHIVA   But darling, I'm awake now!

SHEIDA   When you were asleep, I used to comb your hair every day. Every few days, I would bathe you. Sometimes I even put a little bit of make-up on you, played your favourite music, read you poems, the poems of Forough Farokhzad. I would talk to you all the time. Every year, on the night of the winter solstice, I used to read you poems by Hafez. Oh, I'm so happy that you're awake!

SHIVA   For God's sake, please don't cry Sheida. *(Sheida's sobbing and crying increases.)* Sheida, my dear.

SHEIDA   Listen to me, Shiva, I have something to tell you.

11. A SPECIAL OCCASION

Hasti examines the dress she has on in front of a mirror.

HASTI   Do you mind if I put this on? *(Pause.)* I understand how you feel but I really like to wear it, do you mind? *(Pause.)* Do you want me to take it off? *(Pause.)* Thanks. *(Pause.)* Does it look good on me? *(Pause.)* Sohrab, look first then answer me! *(Pause.)* I suppose it looked better on Parvin, hum? *(Pause.)* Don't try to be nice, I know that you think it looked better on her. *(Pause.)* You loved Parvin more than me, didn't you? *(Pause.)* I don't mind, you can tell me the truth. *(Pause.)* You probably thought she was more beautiful. *(Pause.)* I lied, I do mind! *(Pause.)* You know, I sometimes feel that you still think about Parvin. My words may hurt you but I really wish you would stop thinking about her. *(Pause.)* Please don't lie to me, Sohrab. Don't insult my intelligence.

Lighting shifts. Sohrab enters.

SOHRAB   Hi!

HASTI   Hi!

HASTI Does it look good on me?

SOHRAB Where did you find it?

HASTI In one of the suitcases. I shouldn't have put it on?

SOHRAB I didn't say that.

HASTI Well then, does it look good on me?

SOHRAB Yes, it looks really good on you.

HASTI Did it look better on Parvin?

SOHRAB She never wore it.

HASTI How come?

SOHRAB She was waiting for a special occasion.

HASTI Oh, I'm sorry.

SOHRAB Why?

HASTI I shouldn't have put it on.

SOHRAB Why not? It really suits you.

HASTI But you look annoyed.

SOHRAB Not at all.

HASTI Honey, it's obvious that you are upset.

SOHRAB It's not because of you.

HASTI Then what?

SOHRAB I had bought this for her birthday.

HASTI Oh, I'm really sorry! I'll just take it off and put it back.

SOHRAB Don't, please don't do that!

HASTI I feel really bad. Like I've done something horrible. I wish I'd known. I wouldn't have touched it.

SOHRAB Then I'm glad you didn't know! I'm really happy that you wore it. Please don't take it off!

HASTI But I will never feel comfortable in this dress.

SOHRAB Why not?

HASTI You'd bought it for Parvin.

SOHRAB   Like I said, she never wore it. I hope that you will. And I beg you to never put off anything for later. Don't wait for a special occasion. Every day that we're alive is a special occasion, sweetheart.

Phone rings.

12. SPAIN

Hasti is sitting on the floor, drunk. Sohrab smiling on the sofa looks at her.

HASTI   Well, I have a good feeling about Spain. As if it were my homeland at some point. I feel like I've lived in Spain before. Please don't look at me like that.

SOHRAB   How am I looking at you, sweetheart?

HASTI   I'm not drunk at all and I know exactly what I'm talking about!

SOHRAB   OK, go on.

HASTI   You mean I can't remember what I was talking about?

SOHRAB   That's not what I meant.

HASTI   You are looking at me as if I'm talking nonsense, right?

SOHRAB   Not at all. I'm just paying close attention. You don't want me to look at you?

HASTI   Nope!

SOHRAB   Fine.

HASTI *(choked up)* No, keep looking at me.

SOHRAB   OK, sweetheart.

HASTI *(lying down on the floor)* What was I saying? Don't laugh!

SOHRAB   You were talking about your homeland, Spain.

HASTI *(sits up)* Right. I'm sure I've lived more than once. In this life, I've never been to Spain but sometimes I recall certain memories that I'm sure are not about this life but a past lifetime in Spain.

SOHRAB   And were you as beautiful in your past life as you are in this one?

HASTI   I remember the first time I went to the seaside, when I was a child. I thought the moon was an animal. I remember myself dancing, I even remember the moment of my death. I'm sure I died while giving birth, to a baby conceived out of wedlock. We were going to get married but the man died in the war and I didn't want to abort his child. Sohrab?

SOHRAB   Yes, my love?

HASTI   There is something I want to say, something I have avoided telling you until now. *(Stops talking and drinks.)*

SOHRAB   Well?

HASTI   Nothing, forget it!

SOHRAB   Come on, tell me this thing that you've avoided telling me until now. *(He sits on the floor next to Hasti.)*

HASTI   Nah, forget it!

SOHRAB   I'm begging you, please tell me!

HASTI   I married you because I was sure you are the same man I loved in my past life.

SOHRAB   Why didn't you want to tell me this?

HASTI   Because then I realized you're not that man. No, you're not him.

SOHRAB   And now you regret having married me?

HASTI   No.

SOHRAB   What did he look like?

HASTI   I just remember his gaze, just like yours. His smile, like yours. Oh, Sohrab, I'm so glad that you exist in this world... I love you!

SOHRAB   I love you too, sweetheart.

HASTI   You don't believe in this stuff, do you?

SOHRAB   Why not? I understand what you're saying.

HASTI   But you don't believe it.

SOHRAB   I do.

HASTI   No, you're lying, you don't believe in this stuff.

SOHRAB   I believe in it, sweetheart.

HASTI   Sohrab, you don't believe in this stuff. Just say you don't.

SOHRAB   OK, fine. I don't believe in it.

HASTI   But I believe in it and this belief is so strong in me that I've considered committing suicide.

SOHRAB   No?

HASTI   What, I don't seem the type?

SOHRAB   No.

HASTI   Seriously. I have thought about killing myself a few times. To come back in another body with another name. In the hopes of a better life the next time. For me, this has been the real motivation for suicide. Once, when I was only seventeen, just after my parents' divorce, I was so unhappy that I decided to kill myself. I went to my bedroom, poured a handful of pills in a glass, and filled it with Canada Dry. Then I thought it'd be better to listen to a song before I killed myself. I put a tape of Farhad in the cassette player, stretched out on the bed and fell asleep. *(Laughs.) (Sohrab quietly hides his glass behind himself.)* When I woke up, I thought to myself, well, this isn't so bad and maybe I don't have to kill myself. *(Laughs)* Why aren't you laughing?

SOHRAB   Why should I laugh?

HASTI   Because it's funny. Don't be so serious. *(Sohrab smiles.)* That's nice. But I still think suicide is the best way to die. *(Looking for her glass.)* Hey, where's my glass? Did you take it?

SOHRAB   You really think so?

HASTI   I do. You've never thought about killing yourself?

SOHRAB   No.

HASTI   How come?

The telephone rings. Hasti moves to answer it.

SOHRAB   No, let me answer it. Hello? Hello? *(Beat)* They hung up.

13. NINETEEN EIGHTY-THREE

Shiva and Shirin have embraced each other.

SHIRIN   Sweetheart!

SHIVA   What year is it?

SHIRIN   1983.

SHIVA   Oh, my God! Oh, my God! Oh, my God!!!

SHIRIN   Dearest, oh, my darling.

SHIVA   I'm going crazy, Shirin. I can't believe this. Oh, my God!

SHIRIN   Sweetheart, my dear.

SHIVA   I've been cursed. I'm sure of it.

SHIRIN   This is not a curse, it's a miracle. You think we've had it so easy? You were lucky to be asleep and not experience these terrible times.

SHIVA   What are you saying, Shirin? It's horrible to go to sleep one night and wake up three years later.

SHIRIN   You have no idea how many people would rather fall asleep than endure this situation. I would give anything to be in your shoes. I'm sure Jimmy feels the same way. Seriously, you should be grateful. You have no idea what we're living through: inflation, black market, war—

SHIVA   War?!

SHIRIN   Yes, war. For three years now we have been fighting Iraq for no reason. It started a couple of weeks after you fell asleep again. And nobody knows when it is supposed to end.

Light shift. Shirin puts a cassette in the tape player. Sheida's voice is heard from the tape player.

SHEIDA'S VOICE My dear Shiva, Hi! I hope the day you wake up won't be too late. I hope soon, very soon, one of these days you wake up and never sleep so long again. I'm sure you wish the same thing. When you fell back to sleep again, I burst into tears. I wanted to look after you like before. But the truth of it is that I can't live in this house anymore. I feel guilty. I prefer to go away, far from you all. The only reason I can speak freely now is that you're not sitting in front of me. I will never be able to look you in the eyes. But I want you to know that I have always loved you, my little sister. I want you to know that I really need you to love me too, even though you may think I don't deserve it. I beg you not to blame me. I beg you not to hate me. I beg you to love me. I need your and Shirin's love. I love you, my dearest.

SHIRIN　　　　　I miss her so much. I've only seen her once since she left... Accidentally, we ran into each other on the street. We both burst into tears. She hadn't even called us once since the day she left. We had no idea where she was. I saw her on Vila Street, she had her child with her. Her son is really cute, chubby and—

SHIVA　　　　　Do you mind not talking about her baby?

SHIRIN　　　　　Sorry.

SHIVA　　　　　Have you heard from her recently? Is she alright?

SHIRIN　　　　　Yes, now she calls at least once a week. Plus, a while ago she gave me her number and asked me to call her when you wake up.

SHIVA　　　　　Please don't. I don't want her to know.

SHIRIN　　　　　She said she would never step into this house until you wake up and forgive her.

SHIVA　　　　　I can't see her.

SHIRIN　　　　　It may be asking too much, my dear, but please call her and tell her that you forgive her. She has been punished enough.

SHIVA　　　　　It's not a question of punishment. I'm just not ready to see her yet, to talk to her. It's been three years for the two of you and, I don't know, maybe you've gotten used to it.

But for me, it's as if it just happened yesterday and naturally, I'm still upset with her. Naturally, I don't want to see her. I'm happy she doesn't live here anymore because I honestly don't know what I would say to her.

SHIRIN Sometimes, I think back to twenty years ago, when we were children playing together... It's hard to believe. I miss those days. Remember Sheida back then. Do you remember how sweet she was? You have to agree that she was much nicer than us. I miss how you and Sheida were back then. I miss myself – how me, Shirin was, back then.

14. THIS IS MY SHARE

Shiva is reading from Forough Farokhzad's poetry book.

Shiva

This is my share

This is my share

My share

Is a sky, which the dropping of a curtain seizes from me

My share is going down an abandoned stairway

And leading me to nostalgia and decay

My share is a hopeless wander in the meadow of memories

And dying with the sorrow of a voice that tells me:

I love

Your hands

I will plant my fingers in the flowerbed

I will grow, I know, I know

With inky grains on my palms

Sparrows will lay eggs

In the hallows of my hands.

Jimmy enters.

JIMMY   Hey, Shiva. Aren't you just ecstatic about waking up?

SHIVA   Sure.

JIMMY   So now that you're awake, what would you like to do?

SHIVA   I don't know. I'm scared, Jimmy. What if I fall asleep again? I'm not sure what to do. I keep thinking I have to seize this moment; I have to take advantage of every minute of my life. But then, I don't actually know what to do.

JIMMY   Would you like to go for a ride?

SHIVA   Where to?

JIMMY   Just to see how much everything's changed. I don't know. If you're up to it, that is. If you can stand me.

SHIVA   How could anyone resist you? You're adorable!

JIMMY   At your service! To be honest, I really missed you. Not to toot my own horn but this time, while you were sleeping, I really looked after you. For three years, whenever Shirin wasn't home, I would rush home to make sure somebody's here in case you woke up. I didn't want you to be alone when you woke up.

SHIVA   Oh, Jimmy! The world is a better place with you in it!

JIMMY   At your service day and night! OK, let's go. Just ride with me for a day and you'll be amazed at what sort of people I have to deal with. And I still have that old habit, when someone gets into my taxi, I immediately figure out which animal they look like. Have I ever told you which animal you look like?

SHIVA   No.

JIMMY   You look like a deer[5].

15. THE RHINO & THE GOAT

In the dim light of the room, Shirin has embraced Shiva. Jimmy is laughing.

SHIRIN *(to Shiva)* Don't be afraid, my dear! Now you understand why I say you should be grateful. This is our life. Constant fear of death, constant anxiety. Jimmy, please stop laughing like an idiot!

JIMMY   I can't help laughing; I'm telling myself a really funny joke.

SHIVA   Do share.

JIMMY   I can't. It's offensive.

SHIRIN   Oh, shut up, Jimmy.

JIMMY   But I haven't even started!

SHIRIN   Oh, please offend us!

JIMMY   This guy walks into a—

SHIRIN   Shut up, Jimmy!

Jimmy keeps laughing.

SHIVA *(to Shirin)* Is he really telling himself a joke?

JIMMY   I'm following my late father's advice. His last words to me were, "laugh as much as you can, son." He said if he could live one more time, he would laugh more and take it easy. God bless him.

Jimmy begins humming a song. The sounds of air strikes are heard. Jimmy laughs out loud.

SHIVA   Jimmy! Did you tell yourself another joke?

JIMMY   No. I remembered something I read half an hour ago; it was really funny. I might tell it to you, if you ask me nicely.

SHIVA   Please tell me.

JIMMY   They put a goat into a rhino's cage in a zoo—

Sound of a siren is followed by a recorded announcement.

ANNOUNCER'S VOICE Attention! Attention! This is the White Status siren. This means the danger of air strikes is over. It is now safe to leave the shelter.

JIMMY *(overlapping with the announcement)* They put a goat into a rhino's cage in a zoo —

SHIVA *(to Shirin, overlapping)* Why did you turn on the lights?

JIMMY   They put a goat in a rhino's—

SHIRIN *(overlapping with Jimmy)* That was the white siren.

JIMMY   A goat in a rhino's—

SHIVA *(overlapping with Jimmy)* You mean it's over now?

SHIRIN   Yes, thank God. We survived another one.

Jimmy picks up the phone and dials a number. A woman answers.

JIMMY   Hello? Hi, ma'am. Excuse me but I'm feeling deprived because no one listens to me here. Do you have time for a conversation?

WOMAN'S VOICE You should be ashamed of yourself, in the middle of all this!

Shirin grabs the receiver and listens for a moment then hangs up.

SHIRIN   Jimmy, I've told you over and over that I don't like these stupid games of yours.

JIMMY   It is not a game. I was quite serious. When you don't listen to me, I have to find someone else to listen to me!

SHIVA   Tell me, Jimmy! I am listening. What was the article you read?

JIMMY   It's too late now.

SHIVA   I'm begging you, Jimmy.

JIMMY   You're begging me?

SHIVA   Yes. Thanks.

JIMMY   No problem. They put a goat into a rhino's cage in a zoo, so the rhino wouldn't be alone. The goat being a goat hits the rhino with its horns all day long. The rhino is a tough guy, you know, and not only does he not mind being hit, he even likes it.

SHIVA	Why?
JIMMY	Well you see, no one ever paid any attention to the rhino. And our rhino felt lonely and deprived. When the goat pokes him with his horns, our sad little rhino feels alive. For the first time, someone is paying attention to him. The rhino thinks to himself, I get hit, therefore I exist! Anyway, our bored little rhino now has someone paying attention to him.
SHIVA	And then?
JIMMY	That's all!
SHIRIN	What is so funny about this story, Jimmy?
JIMMY	Well, it's just like our relationship. That's why it made me laugh. In our case, you're the goat and I'm the rhino. Oh, I forgot to mention that the rhino was male and the goat, female. They put them together to mate.
SHIRIN	Is it possible for a rhino and a goat to mate?
JIMMY	Yes.
SHIRIN	That's very strange.
JIMMY	What's so strange about it? Look at us!
SHIRIN	Zip it, you stupid ass!

16. RAMIN

Shiva is on the phone to Ramin. Ramin's voice is heard.

SHIVA	Hi, it's Shiva.
RAMIN	Hello, Shiva! When did you wake up?
SHIVA	On Wednesday?
RAMIN	When you woke up in 1980, I found out too late. I called but they said you were sleeping again. I'm really happy that you called.
SHIVA	I didn't expect to reach you so easily. I called a bunch of people today. But only found a couple of the old gang. Who are you still in touch with?

RAMIN	Mitra and Omid got married. I only hang out with those two from the old gang. And when I'm unlucky, I run into Kayvan.

SHIVA	Why unlucky?

RAMIN	I know everything, Shiva. I know what he did to you.

SHIVA	I don't want to talk about him.

RAMIN	I still love you.

SHIVA	I just called to see how you are Ramin.

RAMIN	And I just want you to know that I still love you.

SHIVA	Thank you.

RAMIN	I'm really happy you called.

SHIVA	Aren't you married yet?

RAMIN	No.

SHIVA	Why?

RAMIN	You know exactly why.

SHIVA	You haven't changed. The thing that really hurts me each time I wake up is seeing how much people have changed.

RAMIN	Shiva?

SHIVA	Yes?

RAMIN	Thank you for calling me. Thank you for remembering me.

SHIVA	I was reading Forough's poetry and it reminded me of you. Do you still know her poems by heart?

RAMIN	Yes.

SHIVA	I always liked the way you read poetry.

RAMIN	Then listen to this one:

They have killed Love, and men who made love.

They have killed songs, and men who sang songs.

They have killed everything that is good in this land.

SHIVA	Forough's?

RAMIN	No. This is by Jesús López Pacheco, the Spanish
poet.	
SHIVA	I'm glad you haven't changed like the others.
RAMIN	Shiva!
SHIVA	Yes?
RAMIN	I would like to see you.

17. ONE MORE TIME

The sound of a telephone ringing is heard in the darkness. Lighting slowly fades up. Shiva is asleep on the sofa. EBI's music is being played on the cassette player.

SHIRIN (*offstage*) Shiva! Shiva! Answer the phone.

The ringing and music continue. Shirin enters, answers the phone. It's Ramin.

SHIRIN	Hello?
RAMIN	Hello, this is Ramin.
SHIRIN	Hello, how are you?
RAMIN	Fine, thank you. May I speak to Shiva?
SHIRIN	Hold on a second. Shiva! Shiva! Shiva, darling!
Shiva! ... Hello? She's sleeping again.	
RAMIN	You mean –?
SHIRIN	Yes, a long deep sleep.

18. JUST DIAL!

SOHRAB	Hello? Hello! Hello?
HASTI (*whispering*) Hang up then dial a number!	
SOHRAB	Why?
HASTI	Just do it, I'll explain later.
SOHRAB	What number should I dial?

HASTI Any number, just dial! Then hang up as soon as they pick up.

Sohrab dials a number.

A VOICE Hello?

Sohrab hangs up.

HASTI I have heard that whenever the phone rings and no one answers, the phone can be turned into a microphone as soon as you hang up.

SOHRAB How is that possible?

HASTI I don't know, this is what I've heard. There must be some way.

The telephone rings.

SOHRAB Hello?

There's no answer. Sohrab hangs up.

HASTI Dial a number.

Sohrab dials a number.

A VOICE Hello?

Sohrab hangs up. The telephone rings.

SOHRAB Hello?

No answer, Sohrab hangs up. Then dials a number.

A VOICE Yes, may I help you?

Sohrab hangs up. The telephone rings immediately. Hasti moves to the phone.

HASTI I am the one they are looking for. *(Picks up the receiver.)* Yes?

MAN'S VOICE Hasti Yekta?

HASTI Who is this?

MAN'S VOICE None of your fucking business! I'm just letting you know to write your will.

HASTI I will. OK, you did your job. Good for you. Now, get lost, you filthy bastard!

Hasti hangs up and sits to watch TV. Sohrab rushes to the phone and dials a number.

A VOICE Hello?

Sohrab hangs up.

SOHRAB It would be best not to provoke these guys.

HASTI But he was talking trash.

SOHRAB It doesn't matter... you should never answer them back or humiliate them. When you humiliate them, you remind them how small they are. And that just provokes them into making more trouble.

HASTI I'm scared, Sohrab! What if they're serious?

SOHRAB Let's leave the country. This is the best opportunity for you to seek asylum somewhere.

19. NINETEEN EIGHTY-SEVEN

No one is on stage. Sound of an explosion. Sound of a telephone ringing. No one answers. Sound of another explosion. Lighting shifts. Shirin and Sheida are on the stage.

SHEIDA I want to see her and talk to her before I leave. I want to say goodbye. I don't care how she treats me.

SHIRIN I'm sure, she wouldn't treat you badly. She's become very reclusive. She doesn't even have the energy to complain. You should have seen her face when I told her it was 1987. It was so sad. She didn't say anything. As if she is in a daze; as if she has accepted her fate. Then she said something that brought tears to our eyes.

SHEIDA What did she say?

The telephone rings. The actors on stage freeze. Sound of picking up of the receiver.

HASTI'S VOICE Hello?

MAN'S VOICE You fucking intellectual! You're still here! What do you want from this country? Get your stupid ass out, you shit!

Sound of phone hanging up. The actors on stage resume.

SHIRIN She said, "I'm sorry to be a burden to you. I'm sure you would have left the country if it weren't for me". She said, "This is terrible, I have no idea what I'm supposed to do in this life. What good am I to anyone?" Oh, Sheida, it breaks my heart to look at her. What if this continues until – I hope that day never comes – but just imagine.

SHEIDA She might not listen to me but you must convince her to—

Sound of telephone ringing. The actors freeze on stage. Sound of picking up the receiver.

HASTI'S VOICE Hello?

MAN'S VOICE Death to the intellectuals! Death to the intellectuals! Death to the intellectuals! Death to the intellectuals!

Sound of hanging up the phone. The actors resume.

SHEIDA She might not listen to me but you must convince her to apply for a passport. Ask Jimmy to take her to the Passport Office. Then as soon as I get to France, I'll send her an invitation letter to come and live with me. I'll send one for you and Jimmy, too.

SHIRIN Have you received your visa?

SHEIDA Yes.

SHIRIN I won't have anyone else here when you leave.

SHEIDA Sweetheart, I'll send you an invitation letter right away.

Lighting shifts.

SHIRIN How's your son these days?

SHEIDA He's very active, asks lots of questions. Sometimes he does things that make me wonder if he's a genius or completely crazy! Just last week, he planted a chicken bone and watered it expecting a chicken to pop out!

SHIRIN   Takes after his parents. You and Kayvan aren't so smart.

SHEIDA   I know. Last night he said something that really threw us off.

SHIRIN   What did he say?

SHEIDA   As the missiles exploded somewhere, he said—

Sound of telephone ringing but no one answers.

SHEIDA   As the missiles exploded somewhere, he said — As the missiles exploded somewhere, he said — *(Sheida repeats the phrase as long as the telephone rings. When the ringing stops, she immediately continues.)* As the missiles exploded somewhere, he said, "Am I going to die, Mommy?"

SHIRIN   You see? What has the world come to when a seven-year old has to worry about dying? I refuse to have a child as long as we live in this mess.

SHEIDA   How does Jimmy feel about it? Doesn't he want a baby?

SHIRIN   Too bad if he does. I'm not like you. I wouldn't be able to cope with my baby saying something like that.

Sound of two missile explosions.

SHIRIN   It would be pretty hilarious if we die today and tomorrow they declare Peace.

20. CLOSED DOORS

Shiva is on the phone to Ramin.

SHIVA   Hi.

RAMIN   Hello, who's speaking?

SHIVA   It's Shiva.

RAMIN   Hi, Shiva. When did you wake up?

SHIVA   Three days ago.

RAMIN   Not the best time to wake up!

SHIVA   What do you mean?

RAMIN   Aren't you sad to wake up to this mess?

SHIVA   Well, I'm just waiting to see what fate has in store for me.

RAMIN   Aren't you afraid?

SHIVA   Well, yes, just a little. I don't want to get hit by a missile in my sleep.

RAMIN   I had a dream about you a while back.

SHIVA   What was it?

RAMIN   I dreamed I was sitting on a chair and you were walking away from me. There was a door across from you. You opened it, there was another door, you opened that one too and again another door ... Endless closed doors ... I watched anxiously as you got further and further away from me; opening one door after another only to be faced with yet another one.

SHIVA   That's horrible.

RAMIN   That you were walking away from me?

SHIVA   No, the endless doors.

RAMIN   Why did you wait three days to call?

SHIVA   I don't know. I wasn't sure if I should call at all. In case you were sleeping.

RAMIN   Can I see you tomorrow?

SHIVA   We're leaving town early in the morning.

RAMIN   You're lucky. I haven't been on a trip in a long time.

SHIVA   I don't dare to sleep. I'm afraid of not waking up for another three years. I want to see the Caspian Sea. I wish it were summertime then I could swim in the sea!

RAMIN   When will you be back?

SHIVA   I don't know. Probably after the missile attacks are over.

RAMIN	Call me as soon as you come back.
SHIVA	Are you still single?
RAMIN	No. *(Long pause.)* Shiva!
SHIVA	Where's your wife now?
RAMIN	She's a nurse. She works the night shift this week.
SHIVA	Don't you love her?
RAMIN	Yes, I do.
SHIVA	Then why do you want to see me?
RAMIN	I've missed you.
SHIVA	OK, take care.
RAMIN	You will call me when you're back, right? I really need to see you, Shiva.
SHIVA	Is it that important to you?
RAMIN	Yes.
SHIVA	I had a feeling I shouldn't call you. That's why it took me three days to call.
RAMIN	Shiva!
SHIVA	I might decide not to see you anymore.
RAMIN	Why?
SHIVA	You're married!

21. GOODBYE UNTIL I DON'T KNOW WHEN

Jimmy and Shiva are sitting counting their scores in a game of cards. They both look tired.

JIMMY   I've got the seven of spades, and here I got one, two three, and six, seven and eight. Well, this makes fifteen points, on top of my 50, that makes 65.

Jimmy yawns and stands up to leave.

SHIVA   Jimmy, let's play another round.

JIMMY   Haven't you had enough of beating me for one night?

SHIVA   Just one more hand, OK?

JIMMY   We're supposed to leave early in the morning.

SHIVA   I know.

JIMMY   OK, so we have a six-seven-hour drive ahead of us. And if you want me to get you there in one piece, you should let me rest. Or else, I might get us all killed.

SHIVA   I wish I could be like you and just relax. I'm tired too but I'm afraid if I close my eyes, I'll wake up three years later.

JIMMY   You're lucky to be able to take a nice long rest for three years. I have to wake up every morning and drive that damn taxi.

SHIVA   Please, stay up with me, Jimmy. Talk to me. Shirin is sleeping now. She can drive tomorrow and you can sleep in the car. I beg you, Jimmy! Please, talk to me, make me laugh. I want to see the Caspian Sea. I don't dare fall asleep.

JIMMY   Don't worry about it. Didn't you fall asleep a couple of nights ago and wake up the next morning? Same thing tomorrow.

SHIVA   That's fine... go to bed, Jimmy. You're too tired to talk to me. Have a good night, Jimmy! Or maybe I should say, good bye until I don't know when.

Jimmy comes back, sits at the table and picks up the cards.

22. THE WHITE CAR

Sohrab is dialling a number. She looks worried. Hasti enters.

SOHRAB   Where have you been? Why didn't you call me?

HASTI   I'm sorry, I didn't have access to a phone.

SOHRAB   Why didn't you take the spray with you?

HASTI   By the time I pull that silly gadget out of my pocket, they would all be done with me.

SOHRAB   That same white car passed by the house again today.

HASTI   Are you sure it was the same car? A lot of people drive a white car.

SOHRAB   It was the same guys. I could pick them out of a huge crowd. Don't go to work anymore.

HASTI   I don't have any more days off.

SOHRAB   They have to give you time off. Tell them your life is in danger. If you don't tell them, I will.

HASTI   Fine, I'll tell them.

23. ONE HUNDRED AND THIRTY-FOUR WRITERS

Hasti is facing a video camera on a tripod. Sohrab is sitting beside the camera, pushes the button on.

HASTI   Last week, two writers were killed. They were among the one hundred and thirty-four writers who had signed the letter on Freedom of Expression. I've also signed that letter and they may kill me one of these days. I can no longer write or read anything. I can only speak. I live in fear of what ... I'd like to start again.

SOHRAB   OK.

Hasti takes off her scarf.

SOHRAB   Are you sure?.

HASTI   Yes.

SOHRAB   OK.

HASTI   Last week, two writers were assassinated. They were among the one hundred and thirty-four writers who had signed the letter on Freedom of Expression. I've also signed that letter and I might be killed one of these days. I can no longer write or read anything. I can only speak. I don't feel safe these days at all even in my own house and if someone rings the doorbell, I don't answer. I live in fear of what might happen an hour from now. I am persecuted simply because of my writing. Strangers call at my house and threaten to kill me. Why don't I apologise or leave the country, I ask myself. It's not because I'm scared of dying. I'm just a human being like everyone else, with all the same fears and anxieties. And I am not ashamed to say that I am afraid. I don't want to lie. I don't want to be a hero. The truth of it is that I really don't want to die. I love life. I love my country. There are so many things I still want to do. (*Lighting shifts to indicate passage of time.*)

I'm working on a play now titled, *"Good Bye Until I Don't Know When"*. It's based on a personal wish. I have always wished to go to sleep for a long time, maybe a hundred years or more, then wake up to a world where things have changed. Honestly, I really envy people who will be born a hundred years from now. I believe humanity moves toward wisdom and away from ignorance. What I'd really like is to return in a hundred years and live in this same body, with the same name and the same job. After everything that's happened, finishing this play has become really difficult for me. I can hardly focus. I've lost all motivation for writing. It's natural to lose the ability to concentrate on writing when you don't know if you'll still be around tomorrow. The few scenes I've written are deeply marked by this situation. I didn't want the play to be depressing and sad. I wanted it to end on a hopeful note. But writing about hope is pretty much impossible for me right now. (*Lighting shifts.*)

I want to feel safe. I wish the best for all writers in the future. I had hoped to see the day when we can write freely, and speak freely. I had hoped to see the day when no one is killed because of their beliefs. I believe that one day, people watching this video will be surprised that a writer was ever threatened with death. I believe that the day will come when people can write whatever they want or at least won't be threatened with death because of their writing.

Silence.

HASTI　　　　　　I'm going to delete it.

SOHRAB   You want to film it again?

HASTI   I changed my mind.

SOHRAB   Why?

HASTI   I don't want them to see me frightened. They want this – they want to see us full of fear.

SOHRAB   That's why we're doing this, to show them you're not afraid.

HASTI   I don't believe they are going to... Nobody's going to... I am not supposed to be assassinated. It's just paranoia. I don't want to record this paranoia.

SOHRAB   You are not paranoid! Two writers were assassinated this week!

HASTI   They are waiting for us to send something like this to the BBC, then they'll pounce. They are looking for an excuse.

SOHRAB   They already have an excuse. Don't be silent. This will be big news all over the world!

HASTI   Yeah, it would be big news. And if I speak out now, they'll get even angrier and continue killing us. I'm not a big fish for them. So, why should I provoke them?

SOHRAB   Don't do that.

HASTI   It's done.

24. A SMILE

Jimmy is on the sofa, covered with a blanket. He looks ill and tired. Shiva enters the scene after another long sleep. She stares at Jimmy, too shocked to speak.

SHIVA   Hi, Jimmy!

JIMMY (*stammering and smiling*) Hi.

SHIVA   What's happened to you, Jimmy?

Jimmy is not able to answer and just smiles.

SHIVA   What is it, Jimmy?

Jimmy is not able to answer and just smiles.

25. WHAT A PLEASANT FEELING!

SHIRIN   Brain stroke. His memory is ruined, that's why he can't talk. Sometimes he remembers a few words and speaks almost without interruption. But he can understand everything we say.

Lighting shifts.

SHIRIN   Now I drive the taxi.

SHIVA   Things must have changed then if you're allowed to drive a taxi.

SHIRIN   It's become just a little easier.

SHIVA   Does anybody bother you?

SHIRIN   At first they did. It was too strange for them to see a woman driving a taxi. For a while I would take Jimmy with me in case they stopped us for questioning, to explain why I'm sitting behind the wheel. He still comes with me from time to time.

SHIVA   Where's Sheida?

SHIRIN   She moved to France with her child, to live with Kayvan.

Lighting shifts.

SHIRIN *(choked up)* I really miss his chattering. Yes, Jimmy, I miss your chattering.

Shiva embraces Shirin. Shirin breaks into sobs.

SHIRIN   I'm sorry, I can't help myself. It will pass. I've held back my tears for so long, I can't hold it anymore. Sorry. Your first day awake and I'm ruining it. Sorry. I can't stop. You're so lucky, Shiva. I'm jealous of you. Many times, I wished I were in your shoes. All those mornings that I wake up to the noise of the alarm clock and feel like crying. I say, oh God, do I have to open my eyes again? How wonderful it would be if I kept sleeping and woke up when everything has changed, when all our problems have been solved. How pleasant it would be to wake up to someone saying: "Honey, life has improved, there is less chaos and violence. Now people are treated with respect."

26. GOODBYE

Shiva dials a number. Sound of busy signal. Jimmy laughs out loud.

SHIVA　　　　What is it, Jimmy? Are you telling yourself a joke like you used to?

JIMMY　　　　No.

SHIVA　　　　You're practising your laughter?

JIMMY　　　　No.

SHIVA　　　　Reminiscing about the past?

JIMMY　　　　Yeah.

SHIVA　　　　Do you remember talking to me about animals, Jimmy?

JIMMY　　　　Yeah.

Shiva dials again. Someone picks up after a few rings.

A WOMAN'S VOICE　Hello?

SHIVA　　　　Hello? Hi, may I speak to Ramin, please?

THE WOMAN　Who's speaking?

SHIVA　　　　I'm an old friend of his. Shiva.

THE WOMAN　Ramin was killed in the missile attacks of 1987.

SHIVA　　　　Oh, my God. Are you his wife?

THE WOMAN　Yes.

SHIVA　　　　I'm very sorry for your loss. You should know that we were just friends. Please believe me.

THE WOMAN　He's dead now.

SHIVA　　　　I don't know what to say. Goodbye.

THE WOMAN　Good Bye.

Shiva starts crying.

JIMMY *(stammering)* SHI...VA!

SHIVA I'm going to bed, Jimmy. Pray that I'll sleep for many years. I pray that I will sleep for a very long time and wake up to see that you are all better. To see Sheida and Shahram are back. To see people out on the streets who are no longer sad and angry. To see people laughing and happy to be alive, happy to have been born here, to be living here. I pray that I will fall asleep. I pray that I will wake up only when it is worth waking up.

27. OH MY GOD!

Shirin enters from Shiva's bedroom. Jimmy is crying.

SHIRIN You scared me, Jimmy! I thought something bad happened to her. Don't cry, darling! She'll wake up again. And by then you'll be all better. Shiva will wake up. We will all be together again. I'm sure things will be better by then. Shiva will wake up and ask us, "How is everything?" And we will tell her everything has changed. Everything is beautiful and nice. She will listen to everything and keep saying, "Oh, my God. Oh, my God." That day will not be too late, oh, no, my dear Jimmy. Believe me. It can't be too late. Shiva will wake up and keep saying, "Oh, my God! Oh, my God! Oh, my God!"

Lighting fades out.

VOICE Dear audience members, the play, *Goodbye Until I Don't Know When* written by Hasti Yekta remains unfinished due to the assassination of the playwright. In memory of this writer and other writers who have been killed around the world, we respectfully ask that you rise to observe a moment of silence.

Lights down.

The End

Mohammad Yaghoubi

Born and raised in Iran, Mohammad Yaghoubi is a playwright, director, screenwriter, theatre instructor, Co-founder and the co-artistic director of Toronto-based NOWADAYS THEATRE company.

His plays have been translated and produced in Australia, Belgium, Canada, France, Germany, Kurdistan, Russia, Sweden, The Czech Republic, Turkey, and the USA.

After moving to Canada in 2015, he founded NOWADAYS THEATRE company, and staged the English premiere of his highly acclaimed play *A Moment of Silence* at 2016 SummerWorks Performance Festival.

In 2018, with the support of Canada Council for the Arts, he wrote his first play in English *Persimmon* which was commissioned by Tarragon Theatre. He has been also awarded a grant by Toronto Arts Council in 2020 to write his second play into English titled *Earworm*.

Recent Credits: The English premiere of his celebrated play *Winter of 88* (Next Stage Theatre Festival, 2020, Factory Theatre MainSpace), *The Only Possible Way* (Canadian Stage, 2019).

Selected *Awards*: The National Theatre Critics Society Award for Outstanding Play for *Drought & Lies;* Winner of the Iranian Playwrights Society and Third place winner of the New Play Contest in Toronto's Fringe Festival for *A Moment of Silence;* The National Theatre Critics Society Award for Outstanding Writing for *Geraniums*.

DOGS AND MY MOTHER'S BONES

Mojgan Khaleghi

Characters

SOUAD – a 55-year-old woman

MAIKA – a 25-year-old woman

HANNAH – a 17-year-old girl

RATKO – a 40-year-old man

HASSAN – a 50-year-old man

RAMIZ – a 20-year old boy

BRANKO – an 18-year-old boy

A VOICE

Three women, Hannah, Souad and Maika stand in the middle of the space.

HANNAH   They shot my mom. For no reason. It was night when we found her body. Without any clothes. Even her wedding ring had been stolen. I had a fever and I couldn't talk. My father picked up his violin. He wanted to sell it because he was afraid I'd die. I was waiting for him to come for three days but then... later... I couldn't even find my father's body ...

Hannah puts on a red overcoat and sits on the bench at the end of the room.

SOUAD   When they attacked, they took my husband away with them. They came into my room and forced me onto the bed. I cannot say how long it took, but they told each other to hurry. I didn't resist at all. The last man said that as I was so calm he wouldn't have to kill me. The door was open. I was afraid my son would arrive unexpectedly and see me in that state. A strange woman dressed me. A red coat, that was all I had to cover myself... After that, I didn't see my son or my husband again.

Souad puts on a red overcoat and sits on the bench at the end of the room.

MAIKA   We were twelve people sleeping close to each other. The pillow was larger than the baby's body. She was asleep. I pressed the pillow onto her face. It's said it's over after six minutes, but I wanted to make sure. I cut the umbilical cord with a knife and then took the bed linen off and washed it. They gave us a blue bag to collect the rubbish. I put it in the blue bag. I called the guard. I was cool. I said I have a bag that I couldn't hold until the morning in my room. The guard approached me. He was wearing a raggedy, red, overcoat.

Maika puts on a red overcoat and sits on the bench at the end of the room.

The sound of the siren is heard. The lighting fades down to black. A voice is heard in the darkness.

A VOICE "My dearest Mom. By the time you receive this letter, I will have been executed. I want you to be strong to bear the pain because I lived as I wanted to. Your boy, Ramiz".

Lights up.

On the bench at the end of the room, where the women were sitting, Hassan and Ramiz are now sitting. They are staring ahead, stunned and motionless.

HASSAN How long before it's done?

RAMIZ Less than an hour.

HASSAN Do you know anyone to write a letter to?

RAMIZ Will they deliver it to them?

HASSAN Maybe.

RAMIZ You know... I killed someone

HASSAN Don't mention that in your letter.

The sound of shooting is heard. Moments pass in silence.

HASSAN Now, no one's left except us..

RAMIZ He was only sixteen years old.

HASSAN His name was the same as my son's: Branko.

Lights out.

Arabic music is heard. When the lights come on, Ratko (a forty-year-old, obese man) stands centre stage on the platform and is teaching Arabic dance. Maika and Souad stand on one side and Hannah stands on the other. They watch him dance. Ratko finishes dancing and looks at the girls.

RATKO This is the last time you see me dancing. Do you understand? You only have until tomorrow to get it right. The authorities show no mercy. If anyone here is not practising, she has to deal with the Commander. Now, who wants to dance? *(Looking at Maika.)* You?

MAIKA Can you let me off today? I'll give you my cigar box.

RATKO *(aside)*   When Maika was brought here, she was mute through fear. She was crying all day long. The bloodshed has made the soldiers so brutal that they don't take any notice of the girls' crying any more. *(To Hannah)* You come here.

HANNAH   Me?

RATKO *(aside)*   Hannah is the same age as my daughter. Only a few days difference in their age, but I have no other choice. I don't take orders from anyone else. *(To Hannah)* You didn't practise yesterday.

Hannah looks at Souad.

SOUAD   Alright, I'll do it.

Souad goes to the centre of the stage. The music starts. Souad stands motionless.

RATKO   Begin!

Ratko starts to dance while he is starting the music.

SOUAD *(turning around)* Is this OK?

RATKO   More!

SOUAD   What about now?

RATKO   More, damn you. Your breasts should be shaking.

SOUAD   Like this? ...Yeah?

Souad shakes her body furiously, at a crazy pace. Maika and Hannah look at her in amazement. The music stops, but Souad is still moving.

RATKO   This is the women's room. That is what the Commander called it. There were nine women here until this week, but now just these three remain. *(To Souad)* ...Continue!

Music is played again.

SOUAD   Do you like this? ...Well, I'm shaking it all for you, aren't I? Or you think that I'm too old to do it? Come on... Come at me with your truncheon. Attack me... But you won't make me a prostitute. I'm not a whore... Mother, help me... *(She cries.)* Ramiz... Where are you, Ramiz?

She falls to the ground from dizziness. Everyone is silent. The music is stopped. A moment later, Ramiz slowly enters the scene, picks up his mother and slowly carries her out with him. Some moments pass in silence.

HANNAH	No news from her son?
MAIKA	Souad is really suffering.
HANNAH	Was it a letter, or something else?
MAIKA	No!

Lights out. In the darkness Ramiz's voice is heard.

RAMIZ Oh, I forgot to say that my family photo will be with me. In the picture, I'm standing between you and Dad and holding your hands. And I'm smiling. Even at the moment when I'll be facing the death squad, I'll always have this photo. I'm not afraid. Your son, Ramiz.

Lights up.

Hannah, Souad and Maika are standing centre stage. Maika has a protrusive belly.

MAIKA I did it once, so I could do it again. Though the first time there were no hard feelings.

SOUAD The baby is so small that he doesn't feel any pain.

MAIKA We have to do it right here. In this room.

SOUAD They seem interested when they see their puppies.

HANNAH	I don't agree with you.
MAIKA	What?
HANNAH	I'll keep it.
MAIKA	You cannot go back on your word.
HANNAH	Just what I said.
MAIKA	Are you scared?
HANNAH	No more than when I was brought here.
MAIKA	You tell him, Souad.
SOUAD	I was told I had a letter.

MAIKA	You're still a kid, Hannah.
SOUAD	Do you want to be a mother, like me?
MAIKA	We'll all do it together. Maika, you and me.
SOUAD	All three of us.
HANNAH	No, no one.

Ratko comes in.

RATKO	You have a letter.
SOUAD	Me? Is it from my son?
RATKO	You, no, it's for Maika.
MAIKA	My father.

Sound of Hassan's voice.

HASSAN   I am writing this letter to you, my dear Maika, without knowing whether you are alive or not.

Hassan enters, stands next to Maika. Souad and Hannah leave the stage Hassan and Maika stand in front of the audience.

HASSAN   The pen is shaking over the paper, I'll be executed in a few hours, but I wanted to use this last opportunity to write a letter to you. Do not be sorry for me, and if you return to the village one day, know that our death has not been in vain. Your father, Hassan.

Maika howls. Lights out.

Lights up. Hassan, Ramiz and Branko are banging their spoons on metal plates. Moments later, Ratko enters with a big pot, on a mobile metal stool.

RATKO   What's wrong with you? If the Commander finds out that you made a racket while eating your food, you'll get a beating.

He takes their plates and pours watery rice into them one by one. They keep away from Ratko and come to the centre of the stage.

RAMIZ	It's your turn.
HASSAN	OK.

RAMIZ Then, it's my turn.

BRANKO I can do it, too.

RAMIZ Then, it's your turn, Branko.

Hassan's spoon is full of rice.

HASSAN Grilled chicken with spicy sauce. Mmm ... no rice.

He eats some rice with his spoon.

RAMIZ Lamb kebabs, sliced onion and olives. Mmm... no rice.

He eats some rice with his spoon.

BRANKO Fish – smoked herring and potato. Mmm...

Hassan and Ramiz look at him. Branko sees them looking.

BRANKO Without rice.

He eats some rice with his spoon.

HASSAN Walnut-topped muffins.

RAMIZ Cream cookies.

BRANKO Apple pie.

RATKO Dinner is over.

HASSAN Iced soda, black, two bottles.

RAMIZ Iced soda, yellow, two bottles.

BRANKO Please buy a pink soda for me, one bottle.

Hassan and Ramiz look at Branko. A pink optical spot can be seen on Branko's face and at the same time, a warning siren can be heard. Hassan and Ramiz recede and sit on the bench at the end of the room.

RATKO *(aside)* He secretly added his brother's name to the rescue list. Last minute, and as the last person. He put the paper in front of the Commander. The Commander looked at it and said that there were seventeen men, but eighteen names were written down there.

BRANKO   He's a cleaner. He was added last week. He should be safe, too.

RATKO   He was added last week — a cleaner. The Commander looked at him. He didn't look angry, then he reached over the other side of the table and picked up a pink marker. I didn't believe that he did this with a pink marker. He may have picked up a black marker, but anyway, he crossed out a human being's life with that marker.

BRANKO   I shouldn't have written his name last on the list. Maybe I should have hidden it somewhere in the middle of the names. Perhaps, if his name had been written somewhere higher up, my brother would be alive now.

The sound of shooting is heard. Moments pass in silence.

HASSAN   Now we're the only ones left.

RAMIZ   He was only sixteen.

HASSAN   Same name as my son's: Branko

The sound of a tapping spoon on a plate can be heard. The three men walk slowly off stage.

The three women enter and stand opposite Ratko while tapping their spoons on their plates. Only Hannah has a protrusive belly. Ratko pours rice onto their plates. They come to the centre of the stage and Ratko goes to the back. The three women turn their backs to the audience. A red circle appears in front of them in the depths of the scene. Sound of a baby's crying is heard. After a while, another baby's crying is also heard. Two blue bags, half-filled, are thrown onto the stage.

Souad and Maika turn towards the audience looking relaxed. A children's song is heard. Souad and Maika start eating rice.

HANNAH   I fell in love with him.

MAIKA   I hate the colour red.

HANNAH   He was the only one amongst them who was kind to me.

MAIKA   If I go back home, I'll put all the red stuff away.

HANNAH	He could have pressed his boot on my chest-like the others, but he never did.
SOUAD	Can you hear that?
HANNAH	Maybe I'll see her again one day.
SOUAD	You know what the bulldozers are doing now?

The sound of a bulldozer engine turning on. Maika and Souad come out from the space slowly. Hannah starts singing a children's song. Branko comes out and approaches Hannah.

BRANKO	Where are all the others?
HANNAH	The school is destroyed.
BRANKO	What about the books?
HANNAH	Burned.
BRANKO	Are you scared?
HANNAH	No.
BRANKO	Give me your hand.
HANNAH	Put your hand on my belly.
BRANKO	It's not my baby. I won't even be allowed to kiss him.
HANNAH	Your face is disappearing.
BRANKO	I cannot find my face.
HANNAH	What would you do if you were me?
BRANKO	I'd throw him in the trash can.
HANNAH	I wouldn't do that.
BRANKO	You're not a hero.
HANNAH	You must go, Branko.
BRANKO	It's your choice, Hannah.
HANNAH	Can you remember my name?
BRANKO	We've seen each other somewhere before, haven't we?
HANNAH	Branko?!
BRANKO	Hannah?!

HANNAH   Hello, Branko.

BRANKO   Hello Hannah. Nice to see you again.

HANNAH   Yes it is.

BRANKO   Give me your hand.

HANNAH   Put your hand on my belly.

BRANKO   It's not my baby.

HANNAH   This is the baby who is talking to you now.

BRANKO   What about you, then?

HANNAH   I'm not here, anymore. Just the baby.

BRANKO   You're lying.

HANNAH   The walls had turned red. That was the first thing Sama saw after her birth.

BRANKO   Who is Sama?

HANNAH   Sama is me, Hannah's daughter. I'm exactly six years old.

BRANKO   Wake me up from this dream.

HANNAH   I can't.

BRANKO   My hand...

HANNAH   My face...

BRANKO   Was there anyone else in the room?

HANNAH   I can't remember.

She gives the rice plate back to Branko and leaves the stage, whispering a children's nursery rhyme. Branko stands still.

Lighting fades softly to darkness. Sound of Branko's voice.

BRANKO   Hannah, my love. I wish we had time to say goodbye to each other. I won't be alive tomorrow, and these words are the last ones I'll say, I'm afraid, but this pain will be over. Kiss you. Branko.

Lights up. The back wall can be seen with a frame of pictures of different men and women. There is a bucket near the wall with a handkerchief hanging on its handle. Ratko comes in with a picture frame.

RATKO   My son, my mother, my grandmother, my uncles, and the girl I loved for many years, were all killed in the war. She wouldn't marry me, maybe because I was too fat. But I cry that she's dead. Every day.

The sound of the opening of an iron door of a cell. Ratko hangs a beautiful girl's picture on the wall.

RATKO   Zeinab was the most beautiful girl in the women's room. The only women's room in a man's camp. There's a small window there.

Every day we watch the gaunt, naked men forced to dig huge pits. Then the bulldozers come with the bodies to fill the pits.

Zeinab asked me to get information about her brother. It cost her five packets of cigarettes. I heard from her brother's friend, Mesha, that he was killed on the first day. Mesha was one of the soldiers in this camp. When he heard about Zeinab, he got a strange look on his face.

Zeinab ran away two days later. It was Mesha who made her do it. First, he traced a cross on his chest with a knife and then he took off his trousers and raped her. Mesha and Zainab and her brother grew up together. They were childhood friends.

Hannah enters.

HANNAH   We're out of soap. What do we wash our dresses with?

RATKO *(aside)*   Hannah was the first woman in the room to be killed. She was lucky enough to be finished off by a shot to the head.

HANNAH   Will you keep a secret if I tell you something?

RATKO   I'm not used to keeping things to myself.

HANNAH   But I'd like to tell you anyway.

RATKO   I'll find you some soap this evening.

HANNAH   I chose a name for her.

RATKO   Polishing the boots is your duty today.

HANNAH   Isn't Sama a nice name?

Ratko doesn't say anything.

HANNAH	If she doesn't like her name, she can change it.
RATKO	You've made your decision?
HANNAH	Isn't Sama a beautiful name?
RATKO	...Yes, Hannah, it's nice.

Hannah begins to say something in English but goes offstage. Ratko soaks his handkerchief in the bucket. Maika comes in, shouting.

MAIKA	How dare you – you are a total bitch, Souad!
RATKO	Please keep your voices down.
MAIKA	She thinks I'm like her.
RATKO	I'll have to report it if another quarrel starts.
MAIKA	You'll report us anyway. Go ahead.

Ratko continues to clean the wall.

MAIKA I tell her not to wear lipstick when she's with them. She chats to them. She says if they think we enjoy it, they can't humiliate us.

RATKO	She's right.
MAIKA	It's none of your business.

RATKO *(aside)* Maika was the second one who was killed. Two shots in her side. She died in pain.

Souad enters, singing a poem in English.

RATKO	Did you get this week's stipend?
SOUAD	We've arranged to do something.
RATKO	You and who else? Hannah won't be admitted.

SOUAD It's another of our ideas. I'll tell you, but don't be a wet blanket.

RATKO	I don't make any promises, but, you can tell me.
SOUAD	We want to run away together.
RATKO	No one can escape these walls.

SOUAD   Maika is taken to the Commander at night; there's even a TV there. He promised her.

RATKO   The Commander shot his best friend in the head.

SOUAD   We can get out of here.

RATKO   But not alive.

SOUAD   I shouldn't have told you anything.

RATKO   No, well maybe you could.

SOUAD   I'm going to teach English. We aren't going to stay in this country.

RATKO *(aside)* Souad was a schoolteacher. She taught English and painting to children. When the soldiers rushed into the women's room, she didn't say anything. So, she was the last one to be shot.

SOUAD   Can you get a pen and paper for me?

RATKO   Are you writing a letter for your son?

SOUAD   No, for my mother.

RATKO   I'll arrange it.

He takes the bucket and goes to exit the stage.

RATKO *(aside, before exiting)* I always read the letters before sending them on. I know it's not right, but I've gotten into the habit of doing it. I need to know that I'm not the most miserable human being on earth.

He goes out. Souad stands on the stage alone. Souad's voice is heard.

SOUAD   "I'm writing this letter to you, Mother, and I hope you are dead. You forced me to become a teacher when I wanted to be a singer. You forced me to marry a man I didn't love. You and father made me remain silent forever. I will never forgive you, Mother. Your daughter, Souad".

The sound of the opening of an iron door. Hannah enters with an old pram.

SOUAD   Where did you find this from?

HANNAH   Everything comes at a price here.

SOUAD   How do you know it will be a girl?

HANNAH   I dreamed about it.

SOUAD   You cannot come with us with a baby.

HANNAH   I won't make any trouble.

SOUAD   That's that then.

HANNAH   We made a promise to each other.

SOUAD   We made another promise and you broke it.

HANNAH   She's my baby. I can keep her if I want to.

SOUAD   Of course you can. Stay here and make her a prostitute like you.

HANNAH   I'm not a whore.

SOUAD   We all are.

HANNAH   You're not allowed to say that.

SOUAD   I'm sick of you, Hannah. I wish you were dead.

HANNAH   Be kind to me, and baby.

SOUAD   I don't want to see you anymore.

HANNAH *(Hannah sees Souad as Branko)* Branko, please.

SOUAD   You'll fall in love with the soldier.

HANNAH   Put your hands on my belly.

SOUAD   She's not my child.

HANNAH   Oh...

SOUAD   You're not worth the effort of me even stamping my boots on your chest.

HANNAH   How dare you?

SOUAD   She shouldn't be born.

HANNAH   You are just like all the others.

SOUAD   I loved you, Hannah.

HANNAH   I just wanna hold her, that's all.

SOUAD   How could you have slept with one of those men who killed me, Hannah?

HANNAH   It was an accident.

SOUAD   I only thought of you when I was being shot, when they pointed their guns at me...

HANNAH   Branko...

SOUAD   You should never say my name.

HANNAH   Your face...

SOUAD   You can see the view through the hole in my head.

HANNAH   Your voice...

SOUAD   You can see my front door through the hole in my chest.

HANNAH   Branko...

SOUAD   Here I'm called seven. For the number of holes in my body.

HANNAH   Can you hear me?

SOUAD   You called me seven as well.

HANNAH   No!

SOUAD   Are you awake? ...Hannah?

HANNAH   I don't know you anymore.

SOUAD   Hannah?... Hannah?

HANNAH   Seven... seven... seven

SOUAD   Open your eyes. *(Calls out to Maika)* Maika, fetch me a soaked towel. She has a high fever.

Maika comes in with a soaked towel.

SOUAD   Wake up, Hannah.

She puts the towel on Hannah's forehead.

SOUAD   She's raving.

MAIKA   It's nothing new.

SOUAD   We need cold water.

MAIKA   We only have tap water.

SOUAD   We shouldn't let her sleep. She may die.

MAIKA   Why?

Souad looks at her.

MAIKA	She's not worth bothering with.
SOUAD	What are you saying, Maika?
MAIKA	Maybe it's better for her.
SOUAD	Are you crazy?
MAIKA	The child won't be born then.
SOUAD	I can't.
MAIKA	You can do it... We can all do it.
SOUAD	Shush! She can hear us.

MAIKA You don't have to do anything. Just leave her, go away.

SOUAD No, Maika.

MAIKA What's stopping you? This is a war.

SOUAD I won't allow it. We can't.

MAIKA Don't act like you're a saint, Souad. What would be worse? Won't you hate yourself if the baby is born and it smiles at you? I would. We'll all die like dogs and be buried beside our mother's bones. This is our destiny. This wound will never heal.

SOUAD Maika!

MAIKA *(shouting)* Don't touch me!

Some moments pass in silence.

MAIKA *(staring at Souad)* You wanted to learn how to scream? Yeah? It's easy, look at me. *(Crying)* I remember my mother's face. She was so scared that she became gaunt – her bony face like a ghoul. I said, I promise we'll meet again. I lied. I was sure the bus would take them all to the big pits. To the same place that these bulldozers want to take us. No one can understand what goes on in the heart of the mother whose daughter is raped all day long in front of her eyes... That child should not be born. This war should not give birth to any child.

Souad looks at Maika with astonishment. Maika removes the towel from Hannah's forehead. The sound of a siren is heard.

Hannah gets up slowly and goes out, like the dead. Maika and Souad go to the end of the stage and sit on the bench. Ratko enters with a postman's uniform.

RATKO *(aside)* Hannah was killed with the first shot, but only the three of us know that Hannah was dead a long time before the soldiers rushed into the room. Unfortunately, her fever was very high, and no one could do anything. *(To Souad)* You have a letter.

SOUAD   Is it from my son? Is he alive?

RATKO   I didn't read your letter.

RATKO *(aside)* Her eyes sparkled with joy when I gave her the letter. A minute later, I was in the hallway when I heard her scream.

The sound of the closing of an iron door. Lights down.

Lights fade up to the sound of the song "Padam Padam", by Édith Piaf. Hassan and Ramiz stand in the middle of the space.

HASSAN   Are you sure no one can hear us?

RAMIZ   Does it make any difference? Tell me, anyway.

HASSAN   Édith Piaf

RAMIZ   Was that her name?

HASSAN   No. The singer. He loved her voice.

RAMIZ   What was her name? Your lover?

HASSAN   That was thirty years ago

RAMIZ   Don't you remember?

HASSAN *(pauses)* I don't remember.

The sound of the song "One Thousand and One Nights" by Umm Kulthum is heard.

HASSAN   It's your turn.

RAMIZ   Umm... Kulthum

HASSAN   You're not so old that you can't remember the name of your first lover, like me.

RAMIZ   You didn't forget it either.

HASSAN   Do you have any news from her?

RAMIZ   Yeah ... I always think about her.

The sound of music stops and all is silent.

HASSAN   Are you ready?

RAMIZ   No, but almost ready.

HASSAN   Did you write your letters?

RAMIZ   Just to my mother.

HASSAN   Is it possible to take a bit longer – one hour more?

RAMIZ   For what? To torment yourself another hour?

HASSAN   I want to make a confession.

RAMIZ   I'm like your son.

HASSAN   With a similar destiny.

RAMIZ   What is your confession?

HASSAN   I'm afraid of death, Ramiz.

RAMIZ   You shouldn't be ashamed of it. I'm afraid, too.

HASSAN   I love life. I don't want to die.

RAMIZ   Think about that girl. About the girl whose name you didn't tell me.

HASSAN   Can you take my hand?

Ramiz slowly takes Hassan's hand.

HASSAN   My legs are locked, I can't walk.

RAMIZ   I'll help you.

HASSAN   Do you think the letter will get to my daughter?

RAMIZ   Maybe

HASSAN   Is she still alive?

RAMIZ   Maybe.

HASSAN   Her name was Svetlana. We fell in love, but I wasn't kind to her.

RAMIZ   You shouldn't think about these things anymore.

HASSAN   All my friends are dead

RAMIZ   Close your eyes. I'll get you out.

HASSAN   Just a moment...

RAMIZ   What happened?

HASSAN   Do you remember the last thing you saw from your house?

RAMIZ   My mom's room.

Some moments pass in silence.

RAMIZ   What about you?

HASSAN   The dining table.

RAMIZ   We got to the door. You have to go from here by yourself. Can you?

HASSAN   My daughter was hiding under the table, terrified, and she looked at me. That's my last picture of home. I have to stay and help her.

The sound of shooting is heard. Lights down.

Lights up. Hannah is seen in the space, alone.

HANNAH   I don't remember my last picture of home, the only thing I remember is being in the kitchen.

I'm in the kitchen. Right beside the cabinet on the left side. The door of the cabinet is loose, and it squeaks when it's opened. Father says the cabinet's squeaking sound is better than that of my violin. Then, my mom laughs. She says, "That's a good excuse for not repairing the cabinet." Mom is standing there next to the worktop near the window. He's making a salad. "Do we have olives, too?" Dad asks. Then he comes over to Mom and puts his arm around her waist. I open and close the cabinet several times, and all of us laugh at the sound of the cabinet's squeaking. We laugh for a long time. There are lots of different kinds of jam in the cabinet. I take the apple jam out. It's made of apples from our courtyard. The apple tree is right in the middle of the courtyard, where the soldier stood. Dad pulled Mom away from the window and the bullet hit the window. I screamed. Mom, Dad and I were clinging on to each other and cowering in the corner of the kitchen. Next to the washing machine. I had been complaining to Mom about throwing my red T-shirt into the washing machine with the other clothes. For a moment, I watched my clothes turning in the washing machine. I saw my mother's scarf. Everything went dark at that moment. The power went out and the attack began.

Blackout. Lights fade up. The three women slowly enter and stand in the middle of the space. Each one is wearing a red overcoat and carrying a suitcase.

SOUAD   I'm in my son's room and I'm tacking up the edge of his Maradona poster to the wall.

MAIKA   I'm powdering my face and I've an appointment with him in the city park.

HANNAH   I ... I'm not there.

The sound of a violin. Ratko enters.

RATKO   I'm the only witness to these events. But if I were alive, I'd certainly testify in court that they never happened.

I was the last one to be killed in this camp. They promised me that I would be safe, but then this is war time. They didn't need to take me with them.

Hannah's voice is heard in the darkness.

HANNAH   "I write this letter to you, my beautiful daughter. I do not know who your father is. Nor do I know where he is, nor what he is fighting for. He was not born to fight, and I know this more than anyone else.

Maybe I'll see him again one day if I'm still alive, but if I die, I hope my grave will be nameless. I have come to hate my name. Like all the women in the women's room. Hope to see you again one day, my dear Sama. Your mother, Hannah.

Lights down.

The End.

Mojgan Khaleghi is a writer and director who has been focusing more on directing in recent years, and she recently completed her latest documentary film.

She also directed the hit play *You Are Busy Dying* at The City Theater Complex in Tehran. As an actor she performed in *Blind Owl* and has worked with famous stage directors and movie makers like Ebrahim Hatami Kia, Mohammad Yaghoubi and Hadi Marzban.

In an interview with Iran Theater she said that she will direct the show *Dogs and my Mother's Bones* at City Theater Complex after the coronavirus pandemic. The subject is the Balkan Wars in the early 1990s, focusing on women's issues in war and the challenges and abuses they faced.

About the Play
Torange Yeghiazarian

In the fall of 1963, the U.S. government sent Duke Ellington and his orchestra on a three-month State Department goodwill tour. The band visited, in order: Syria, Jordan, Afghanistan, India, Ceylon (now Sri Lanka), Pakistan and Bangladesh, Iran, Iraq, and Lebanon. Shows in Turkey, Cypress, the United Arab Republic, Greece, Egypt, and Yugoslavia were cancelled after the assassination of President Kennedy. The Far East Suite (1966), including the song *"Isfahan,"* arose from the sights and sounds Ellington and his co-composer, Billy Strayhorn absorbed during this trip.

On New Year's Eve 1963 – 64, Iranian film star, Vida Ghahremani and her husband, David Yeghiazarian opened Cuccini, one of the first night clubs in Iran. There, they introduced Iranian audiences to live music inspired by American Rhythm & Blues, Rock 'n' Roll, and Jazz. Some of the most prominent and popular Iranian pop stars began their career at Cuccini.

While this story is inspired by actual events, certain characters, characterizations, incidents, locations and dialogue were fictionalized or invented for purposes of dramatization. With respect to such fictionalization or invention, any similarity to the name or to the actual character or history of any person, living or dead, or any product or entity or actual incident is entirely for dramatic purposes and not intended to reflect on any actual character, history, product or entity.

Much of the tour information is derived from *Duke Ellington's America* by Harvey G. Cohen, University of Chicago Press, 2010.

The blog quote is from *Take The "A" Train* by Ehsan Khoshbakht, http://ehsankhoshbakht.blogspot.com/2013/01/DukeIran.html

Thanks to Vida Ghahremani, Shahbal Shabpareh and Aryo Khakpour for their research help.

ISFAHAN BLUES

Torange Yeghiazarian

Developed in collaboration with Vida Ghahremani, L. Peter Callender, Nakissa Etemad, Laura Hope, and Marcus Shelby.

Co-produced by Golden Thread Productions and The African American Shakespeare Company in San Francisco. The play opened on May 3, 2015. It was directed by Laura Hope.

Characters

RAY – 50, American Jazz composer and pianist

BELLA – 70, Iranian ex-pat

YOUNG BELLA – 26, Iranian film star and night club owner

FARID – 24, the night club headliner

SARHANG – 50, chief of security SAVAK (also plays Café Owner, Man 1 or Man 2)

MIRZA – 30, the Maitre D/head waiter (also plays Policeman, Gendarme, U.S. Security Officer)

LOAN SHARK – 40, tall, hefty (also Capitaine, Man 1 or Man 2)

POLICEMAN – mousy, apologetic (also plays Gendarme, U.S. Security Officer)

CAFÉ OWNER – surprisingly refined

MAN 1 & MAN 2 – menacing, entitled

GENDARME – sincere, committed to the law

CAPITAINE – Police Captain, small physique, large ambitions

U.S. SECURITY OFFICER – sophisticated, cold

Recorded Voices: NEWSREEL – official tone, typical 60s newsreel; **CONCERT ANNOUNCER** – warm, excited

NOTE: Ensemble can be performed by three men

Time

November 1963; and now

Place

Tehran to Isfahan, Iran and Los Angeles, CA

Note:

/ followed by a second / indicates overlap of dialogue

Setting

The set is a versatile open space that can fluidly transform from interior of a night club to road trip to roadside café, police station and concert hall. Interior of the night club is black and white; the walls are painted with famous album covers of Janis Joplin, The Beatles, and Ray Charles.

A platform upstage implies a stage. An upright piano is to one side, a full ashtray on top, a tumbler next to it. Bella is stationed at the piano but it's clear that she is not in the club. The car is implied using chairs from the club. The roadside café and the police station (Gendarmerie) are stark and minimal: one table, 3 chairs.

A large white wall space is used to project images of the actual club, silhouettes of a drum set, mic stands/speakers, city sights, and actual archival footage from 1963. The projections are the main source of colour.

Costumes

Men are dressed in black suit and tie, white shirt, and hat. Farid and Ray wear turtleneck shirts. The night club waiters wear white gloves. Young Bella is dressed in a Jackson Pollock-esque colourful fitted open-neck satin dress and stilettos. Her hair is elaborately coiffured. Bella wears a loose North African/Indian style brocade dress. She is barefoot.

SCENE 1 – CLUB CUCCINI IN TEHRAN

In darkness, energetic music comes up, e.g. "Take the 'A' Train."
Voiceover archival footage/images of the 1963 Ellington tour.

NEWSREEL (V.O) Capacity audiences cheered the Ellington band in Tehran, the orchestra's first stop in Iran, the seventh country in the band's three-month State Department Goodwill tour. Eager to surpass the Soviet Union in the Arts Race, the Kennedy Administration's cultural campaign is carefully designed to gain support for its foreign policy objectives in each particular country. The State Department is building its arsenal of persuasion with Mr. Ellington's refined image and eloquence. Representing both American opportunity and culture, Mr. Ellington is arguably America's most fitting ambassador.

Spot light on Ray. Music shifts to Civil Rights anthems.

RAY　　　　　It was 1963. The year that changed the game. The March on Washington proved once and for all that we were the cause, and not just the Black cause but America's cause. The movement was one thing before the march, and an entirely different thing after. I was there. Everybody was there. We mattered that day, on the national scene. Not just in the south. Not just among the radicals and the activists but everywhere in the nation.

The apex of the movement. And for a moment I thought to myself that maybe, just maybe it would mark the end of the beatings, the burnings, the dogs. But two weeks later – well, you know what happened two weeks later. And I knew then that we had lost. That America was not ready to accept the Negro as an equal. The burning of that church with those four kids in it was going to mean the defeat of non-violence.

Lights up on Bella sitting at her station plucking her eyebrows against a round mirror.

BELLA　　　　　Get to the point.

RAY　　　　　This is the point.

BELLA　　　　　Your visit to Iran.

RAY I'm getting there. But first I have to get into the groove, you know. Connect emotionally, isn't that what you actors say?

BELLA I wouldn't know.

RAY So, you're not an actor anymore? I never stopped being a musician even though I stopped playing for a while.

BELLA They forced me to stop. You chose to stop. There is a difference.

RAY Ah... the illusion of choice, but we still have to live with the decisions we make.

BELLA Can we get back to the tour?

RAY Oh, now you want to get back to the tour. Fine. *(Gets into the groove again.)* I didn't want to leave the U.S. after what happened in Alabama. The bombing of the 16th Street Baptist Church in Birmingham left us all in shock. I could not get the faces of those four girls out of my mind. It was a crucial time for the Civil Rights Movement and I needed to stay and lend my support. But the State Department sent us on another tour. I mean we had just returned from Europe, promoting American ideals of democracy and freedom while our brothers were being killed in the streets!

(Lights up another cigarette.) Dizzy had agreed to a State Department tour back in '56 but refused to go this time. Duke had wanted the tour for a long time. He might not have said it in public but he was livid when they sent Benny Goodman to the Soviet Union in '62. Duke wanted to be the one to represent Jazz, and America, which to him were one and the same. So when the invitation came, Duke accepted. Who were we to argue? His little minions! Don't get me wrong; we were grateful for the gigs – and the money that came with it. *(Puffs out smoke.)* Duke was the boss. I had my own reasons for wanting it that way. Let's just say I appreciated my privacy. Something Duke had none of. He lived his life in the lime light. He had made that choice, and he was great at it. I asked him about the tour, how can we leave now? When our brothers are marching! He gave me that brilliant smile and said, "You can do more for the people if you're the best at

what you're doing and you conduct yourself admirably." He didn't much like walking but more to the point, he loved America too much, and as we all know, love is blind.

BELLA   Tell them why you were angry in Iran.

RAY   I wasn't angry in Iran. I had a lovely time.

BELLA   You have selective memory.

RAY   No, you're the one with selective memory. People say I never get angry. The Robot, remember?

BELLA   You did not want to be in Iran then. And I don't want to go to Iran now.

RAY   You are mixing up the issues. I didn't want to go on tour again. That's all. I did not want to be a trophy for a government that was oppressing my people.

BELLA   That's exactly how I feel now.

RAY   I know. *(Beat)* I did yell at a few people in Isfahan – I do recall that – but I was just trying to protect you, sweetheart.

BELLA   Ah, I love that word. You stole my heart that first time you called me sweetheart.

RAY   Ooo, then shall we begin our journey there?

BELLA   Yes! But please skip the bad parts.

RAY   May I just tell the story?

BELLA   I don't know.

RAY   What do you mean you don't know?

BELLA   You're dead!

RAY   Oh, you had to bring that up! *(They laugh.)*

Transition to the hustle and bustle of Cuccini. Patrons at the tables, waiters dressed in black suits, black tie, white gloves are rushing around, kitchen door swings open and closed. Bella watches from her station. Young Bella sitting at a table with Sarhang (the Colonel) dressed in a suit and tie. His hat is on the table. The band is implied through projections/silhouette.

SARHANG *(screaming at first over the noise, then the music gradually subsides)* I told that mullah turd to take off his turban and keep it between his knees.

YOUNG BELLA Who? Which mullah?

SARHANG   Some numbskull nobody named Khomeini. The whole trip he sat like that. I kept checking in the rear view mirror and I tell you the fucking vermin did not move, not even a millimetre!

YOUNG BELLA All the way to the prison?

SARHANG *(nods proudly)* One look at this here *(pats his chest pocket)* and he knew exactly who he is dealing with.

YOUNG BELLA *(lowers her voice)* You're wearing your gun strap here? Sarhang-joon, I beg you.

SARHANG   These lousy mullahs need to be taught a lesson. I would have executed him – not personally, of course, but if I were in His Majesty's shoes...

What is prison? The piece of shit will be out again in a few years with an even bigger turban! *(Empties the rest of the whisky from the bottle into his glass and gulps it down.)*

YOUNG BELLA *(waving to the waiter, Mirza)* Water!

Farid the band leader addresses the audience while he plays. During his intro, Young Bella notices Ray and Mirza standing at the entrance. Ray seems agitated, lights a cigarette. Young Bella excuses herself and walks to them. We see their conversation in the distance. Ray introduces himself. Young Bella shakes Ray's hand enthusiastically and ushers him to her table. Mirza leaves.

FARID   Ladies & gentlemen, we are very happy to perform for you tonight. The young lady sitting over there asked me to introduce this handsome guy. *(To bass-player)* I don't know, should I introduce you? *(Bass-player shows off)* Alright! On the bass, ladies and gentlemen, Andranik the mustachio! And in case you're wondering about me – *(shows off on guitar)* I'm Farid, your Chaker on guitar.

Audience applause. Music gradually fades to the background.

YOUNG BELLA Sarhang-joon, meet Raymond Hamilton. Mr. Hamilton is a very famous American Jazz musician, here to give a concert.

SARHANG *(stands and gives a handshake)* How do you do. / You will be playing here tonight?

RAY / How do you do. *(Handshake.)*/ Oh no, we performed at University of Tehran earlier tonight. And tomorrow, we will be on our way to Isfahan.

SARHANG Isfahan-Nesfe-Jahan!

Ray looks perplexed.

YOUNG BELLA It is a Persian saying. Isfahan is so beautiful that we say it is half the world. Isfahan-Nesfe-Jahan! *(Ray nods appreciating the info.)* What instrument do you play?

RAY Well, the piano. I also compose. And sing.

YOUNG BELLA My God, you are amazing! What other countries have you been touring to?

RAY Oh my, we've been to so many... Jordan, Lebanon, Afghanistan... We were just in India and Pakistan before this. In Delhi we heard a twenty-piece orchestra that used not one instrument familiar to us! It's been an extraordinary experience.

YOUNG BELLA That is incredible. I love travelling.

RAY You know Duke Ellington? You know Jazz?

YOUNG BELLA Of course! We love Jazz music: Louis Armstrong, the Beatles, Wilson Pickett, Ray Charles! We have a Jazz band of our own here. Look: Black Cats!

RAY That's your Jazz band?

YOUNG BELLA Aren't they great? *(Beat.)* This is so exciting. Duke Ellington in Iran! Where is Duke Ellington? The rest of the orchestra?

RAY At the hotel. Duke is a bit under the weather and the others are, uhm – resting. I'm here as their representative.

YOUNG BELLA We are so honoured to have you! You are our guest! *(To waiter)* Ye botri Johnny Walker, lotfan. [A bottle of Johnny Walker, please.]

RAY Johnny Walker?

YOUNG BELLA You don't like it?

RAY Oh, I like it. Thank you. I appreciate the opportunity to meet some local artists, musicians.

SARHANG Then you have come to the right place, sir. You will not find a more artistic place than this dancing club right here. I am pleased that the U.S. Embassy approved the list of local establishments we submitted.

RAY The hotel front desk recommended this place.

SARHANG I see...

YOUNG BELLA That is wonderful. We have not even had our official opening yet. Welcome to Cuccini!

SARHANG It is exhilarating to see Iran restored as the bastion of art and culture. What is your itinerary, sir? Will you be going to Shiraz as well? Magnificent city and the heart of the Persian Empire!

RAY Tomorrow we leave for Isfahan and then to Abadan, in the south, I believe.

Young Bella nods approvingly.

SARHANG Interesting, very wise choice on the part of the organizers. As you may know, Abadan is the center of Iran's oil industry and host to a significant international community of experts and engineers. *(Mirza delivers a note on a small tray to Sarhang)* Pardon me, the office is calling.

Sarhang rises, bows to them and leaves.

RAY *(to Young Bella)* The office? After midnight?

YOUNG BELLA Security never sleeps! He might be back. His office is just across the street.

RAY He certainly asks a lot of questions! Does he own the place?

YOUNG BELLA Sarhang? *(Laughs.)* No, he is just one of our regulars. *(Whispering.)* And to be honest, we are obliged to let him in – you know, because of who he is – Head of SAVAK, the CIA of Iran.

RAY Oh Christ, is he going to report me?

YOUNG BELLA Report you on what? No! Please be comfortable. Sarhang is a friend of my father's.

RAY Is that a good thing?

YOUNG BELLA Of course! *(Leans in)* It means, he has my back. Like an uncle. *(Smiles warmly)* I am so happy you are here.

RAY Thank you. It's good to have friends in high places!

YOUNG BELLA Exactly! Anyway, Cuccini belongs to me and my husband. But all of our friends helped decorate it: Farshid is Iran's best graphist, he made the stained glass lamps, the famous architect, Edmond, painted the zebra hallway, and Mohammad, our DJ, installed the burlap on the ceiling, for acoustics! There is no other club in Tehran that offers live music every night. We wanted to build something special: artistic and modern. This is our, how do you call it, trial run. Our official opening will be in two months, on New Year's Eve. We are planning a big party.

RAY It's a lovely space. And I certainly appreciate the live music. Your Maitre D' however, is a different story.

YOUNG BELLA Oh, you mean because he would not let you in?/ I am sorry.

RAY Yes. / First I thought it's a Whites-only club.

YOUNG BELLA What? We don't do that in Iran!

RAY Are there many Blacks in Iran?

YOUNG BELLA No, not really.

RAY I thought as much. Your Maitre D' explained that the club only allows men that are accompanied by women. This is also a type of preferential treatment. Isn't it?

YOUNG BELLA But we have to! Believe me. Otherwise this place would become a – what do you call it? Pick-up joint!

RAY Your English is very good.

YOUNG BELLA Thank you! I watch a lot of American movies. You know, in Iran, we love Blacks! *(Ray laughs, amused.)* Sidney Poitier, Harry Belafonte, Nat King Cole...

RAY Raymond Hamilton...

YOUNG BELLA Yes, and now, Raymond Hamilton.

Ray/Young Bella laugh.

RAY You know, I spoke with Harry Belafonte recently. At a major march in Washington.

YOUNG BELLA You were there? Oh, we watched it on television here. Harry Belafonte's speech was very good. And King, the leader of the march, he was so inspiring, I cried.

RAY You did? *(Bella nods.)* You watch American news here? You have television?

YOUNG BELLA Of course! We are very modern. Tell me; were you there when Khrushchev went to Harlem to visit Fidel Castro? They were both there for the UN meeting but Castro changed his hotel to Harlem, in support of your freedom movement! It was in all the news. They walked together down a wide street, shook hands and spoke to everyone. It was wonderful...

RAY My goodness, are you a fan of Mr. Khrushchev and Mr. Castro?

YOUNG BELLA Not Khrushchev. But Castro – he is so handsome. And he speaks with so much passion about freedom and the people! My husband becomes very jealous when I rave about Castro, and Che Guevara.

RAY I can understand why. Where is your husband? Is he here?

YOUNG BELLA *(sighs)* No, he left. He will be back.

RAY *(sensing there is more to it)* Is something wrong?

YOUNG BELLA Oh, it's nothing. He was upset because I received a new film offer.

RAY You're an actress. Of course!

YOUNG BELLA *(beaming)* I made my first film when I was 17, and they threw me right out of high school because of it! *(Laughs heartily.)*

RAY But why? That's terrible!

YOUNG BELLA I did not care. My parents supported me and that is all that mattered. My father, he always treated me like a princess; he took me to meet the director for a, how do you say it?

RAY Screen test?

YOUNG BELLA Yes. The director was Armenian, Sam-vel Khatchikian. He and my father smiled and shook hands and it was all settled. My first film! That was almost ten years ago.

RAY They expelled you for acting?

YOUNG BELLA Well, the film ended with a kiss. The first kiss in the history of Iranian cinema!

RAY How scandalous! Who was the lucky guy?

YOUNG BELLA Nasser Malak Motiyi.

RAY Can I see any of your movies?

YOUNG BELLA One cinema still shows my film from two years ago – *Fire and Ashes*. You want to see it?

RAY I would love that. Are there subtitles?

YOUNG BELLA No, but I can tell you the story: My husband dies, then I fall in love with a musician who looks exactly like my husband.

RAY Who plays the musician?

YOUNG BELLA Vigen. You know Vigen? He is Iran's Sultan of Jazz.

RAY Sultan of Jazz? That's – a very grand title.

YOUNG BELLA He was the first person to play the electric guitar in Iran.

RAY The electric guitar?

YOUNG BELLA Yes. Our pictures were on the cover of every magazine when the film came out! *(Enjoying it.)*

RAY   I am honoured to meet such an accomplished artist.

YOUNG BELLA Yes, you will. Vigen usually comes to Cuccini to relax after his other engagements.

RAY   Sweetheart, I was speaking of you.

YOUNG BELLA Oh. *(Suddenly shy)* Thank you.

RAY   I hope the school principal that expelled you was fired.

YOUNG BELLA *(sigh)* No. Unfortunately, the school administration agreed that my film was shameful and it humiliated the school...

RAY   Ah, shame, the implement of the pious.

YOUNG BELLA You do not believe in shame?

RAY   No shame, and no regrets! *(They laugh.)*

YOUNG BELLA I like that. Are you hungry?

RAY   The young man playing / the guitar is excellent.

YOUNG BELLA / Our Schnitzel is very popular!

RAY   He looks like he could be from Harlem.

YOUNG BELLA Farid? Yes! My discovery!

RAY   Is he Iranian?

YOUNG BELLA Yes, from the South. I'll ask him to join us. *(Gestures to waiter.)* Mirza! Please set up Farid's vodka and mazeh [appetizer] here and ask him to join us after this set. *(To Ray)* What would you like to eat? We have an excellent menu.

RAY   Thanks, I'm OK. But you know, Duke has been suffering from the lack of a good steak. India was particularly difficult. Do you by any chance have steak?

YOUNG BELLA Of course! Shall we send him a bottle of whisky too?

RAY   No, all he needs is a glass of hot water and a big juicy steak. And baked potato, if you have it.

YOUNG BELLA We have it. Our menu is all European.

She gives the order to Mirza. Mirza refreshes the ashtray ceremoniously, nods, and walks away.

RAY No Iranian food?

YOUNG BELLA No! People can eat Iranian food at home. Here, we give them something special.

RAY I would love to try Iranian food. What is it like?

YOUNG BELLA Maybe we take you to a Chelo Kabab for lunch tomorrow?

RAY I think we leave for Isfahan at noon. Can I have it for breakfast?

YOUNG BELLA *(laughs)* No, you can't have Chelo Kabab for breakfast! You leave tomorrow? That is too bad. I wish I could meet Duke Ellington.

RAY Come to Isfahan with us. I'm sure Duke would love to meet an Iranian actress. Particularly one as lovely as you.

YOUNG BELLA Oh, it would be great to watch your concert.

RAY No, I mean travel with us, the orchestra. And bring the guitarist.

YOUNG BELLA Really? They allow that?

RAY Strictly speaking, no. But that makes it even more exciting. Right?

YOUNG BELLA Oh, you are a trouble-maker!

RAY To be honest, *(Confiding)* I had to sneak out of the hotel just to find a place to relax. You see, the State Department dictates every element of our itinerary down to the minutest detail. We can't even go out for a walk alone. There is an escort officer that follows us everywhere. It makes me feel like a prisoner!

YOUNG BELLA Sounds unbearable. But how does Duke Ellington react to your rule-breaking?

RAY He always protects his artists above everything else.

YOUNG BELLA This is very important. My husband is the same way. *(Whispering)* Just yesterday, he had to intervene on behalf of Farid, the guitar player, to secure his release from prison.

RAY Oh my! What had he done – murder?

YOUNG BELLA *(laughing)* I don't know exactly.

RAY He looks so innocent.

YOUNG BELLA He is very charming. You will see.

Lighting shifts to Bella and Ray at Bella's station.

RAY Farid was quite charming indeed, and a big flirt!

BELLA I thought I only had to protect him from women!

RAY Sweetheart, you know you are my one and only.

Bella wipes away a tear. Ray reaches in his pocket and offers a bar napkin.

RAY What's the matter, Bells?

BELLA Thanks. *(Wipes away her tears.)*

RAY Describe it to me.

BELLA It's this damn tribute. I wish they'd just leave me alone.

RAY But it's wonderful that people want to honour your film career.

BELLA But the tribute is in Iran!

RAY Do they still show your films in Iran? I thought they would be banned after the revolution.

BELLA Are you crazy? Of course they are banned. They wiped me off the history of cinema for thirty-five years and now suddenly they want to honour me? They don't know the meaning of that word!

RAY Who exactly are *they*? *(Smiling)* These damn people who want to honour you?

BELLA A film historian and his students. Rayhaneh met them at a café in Tehran. They started talking – she told them who her mother is and the teacher went crazy!

RAY   Rayhaneh?

BELLA   Yes. My daughter.

RAY   Ray-haneh? You did name her after me! *(Bella smiles pleased that he remembers.)* Does she like Jazz? *(Bella nods.)* Does she play the piano?

BELLA   The saxophone.

RAY   The saxophone? Like Johnny Hodges. Oh, I can still hear his marzipan tone. Sweet and delicious.

BELLA   She grew up listening to your music.

RAY   My music. It feels good to say that: My music. My body of work. See, some things do last.

BELLA   Nothing lasts in Iran. Those mullahs destroyed everything. One day I was a film star, the next day I had to hide in the basement. Some revolution!

RAY   The mullah that Sarhang arrested that night, was he the same Ayatollah Khomeini that took over in '79?

BELLA   Yes but Khomeini wasn't an ayatollah back then and we didn't take him seriously. We were so naïve. Sarhang was right – he did return with an even bigger turban.

RAY   Whether it's a turban or a collar, you give religion the power to govern and you get yourself into a big mess of trouble.

BELLA   I hate those mullahs!

RAY   But you're not going back to visit the mullahs, you're going to be honoured by film-lovers who know and respect your work.

BELLA   Look at her email – she thinks I hate Iran.

RAY   No one who's been to Isfahan can hate Iran. It's a city to fall in love in.

BELLA   I never told her about our trip. Maybe the next time we Skype...

RAY   You didn't tell her about me?

BELLA I told her about your music, but not the trip. The only other person who knew about our trip was my husband.

RAY Don't forget the Gendarme!

Bella rolls her eyes. Lights shift to the club. Farid finishes his set.

FARID *(with a final guitar flourish)* Thank you, ladies and gentlemen. We're going to take a short break. Don't go anywhere – we'll be right back.

Applause. Sarhang appears at the door.

YOUNG BELLA *(to Ray)* What did I tell you?

SARHANG *(takes off his hat and sits at the table panting)* Riots in Qom. Apparently Khomeini issued a statement before we hauled his ass out of his masjid! Orders have been issued. Shoot on sight. Ask questions later.

YOUNG BELLA Sarhang-joon, should you be telling us all this?

SARHANG This is our sanctuary, Bella-jan. If I cannot speak freely here, where can I be myself? *(To Ray)* This is a very special place – Cuccini. *(Whispers.)* Communists, nationalists, and industrialists, all gather here. A sort of meeting of the minds. Very unique in today's political atmosphere.

Farid, dressed in a fitted white turtleneck sweater, black pants & white belt, approaches the table. He is dismayed to see Sarhang there.

FARID *(warmly)* Salam! The gang is all here. *(Rubbing his chin.)* How's that left knuckle, Sarhang?

SARHANG *(scuffs)* You would be wise not to –

YOUNG BELLA *(places her hand lightly on Sarhang's shoulder to stop him from going on)* Farid-joon. Guess what?

Duke Ellington is here!

FARID This isn't Duke Ellington.

RAY Hello. I'm Raymond Hamilton. My friends call me Ray.

FARID Hey, Ray. *(Shakes Ray's hand)* What's up? *(He sits down.)*

RAY   I'm a member of the band. We performed at Tehran University earlier today.

FARID   Cool. What's your instrument?

During this, Farid prepares his vodka shot and appetizer: carefully pours vodka in hollowed cucumbers and rests them on ice in the bucket.

RAY   The Piano.

FARID   Oh yeah? The guitar is my kick.

RAY   Yes, I've been watching you.

YOUNG BELLA You should play for us!

RAY   What, now? No, I can't.

FARID (*drinks a shot of vodka*) Beh salamati! To your health.

SARHANG   Those mullahs would shut you down if they had the power. They are not too fond of dancing music and alcohol.

RAY (*to Farid*) Is this an Iranian tradition?

YOUNG BELLA (*to Sarhang*) Sarhang-joon, please. You know I don't like discussing politics.

FARID   It's my tradition, cause I'm a cool cat! You dig?

RAY   I do. (*Amused*) May I? (*Tries one of the cucumber shots.*)

SARHANG (*to Young Bella*) I'm protecting you. This generation. And our future.

YOUNG BELLA (*to Sarhang*) Merci.

SARHANG   Your husband understands.

FARID   That's what Bella calls me – black cat!

RAY   Ah, the name of the band.

FARID   That's right.

RAY   Duke calls me Ray the Robot.

FARID   Ray the Robot?

YOUNG BELLA Why? That is a crazy name for a musician.

RAY Did you ever see Forbidden Planet? Robbie the Robot saves the women and children. That's me. Always protecting women and children.

YOUNG BELLA Really...

FARID Duke likes space films?

RAY Sure he does.

FARID That's cool. *(Downs another shot and holds up the cucumber.)* How do you like my cucumber shots?

RAY Refreshing. Do you eat the cucumber?

FARID Dip it in this yoghurt first, to cut the vodka.

RAY A yoghurt chaser! *(Complies)* Mmm, tasty.

FARID *(smiles approvingly)* Bravo. You do that like a professional. How long have you been in Iran?

RAY Oh, we just arrived last night.

FARID You are doing very well. This song is for you. *(Takes another shot then goes to the stage.)* Ladies and gentlemen, we have a very special guest tonight. Someone from Duke Ellington's orchestra.

Applause, it appears from the uproar of the audience that some are aware of the orchestra's visit, maybe even attended the concert earlier in the evening. Bella and Ray make eye contact, an overlap of past and present. Bella watches and hums along with Ray.

FARID *(plays his guitar and sings on stage)* Cigarette smoke, flying over the piano. There he stood, the handsome Italiano. And I thought maybe, for one moment – This is the end of my torment. *(To Ray)* Maybe Mr. Ellington should hire me?

RAY I feel genuinely threatened!

FARID Raymond Hamilton, Ladies and Gentlemen.

Applause. Ray stands up and bows. He is reluctant to join Farid and sits back down. Ray and Bella lock eyes. Farid senses Ray's hesitation and ends the song quickly.

FARID *(sings)* But oh no, it was not to be.
   I am cursed
   to always be free.
   This recipe never fails.
   Back to Jazz and, cocktails.
   Get lost in Jazz and, cocktails. *(Beat.)*

More applause. Ray extends his hand to shake Farid's hand, but Farid embraces him warmly and kisses him on both cheeks. Young Bella stands cheering; she is called away by Mirza. Ray and Farid take one more bow then head to the table. Recorded pop/R&B music comes on and fades into the background. Ray & Farid sit at the table.

FARID   Hey man, I'm sorry if I made you uncomfortable. Just wanted to jam with you a little.

RAY   Oh, I injured my hand and haven't played lately. That's all. *(Beat)* I'm astounded that so many people recognized the song. It's my composition.

FARID   Really? It's my favorite! But the album only says "Duke Ellington."

RAY *(shrugs)* The audience response was so lovely, it deserves a toast. *(Pours vodka)* How do you say "to your health?"

FARID   Beh salamati!

RAY   Beh salamati!

FARID   Cool. How was your concert, Ray?

RAY   Lovely. The audience was very excited. Duke held a workshop before the performance and the students fawned over him enthusiastically. He loved it.

FARID   How does it feel to play jazz for a non-American audience?

RAY   It's interesting that you ask because I frequently feel more appreciated outside the U.S. *(Beat.)* There are clubs and concert halls in the U.S. that are still whites-only. They make us enter from the back when we perform there! It's very discouraging. *(Takes another shot.)* What's the point of playing music under such circumstances?

FARID   It's a shame the way they treat you in America; I don't know how you put up with it. *(Pours both of them another drink.)*

RAY   Well, I for one, refuse to put up with it anymore. *(Beat.)* I'm surprised that you understand.

FARID *(nods)* We have more in common than you think. *(Beat.)*

RAY   May I ask you a question?

FARID   Be my guest.

RAY   What do you call Duke Ellington's music?

FARID   What do I call it? Jazz.

RAY   What do you call the music of the Beatles?

FARID   Rock and Roll.

RAY   And Ray Charles?

FARID   What is this, a test?

RAY   No, I'm only asking because earlier Bella referred to all of those as jazz music.

FARID   Oh, I see. OK, this is the story: the word for the drum set in Persian is jazz, pronounced jaws, and all contemporary western music, Jazz, Pop, R&B, Rock and Roll, it's all called jazz music in Persian.

RAY   That is bizarre!

FARID   And this is only your first day in Iran!

RAY   I can't wait to learn more about the local customs!

Loud commotion at the entrance as Young Bella and Sarhang return to the table. Policeman and Loan Shark enter. Loan Shark points to Young Bella then approaches with determination.

LOAN SHARK I'm shutting you down! No more of this, today-tomorrow game-playing!

YOUNG BELLA What is going on?

POLICEMAN I am very sorry, Bella khanoom but we have orders to close Cuccini. *(Waves a piece of paper.)*

SARHANG   Let me see that! *(Grabs the paper.)*

YOUNG BELLA My husband isn't here. I'm sure he can take care of whatever the problem is when he comes back.

LOAN SHARK He's not coming back! I'm going to pull him away from his gambling table with his tail between his legs! *(Both Bellas stand motionless, visibly shaken.)* That's right! I know where to find him!

You think I'm going to sit around and wait while your fancy husband gambles away my money? This place is mine! Mine!!! Do you hear me? I'll tear it down and build something respectable in its place.

SARHANG   Get a hold of yourself. What's the point of screaming at the lady in public? She is not responsible for your money.

LOAN SHARK   All you people make me sick! Living like Hollywood stars and not a papasi [penny] in your pocket.

POLICEMAN   I'm sorry, Bella khanoom but I have to shut you down.

YOUNG BELLA What? Right now? With all these people here?

LOAN SHARK   Of course! Public disgrace is the only way to teach you people a lesson!

FARID   Hey man, calm down. Can't we talk about this like civilized people?

LOAN SHARK   Are you calling me uncivilized?

Loan Shark throws a punch at Farid. Farid ducks. Sarhang is hit.

SARHANG   What– you son of a–! *(punches the Loan Shark. Loan Shark punches Farid, then reaches for Sarhang's collar. Ray tries to separate them.)*

SARHANG   You have any idea who I am? *(Reaches for his pocket.)*

YOUNG BELLA *(noticing Sarhang's hand)* No! Stop it. Stop it now! Fine. We'll shut down. *(Announcing)* We're closed everybody, please leave! You heard me! Good night, everyone! *(To the Policeman.)* Give me that piece of paper.

LOAN SHARK   Not too fancy now, are you!

YOUNG BELLA *(to Loan Shark)* You too. You accomplished what you came here to do. Now get out!

LOAN SHARK   You haven't seen the last of me yet! Your signature's on a few of those promissory notes too!

Young Bella stares down the Loan Shark. Cursing under his breath the Loan Shark walks away. Policeman herds the patrons out. Farid sits down. Ray fills a napkin with ice and holds it over Farid's bruised face.

YOUNG BELLA I am sorry you had to see this. *(Sits, exasperated)*

RAY   Don't worry, sweetheart. I'm certainly no stranger to bar brawls.

SARHANG   Bella-jan, I will make a few calls.

YOUNG BELLA Merci, Sarhang.

SARHANG   Well, I hope the rest of your visit is less eventful.

RAY   I should be going as well.

YOUNG BELLA No, please stay! We will drive you to your hotel.

SARHANG   My car is outside and I would be happy to –

YOUNG BELLA *(to Ray)* Please, don't go. Not like this.

RAY   Sure, I can stay a little longer. *(To Sarhang.)* Thank you for your offer. *(To Young Bella.)* Are you certain it's not too much trouble for you?

YOUNG BELLA Yes, of course. No trouble at all.

SARHANG *(to Young Bella)* I am sure what he said about your husband is not true. *(Beat.)*

YOUNG BELLA Good night, Sarhang. *(Beat.)*

SARHANG   Good night. *(Puts on hat, exits.)*

FARID   I need more vodka. Mirza!

YOUNG BELLA I think he left.

FARID   He would never do that.

Mirza appears. Farid points to his empty vodka bottle. Mirza nods. Ceremoniously empties the overfilled ashtray and leaves. The three of them chuckle.

FARID   You gotta hand it to him – your husband trained these waiters right!

YOUNG BELLA   He runs the place like an army barracks. I hate him!

FARID   C'mon ...

YOUNG BELLA   You heard them! Apparently, everyone knows where to find him! *(Sighs.)* He will never change. Never! *(In tears.)* I am such a stupid fool. The film was just an excuse. Anything so he can get mad at me and storm out! I am nothing to him. After everything we have been through together. Nothing.

Mirza returns during Young Bella's speech with a fresh bottle of vodka. Farid pours two glasses and offers one to Young Bella, she passes. Farid offers the shot to Ray who takes it appreciatively.

RAY   You should drop him like a hot potato. That's what my grandma would say. *(Imitates Grandma.)* That boy's a nuisance! You ought to drop him like a hot potato! You know, when I complained about bad partners – business partners.

YOUNG BELLA *(breaks down)* Oh, what am I going to do? Shut down and we have not even officially opened! What if that loan shark comes back for me? Did you hear the horrible things he said?

RAY   There, there. *(Comforting Young Bella)* Don't listen to those goons, sweetheart. They don't understand people like us. We create beauty in the world. And they resent the power beauty has over man's soul, a power they must either possess or destroy. You can't let them push you around and you mustn't let them change you. Another thing my grandma taught me – be who you are, fully and proudly!

YOUNG BELLA   I am an actress. That is who I am! And I want to do the film – it will not get in the way of running the club or hurt the baby.

RAY You're pregnant?

YOUNG BELLA The last time I was pregnant I was in *Tomorrow is Bright*. Nobody even noticed, except for throwing up on Fardin once. *(Laughs)* My leading man. He was a sport about it. *(Beat.)* This one is only a 12-day shoot. I will be back before the opening. Well, if there is going to be one.

FARID There will be an opening, Bella-jan. Don't worry. Your husband will clear up this mess.

YOUNG BELLA Why has he not returned? It is one o'clock in the morning!

FARID He'll be here. *(To Ray)* Best New Year's Eve party in town. You should come!

RAY I'll fly in for it!

YOUNG BELLA *(appreciatively)* You will?

SARHANG *(out of breath)* Oh, I am glad you are still here. This is serious. Very serious, indeed. This time, your husband has stepped on the wrong man's toes. They have issued a warrant for his arrest.

YOUNG BELLA How much do they want?

SARHANG It is not about money. That loan shark is just a lackey. *(Pointing up with his finger.)* This goes up – way up – to you know where. *(Waving his head in dismay.)* I am afraid it is out of my hands, Bella-jan. He went too far this time. Too far, I tell you.

YOUNG BELLA What are you talking about, Sarhang? What way-up? What did he do? Whose toes did he step on?

SARHANG It is bad, very bad indeed.

YOUNG BELLA What? What is going on?

SARHANG *(whispers)* The prince is involved.

YOUNG BELLA Which one?

SARHANG Which? Eh, the one that looks like Tyrone Power.

YOUNG BELLA My husband borrowed money from the prince?

SARHANG No, it is not about money, I am telling you!

YOUNG BELLA Then what?

SARHANG The young lady who shall remain nameless – the companion to the prince? Well, apparently she and your husband – eh, in other words she is no longer – eh, allegedly she has recently become – attached to your – *(Young Bella is speechless.)* Do you understand? They want to teach him a lesson.

FARID Good luck with that!

SARHANG This is no game, young man. These people take such things very seriously.

FARID I wish they would take the needs of the people more seriously.

SARHANG This is no time for your political slogan-throwing!

YOUNG BELLA Stop it! Both of you!!

MIRZA *(carrying a tray of covered food, like a hotel's delivery tray)* Excuse me, Bella khanoom. Musa Khan is asking if you still would like the steak dinner for Mr. Duke Ellington. *(Beat.)*

SCENE 2 – ROAD TRIP

Ray walks up to Bella at her station. During their conversation, the stage shifts from the club to a road trip. The actors face the audience to imply car. Images are projected to imply the road/ travel. Farid is driving, Young Bella in the back seat. Ray sits in the front passenger seat; he fluidly exists between the past and the present.

RAY How am I doing?

BELLA Magnificently! *(Ray kisses her hand.)* You never told me. Did Duke like that steak dinner?

RAY He loved it! He loved having a real steak and baked potato for breakfast. It brought him back to life!

BELLA I'm glad.

RAY Why the gloomy expression, Bells?

BELLA   Look, Rayhaneh emailed more pictures.

Projected image of Cuccini, spelled "Couch-innie", Tehran in present day. A grinning doorman stands in the background watching them.

RAY   It's the club! I recognize the zebra entryway.

BELLA   She says it's an event hall now. The students want to hold the tribute there.

RAY   Oh my, wouldn't that be lovely? A homecoming. I can see it now/ your name on the —

BELLA   Are you crazy? / Do you really expect me to celebrate at the club they confiscated from us?

RAY   Who confiscated it – the mullahs?

BELLA   No, those damn loan sharks. They eventually shut down Cuccini for good and threw my husband in jail. Then they had the nerve to turn that beautiful place into a cheap cabaret with belly dancing and bad music.

RAY   And after the revolution it became an event hall?

BELLA   That's what Rayhaneh said in her email. What do they do there – religious sermons and chest-beating parties?

RAY   The zebra motif might be a little odd for religious events. *(Beat.)* What exactly is Rayhaneh doing there?

BELLA   Research! She is so excited, as if she forgot everything we went through because of the revolution and those mullahs. Here. Read her email.

RAY   I don't remember you being this bossy.

BELLA   You have selective memory.

RAY   You're one to talk.

BELLA   Are you going to read her email or not?

RAY   "BibiBells" – Bibibells?

BELLA   I'm her BibiBells.

RAY   Aw... "BibiBells, guess where I am! Cuccini! The film professor who has collected all your films wants to hold the tribute here." A collector? He has collected all your films, Bells. That's incredible!

BELLA   One person remembers me. Incredible!

RAY   "The event is scheduled for next week. We'll send you a ticket. Pack your bags. I miss you. Boos, boos!" Next week? Why so soon? You have to get ready!

BELLA   They burned my films, Ray. They banned me from acting, and called me a disgrace to Iranian women! They said my films offended the modesty of the people.

RAY   Offended the modesty of the people? What does that even mean?

BELLA   It's some Islamic Republic mumbo jumbo. How can I go back to that?

RAY   But this is your chance to prove them wrong! When they see one of your films they'll begin to understand what a marvellous actor you were. Maybe they can show *The Midnight Terror?* That's the one I saw in Abadan.

BELLA   You never told me you saw one of my films.

RAY   You think you're the only one with secrets? *(Beat.)* Why should they get to define the Iranian woman? You go there and show them what a remarkable woman and brilliant artist you are!

BELLA   I don't know if I can. *(Ray gently caresses her face)* How did we do it, Ray? How did we find the answers back then?

RAY *(smiles)* We went on a journey.

Lighting shift to the car. 1960s pop music playing.

FARID   Here we are.

RAY   Is this the hotel? *(Checking his itinerary.)* Intercontinental on Farah Street.

FARID   Yes, sir! Hotel Intercontinental. Where only foreigners and the very rich can afford to stay!

YOUNG BELLA Farid!

RAY　　　　　It's OK. I get it. I'm no friend of "the man" either! You see that, right? We're on the same side.

FARID　　　　If you say so.

RAY　　　　　I do. We'll talk more when I see you in Isfahan. Thank you for dropping me off.

FARID　　　　She won't come, you know.

RAY　　　　　Who? What? Why not?

YOUNG BELLA I should go home to my husband.

RAY　　　　　Isn't he spending the night with the prince's girlfriend?

YOUNG BELLA That's my business!

RAY　　　　　You're right. I'm sorry.

FARID　　　　C'mon, let's forget about all that. If we leave now we'll make it to Isfahan before lunch.

YOUNG BELLA I can't just drive away with you! What will people say?

FARID　　　　Since when do you care about that?

RAY　　　　　Fly with the orchestra. That invitation still stands.

YOUNG BELLA Traveling with thirty men in a small plane is not my idea of a good time. Even when we have to travel for a film, I ask to go separately by car.

FARID　　　　Then let's go by car! One man, one Paykan. We can fly faster than any private jet.

RAY　　　　　Sounds irresistible! What's a Paykan?

FARID (*dramatically*) My chariot!

RAY　　　　　Impressive! What more is there to think about, Bells? Sometimes a journey can help clear your mind. You should try it. (*Pause.*) See you in Isfahan?

YOUNG BELLA (*challenging Ray*) Only if you come with us.

FARID　　　　Yes! That is a brilliant idea!

RAY　　　　　I can't. I have to stay with the band.

YOUNG BELLA I thought it made you feel like a prisoner.

FARID   You wanted to learn more about the local customs. Here is your chance! *(Waits.)* Ray, you wanna ride my impressive chariot? *(Beat.)*

RAY *(to the audience)* Maybe it wasn't the smartest idea – travelling with a married woman in a foreign land. I could tell myself it was because of that flirt, Farid; he was so exotic! Or I could site my deep indignation for the escort officers and the endless barrage of rules the State Department inundated us with. Mingling with the locals without an official chaperon was a definite no-no, which made it even more irresistible. *(Beat.)* But the truth is that it was because of her.

(To Bella) Something about you made my heart beat faster. You seemed fearless. You inspired me. And that is a rare thing. I had never felt that way about a woman before.

(To the audience.) You are a sophisticated audience – you understand what I'm saying. Yes? And that's exactly what I said...

(Back to the scene) Yes! Let me run up and get my things. I ditched the escort officer once, I can do it again!

YOUNG BELLA Excellent! *(Offering the covered plate.)* Don't forget this!

RAY   Right. *(Grabs plate and runs off.)*

FARID   See you soon! *(Waits in silence, then abruptly.)* Should we call your husband?

YOUNG BELLA Are you trying to get us both killed? For once, let him be the one waiting for me all night.

FARID   He loves you – you know that.

YOUNG BELLA This is love? No, thanks.

FARID   I'm sure Sarhang got the story wrong.

YOUNG BELLA Sarhang never gets anything wrong.

FARID   He does have a tendency to blow things out of proportion.

Young Bella wipes away a tear.

FARID   Come on... your love is legendary! Didn't your husband try to kill himself when your parents refused to let you marry him?

YOUNG BELLA I wish he had succeeded!

FARID   You don't mean that.

YOUNG BELLA This isn't just another one of his stunts! He has jeopardized everything this time. You know how many people we borrowed money from just to get Cuccini off the ground?

FARID   You'll pay them all back. Cuccini is already a huge success; long line around the block every night.

YOUNG BELLA You don't understand. It's not about the money. I couldn't care less about that. We made each other a promise, to protect each other. Against those goons, as Ray calls them. Well, where is he? Why has he left me vulnerable? How can I ever trust him again?

FARID   What? No... all he thinks about is protecting you, day and night!

YOUNG BELLA That's not protecting, that's suffocating! Why do you defend him?

FARID   I've never met anyone like him. He is a true friend. The only one I would call in times of distress.

YOUNG BELLA Yes. He is kinder to his friends than to his wife.

FARID   Your husband –

YOUNG BELLA Stop talking about him! I can't take it anymore! *(Silence.)* I'm so sorry about Sarhang. He said he went easy on you.

FARID *(rubbing his chin)* He didn't break my jaw this time, if that's what you mean.

YOUNG BELLA What was it this time?

FARID   Now, he thinks I'm an Islamist sympathizer.

YOUNG BELLA Didn't he see all those Marx and Engels books in your apartment?

FARID   I have a diverse library!

YOUNG BELLA I think you just like to piss him off!

FARID True. It makes for a little amusement in life.

YOUNG BELLA I wish it wasn't necessary.

FARID What?

YOUNG BELLA SAVAK. KGB. CIA.

FARID You think it's necessary? Really?

YOUNG BELLA Shah has a lot of enemies. People who don't want to see his progress plans succeed.

FARID Now you're just being naïve. The CIA propped up the Shah and they'll kick him out the minute he's not useful to them anymore.

YOUNG BELLA My God, you're so cynical!

FARID I live in the real world, baby.

YOUNG BELLA What world do I live in?

FARID You live in a dream world where everyone is as honest and direct as you are. This is why I love you.

YOUNG BELLA I love you too, Mr. Farid. So don't go get yourself killed for some stupid political book, OK?

FARID Yes, ma'am! *(Silence. They wait.)* He's not coming.

YOUNG BELLA We'll see. Just wait.

FARID The Americans keep their people on a very tight leash. They think we're savages.

YOUNG BELLA I think that too sometimes.

FARID Yes, but your opinion is based on years of first-hand experience. *(Beat.)*

YOUNG BELLA *(laughs)* Let's not tell him that. *(Silence. They wait.)* You think it's a good idea? *(Pause.)* To travel with an American.

FARID He seems different.

YOUNG BELLA You like him.

FARID You have a husband!

YOUNG BELLA Do I?

RAY *(jumps in)* Let's go.

FARID   Here you are!

YOUNG BELLA Is somebody chasing after you?

RAY   Not yet!

FARID   Alright, here we go! This old Paykan may not be as fancy as your husband's Buick but it does have a record player! *(Inserts a 45 record into the player: Louis Armstrong.)*

RAY   Oh yeah!! *(Mimics Armstrong.)* It don't mean a thing if it ain't got that swing! Doowop, doowop, doowop... We're swinging to Isfahan now, baby, oh yeah!

FARID   Cool! Say goodbye to Tehran!

YOUNG BELLA Goodbye Tehran. Hello, open road.

Lighting shifts. Bella at her station.

BELLA   You love playing Louis Armstrong!

RAY *(approaches Bella as he mimics Armstrong)* Doowop, doowop, doowop... It makes no difference if it's sweet or hot, just give that rhythm everything you've got... Doowop, doowop, doowop ... I needed to get out of that hotel fast!

BELLA   Farid was ready to give up on you but I knew you would come.

RAY   I'm so glad you waited for me.

BELLA   We were like two caged birds fleeing... so carefree and naïve. I want to remember those feelings... All I feel now is anger, bitterness.

RAY   Sweetheart, I understand your anger. Those final years of my life, I was livid! So much changed after I left Iran. The day John Kennedy was shot we were in Turkey. Ellington wanted to dedicate that night's concert to Kennedy but we were told the tour had been cancelled. When we landed in New York, the man at customs said to me, welcome home. And I just stared at him. Home? *(Beat)*

BELLA   Same thing happened in Iran. Riots, burning buildings, threats. So many people were assassinated. We lost all the progress of the 60s and 70s when Khomeini returned in 1979. But like idiots, people voted 'yes' to the Islamic Republic. I could not believe it.

RAY I know what you mean. The night Dr. King was killed, there were riots everywhere. I didn't recognize my country or my people in those days.

BELLA How do you think I felt when my own friends started to turn on me? We had to secretly leave the country. The war with Iraq had just started and all the borders were closed. My husband carried Rayhaneh on his shoulders for hours until we reached the pickup truck on the other side in Pakistan. *(Beat.)* I don't even recognize my country anymore. Who are those people? It's like my country was invaded by foreigners.

RAY You don't feel like a foreigner here in the U.S.?

Beat.

BELLA At least I can live my life here. There, I would have to pretend to be somebody else.

RAY I know how that feels. *(Beat.)* But Bells, this tribute is a private event, organized by people who already know and respect your work.

BELLA But those are the same people who keep the Islamic Republic in power!

RAY True, but I would hate to be judged based on the policies of my government. Did you think of the American government when you first met me back in '63?

BELLA No. I saw an artist.

RAY There you go.

BELLA But I can't do that with those monsters! Do you know how many people they have killed? Between the war and all the executions? I can't separate the people from the government. It's not that easy.

RAY I understand, sweetheart. There is nothing harder than leaving your home.

BELLA   Los Angeles is my home now... I don't want to leave here.

RAY   That's alright. Just email Rayhaneh and say you can't go.

BELLA *(hesitates)* I don't know how to use email. *(Beat.)*

RAY   Oh, sure.

Lighting shifts to driving in the car.

RAY   It took a lot of courage for me to leave my family home in Pittsburgh. Lord, was I petrified! It was my first trip alone, and I only knew two people in New York. Duke had sent me a train ticket and twenty dollars pocket change. The rest was to be determined upon arrival! It all could have gone very wrong.

FARID   Yes, but you had excellent directions.

RAY   That's right.

FARID *(sings)* You must take the 'A' Train, to go to Sugar Hill way up in Harlem. *(Ray joins in.)* / If you miss the 'A' Train, you'll find you've missed the quickest way to Harlem. *(Laughing.)*

RAY *(joins in)* / If you miss the 'A' Train, you'll find you've missed the quickest way to Harlem. *(They laugh.)* And I wasn't pregnant!

YOUNG BELLA I won't keep it.

RAY *(shocked)* Is that legal here?

YOUNG BELLA My doctor will do it. She has done it before. *(Farid clears his throat)* Oh, it's no big secret. I can't pop out a baby every year!

RAY   Little Miss Bells, I'm astonished!

FARID   This is why I'm never getting married. Who knows what a woman will do with your seed! They can get pregnant without telling you, and they can have an abortion without telling you. There is just too much uncertainty, man. I'm waiting for the day some random kid walks up to me and calls me Dad!

YOUNG BELLA Well, there is an easy way around all that uncertainty, you know.

FARID   Oh yeah? What?

YOUNG BELLA Keep it in your pants!

RAY   Easier said than done, I'm sure.

YOUNG BELLA Farid's being dramatic. The simple truth is no woman in her right mind would marry a musician. They're heart-breakers, wanderers, everyone knows this!

RAY/FARID *(together)* Hey!

YOUNG BELLA Ray, are you a Don Juan like Farid?

RAY   Well, I don't have his looks so I'm afraid there is not as much demand for me.

YOUNG BELLA I find that very hard to believe.

FARID   When I lived in London, women paid no attention to me. As if I wasn't even there.

RAY   The British are very cold.

YOUNG BELLA When I was visiting North Carolina with my husband, the newspapers called me the Iranian Elizabeth Taylor! People at the market asked for my autograph.

RAY   I can see that.

FARID   That must have been a trip.

YOUNG BELLA What? You don't believe me?

FARID   I believe you, baby. That's why your husband gets into fights all the time.

RAY   Is that right?

YOUNG BELLA He just likes to fight. He was a boxer. Still having a hard time ending the day without smashing somebody's face!

FARID   But he does it with style.

RAY   How is he going to feel about you travelling with two men?

FARID   I'm one of her approved bodyguards, you see. This is how it works: Bella is a busy woman but for obvious reasons cannot go anywhere alone. The three of us, me and her two brothers, share babysitting and protection duties. Each of us has a unique secret weapon. One of her brothers is in military school and scares intruders with his uniform. The other brother is wily and tricks the unsuspecting public away. And I, of course, use my extensive charm to focus attention away from her.

RAY Where is the husband during all this?

FARID Waiting by the phone, in case somebody looks at Bella the wrong way and we call in for help.

RAY Oh my, I'll have to watch myself! *(Young Bella smiles)* Why do I get the feeling we are preparing for battle?

FARID Don't worry – nobody can touch you in Iran.

RAY How do you mean?

FARID Iranian law has no jurisdiction over Americans so you can get away with anything. It's a sweet little treaty we just signed, The Capitulation Law!

RAY Sounds like something from colonial times.

FARID We're living it, brother.

YOUNG BELLA Don't get him started, please.

RAY Was Iran ever colonized?

FARID Not formally. But the British and the Russians sucked the juice out of us for centuries.

YOUNG BELLA You see, Ray, Iranians are a very hospitable people. Whenever a foreign power invaded Iran, instead of fighting them, we welcomed them, and showed them such a good time that they eventually gave in to our ways.

RAY You kill them with kindness.

YOUNG BELLA Correct. Take Alexander the Great. He invaded half the world but died in Iran. You know why? Because we gave him so much wine and women, the poor man eventually had a heart attack!

RAY Thank you for the warning.

YOUNG BELLA *(laughs heartily)* And Isfahan is most famous for its hospitality!

RAY   Is there any hospitality before Isfahan? I could use a wash and some nourishment. Not as much as Alexander but...

FARID   Yes! I'm starving.

YOUNG BELLA   Where is that Kaleh-Pacheh place near Saveh?

RAY   A what?

YOUNG BELLA   You're not vegetarian, are you?

RAY   Pshaw, wouldn't survive a day without meat!

YOUNG BELLA   Thank God!

FARID   This is the real deal, man. Head and Hooves!

RAY   Head and what?

FARID   Hooves!

RAY   You're joking, right?

FARID   It should be right around here. Let's see...

YOUNG BELLA   I see it! Right there! Tabakhi-yeh Saveh. Right there! Park right there!

FARID   OK, OK! I'm parking, I'm parking!

YOUNG BELLA   This is the perfect food for five o'clock in the morning! See, you wanted to try Iranian food, and here it is.

RAY   Are you sure? Why don't I– ?

FARID   What are you waiting for? Come on! No time to lose!

Farid grabs Ray's hand and pulls him out of the car. They walk away laughing. Young Bella follows, struggling to walk on the gravel road with her high heels.

Bella puts on a jazz record. Various images of heavily made-up sweaty drunk party people projected.

RAY   You and your hospitality!

BELLA   You wanted to try Persian food.

RAY   I should have been more careful...

BELLA   I wish Rayhaneh would be a little more careful. Look. *(Pointing to the laptop)* Rayhaneh went to an underground jazz concert in Tehran. At someone's home. She said there was alcohol and hashish and all kinds of things.

RAY Was it a Halloween party?

BELLA No, they wear that much makeup all the time. Having fun is illegal above ground, so they have to exaggerate their fun underground.

RAY What is this?

Image of Ehsan's blog is projected.

BELLA Read it.

RAY "Far of the Middle: Ellington's 1963 State Department Tour." Here is the map of our tour, all the dates. Who wrote this?

BELLA A young man Rayhaneh met at the concert. He is an architect by day and a jazz-lover by night. She says there are so many artists and musicians in Tehran she is getting dizzy.

RAY Oh my, this is making me dizzy! *(continues to scroll on the laptop)* "Ellington's music became that rare imaginary moment when gunfire stopped and a bird started singing over the battlefields of the Middle East." *(Stunned.)* Who is this kid? He writes about our music with such eloquence. *(Beat.)* I thought you said music is banned in Iran. How did they go to a jazz concert?

BELLA Underground! Everything is OK underground. To live in Iran you have to live a double-life: your private lifestyle, underground; the government's lifestyle, above ground.

RAY All my life, I tried to avoid that. But sometimes, it wasn't possible.

BELLA Avoid what?

RAY Living a double life. Usually, it would be because of some well-meaning white folks at an Upper East Side dinner party. They would be enraged about segregation and inequality. Speaking in "general" terms but keeping their eyes on me all the while. I would quietly sip on my gin and tonic and refuse to give them the benefit of my opinion.

BELLA   You always gave me the benefit of your opinion.

RAY   You're different, Bells. *(Bella is pleased, smiles.)* You know what I see when I look at these images? I see you, your fearlessness! There were so many reasons for us not to go on that trip together, but we did. We took a chance.

BELLA   But there were consequences.

RAY   There always are, Bells. Life has consequences! Reliving those moments now, I realize that we trusted each other implicitly – much like Rayhaneh trusts her new friends. I find that remarkable. We really had a beautiful thing going.

BELLA   Until we were arrested!

RAY   ----

End of Scene.

Intermission.

SCENE 3 – KALEH PACHEH DEBATES

Lighting shifts to interior of roadside cafe. Classical Persian music is heard from an old radio. Young Bella, Farid and Ray sitting at a table.

Café Owner wears loose long shirt over loose cotton pants, a long vest, a small round felt hat, and a rag thrown over his shoulder. He serves tea, with a tray of Lavash bread. He holds a half-smoked cigarette between his lips and mumbles his questions and comments indecipherably.

RAY   What did he say?

FARID   Do you want any cheese?

RAY   Sure. Is this sugar?

FARID   No, wait. That's salt. *(Waves his hand to the Café Owner. He speaks in a regional dialect.)*

RAY *(noticing the newspaper covering the table)* Is this the morning paper?

YOUNG BELLA They just use it like a table cover. I doubt this old man ever reads the news.

FARID Now, careful not to stuff yourself because Kaleh-Pacheh is very filling.

RAY The smell alone is overwhelming.

FARID It's the only thing they make here.

YOUNG BELLA It will take three days to wash the smell off your clothes!

RAY Great! I'm sure the people at tonight's concert will appreciate that.

YOUNG BELLA Don't worry, you will fit right in!

FARID *(to Young Bella)* Are you calling my people stinky?

YOUNG BELLA Let's just say they don't take a bath as often as they should.

FARID We like to feel natural. *(Young Bella rolls her eyes.)*

RAY Now, tell me again what this specialty dish is?

FARID Sheep's head and knuckles.

YOUNG BELLA It's like pig's feet. You eat that, right? It was a favourite in North Carolina.

RAY I'm from Pittsburgh.

YOUNG BELLA Don't all blacks like that stuff? Smashed corn and fried chicken? It's all we ate at Fort Bragg. And washed it down with lots of cold beer! *(Laughs.)*

FARID *(disapprovingly)* All blacks?

YOUNG BELLA It's true!

RAY Fort Bragg?

YOUNG BELLA My husband was in the Air Force. His platoon trained in Fort Bragg.

RAY American Air Force?

YOUNG BELLA/FARID *(together)* Iranian Air Force!

RAY Am I to understand that Iranian military personnel are trained in the U.S. by American military personnel?

(Farid and Bella wait not understanding the problem.) I mean, why?

YOUNG BELLA This is part of our partnership / with America!

FARID / This is how America takes back all the oil money! The Shah just spends it on arms and military training

YOUNG BELLA Keep your voice down.

FARID Nobody's here. *(To Ray.)* Yes, Bella's husband was trained with American Marines, Special Forces. He was a commando!

RAY My my, a boxer and a commando. Tough act to follow.

FARID Not to mention, night club-owner, designer, music producer and poet!

YOUNG BELLA Hey, I painted all the wall posters. The whole design concept was mine! And I discovered you! Don't forget that!

FARID OK, you win.

Café Owner brings sugar and cheese to the table. A mumbling of thanks.

FARID *(stands up)* My turn to wash my hands. *(To Ray)* Where was the bathroom?

YOUNG BELLA It's outside to the left.

RAY You'll need a net to protect yourself from the flies. And careful not to fall inside!

FARID Don't worry, I'm used to the fly-infested hole in the ground. *(Exits.)*

YOUNG BELLA You have nothing to complain about. Can you imagine me, with this dress, trying to use that toilet?

RAY No, actually. I cannot.

YOUNG BELLA I have to pull up my skirt and put one foot on one side, then very carefully put the other foot over on the other side, then –

RAY You know what? That's OK. There are certain local customs I don't need to learn about.

YOUNG BELLA *(laughs)* Ray?

RAY   Yes, Bells.

YOUNG BELLA Are you married?

RAY   No.

YOUNG BELLA Ever been in love?

RAY *(sighs)*   Yes.

RAY   With a woman? *(Beat.)*

RAY   Well, not yet.

YOUNG BELLA Oh my God! Does Duke know?

RAY   All my friends know.

YOUNG BELLA Is it OK? I mean, do people bother you?

RAY It's not easy, but I manage. I mostly socialize with a small circle of trusted friends and colleagues and we accept each other as we are.

YOUNG BELLA I think you are beautiful.

RAY *(moved)*   Thank you.

YOUNG BELLA What's the real story behind Ray the Robot?

RAY What – how did you know? *(Young Bella smiles.)* Soon you'll know all my secrets. *(Young Bella waits eagerly.)* Well, I was quite expressive as a child. I would play the piano passionately, completely unaware of my facial expression and body movement. Then one night, I was playing an out-of-town gig, and I overheard a group of people sitting in the front row talking about me.

YOUNG BELLA What did they say?

RAY The same old stereotypes. My long arms, big round eyes. Apparently, I would 'jump off' my seat. It was unimaginative. Maybe it hurt more because of that.

YOUNG BELLA People think artists have no feelings. They talk about us as if we are not even human.

RAY   Exactly!

YOUNG BELLA Sometimes I feel that I am living someone else's life. Have you ever felt that way?

RAY Constantly.

YOUNG BELLA Really? You surprise me.

RAY Honestly. I go where they send me. I play the music they give me. I compose whatever they tell me to compose.

YOUNG BELLA Oh, it is crazy. I am so happy now to be away from everyone. My father, my husband, my director! They are always watching me. Always telling me do this, do that.

RAY We must enjoy these precious moments indeed.

YOUNG BELLA Will you be this nice to me when I visit you in America?

RAY When you visit me in America? Why, yes. I will certainly be this nice, if not nicer.

YOUNG BELLA You promise?

RAY Scout's honour.

FARID *(appears out of nowhere)* What did I miss? Hey, you didn't touch the cheese yet.

YOUNG BELLA We were waiting for you.

FARID Ray, let me show you how it's done. *(Demonstrating)* Look, put a piece of cheese in the middle, spread it with your thumb then roll the bread like this. And in your mouth!

RAY *(copies Farid)* I like this type of bread that you can roll.

FARID Rock and Roll!

YOUNG BELLA It's called lavash bread.

RAY *(bites)* This is tasty cheese!

FARID *(to Young Bella)* Why aren't you eating?

YOUNG BELLA I don't want to fill up with bread and cheese.

FARID It must be tough maintaining that figure.

YOUNG BELLA Shut up!

FARID So, did you solve the world's problems?

RAY Was that our mandate while you were washing your hands?

FARID　　　　　No, Ray, your mandate is to list man's greatest achievements of the 20th century!

RAY　　　　　That's easy. The modern man's greatest achievement is that we have actually invented the means to annihilate ourselves!

FARID　　　　　That is a gloomy thought! But I have to agree with you.

YOUNG BELLA　No, the modern man's greatest achievement is Jazz! It's America's gift to humanity!

RAY　　　　　I wish Americans were as enthusiastic about Jazz as you. Frankly, most Americans still consider it jungle music, nothing to be proud of.

YOUNG BELLA　How can you listen to Louis Armstrong or Ella Fitzgerald and not feel proud to be American?

RAY　　　　　Easy. White America has dehumanized us for centuries. Slavery may have been abolished a hundred years ago but segregation continues to humiliate and exclude Black America. And it's not only in the south. The north is simply more insidious: on paper we have equal rights but in practice, we are left out just the same.

YOUNG BELLA　Do you think Martin Luther King will succeed in changing things?

RAY　　　　　I used to. But now I've lost hope in the non-violent movement. The problem is much deeper. I mean, sometimes I feel like a foreigner in my own country. Our story is completely excluded from history books. Can you imagine if our contributions were actually taught as part of the normal curriculum of schools across America? *(Passionately.)* Listen, our crisis in America today is not a Negro crisis, it's a crisis of identity. My being who I am, my having rights as a full citizen, a complete human being, is perceived as a direct threat to White America. *(Beat.)* But how can our existence be mutually exclusive? *(Farid and Young Bella nod in agreement.)* In today's America, I'm forced to live a kind of double life – a public persona that I've adopted for the benefit of white folks – and a private life for my own benefit, where I behave as I am.

YOUNG BELLA That is very convoluted.

RAY Schizophrenic, in fact!

FARID The upper classes control everything and the only way to benefit from the system is to play their game: become another cog in the machine.

YOUNG BELLA You want to establish socialism in Iran? Are you crazy? The Soviet Union would swallow us up just like that!

FARID That is just a scare tactic. America is fighting Communism so we all have to fight it with them.

RAY You're not afraid of Communism?

FARID Listen, the real enemy is ignorance. In Iran and in America.

YOUNG BELLA But in America they're separating Whites and Blacks. You never see that here.

FARID We had slavery.

YOUNG BELLA We who?

FARID In Iran. There was slavery in Iran. And even today, the way the poor are treated, taken from the village and sold to rich people in the city.

YOUNG BELLA Money separates, yes, and education, but not the colour of your skin.

FARID I was teased in school because of the colour of my skin. The kids used to call me Kaka-syah.

RAY What does that mean?

FARID Black slave!

YOUNG BELLA It's not the same thing!

RAY Oh, my. I'm so sorry. *(To Young Bella.)* But you said there are no blacks in Iran.

YOUNG BELLA Well, there aren't. Not like America.

FARID My ancestors are from Africa, brought to Iran on Portuguese slave ships.

YOUNG BELLA Four hundred years ago!

RAY That's incredible. I didn't realize there was slavery in the Middle East.

FARID Sure. You had merchant ships – they traded slaves same as saffron and gold.

RAY My grandmother was born on a plantation. Her family moved north after the emancipation.

YOUNG BELLA There is no parallel! In Iran, you could start as a slave but receive education and have the opportunity to rise in society. It was not like that in America. *(Beat.)* Farid, just because you sing like Ray Charles, it does not mean you lived his life!

Café owner places three bowls on the table.

FARID Well, well. Here we go.

YOUNG BELLA Thank God. I thought I was going to pass out. *(Rubbing her belly.)* Here is your first Kaleh Pacheh!

Farid and Ray stare at Young Bella. She ignores them and begins eating voraciously. Café owner mumbles something to Farid.

FARID *(he nods and smiles and then to Young Bella)* He wants your autograph!

YOUNG BELLA *(to Ray)* Careful! It's very hot. *(To Farid.)* He recognized me?

FARID He says he sent his daughter to acting school in France after seeing your film, *The Midnight Terror*.

YOUNG BELLA My God! *(To the café owner.)* Jeddi? [seriously?] That's wonderful.

Café owner presents a magazine with Bella's picture on the cover and a pen.

YOUNG BELLA *(takes the magazine, signs the cover and gives it back.)* Befarmayin [here you go].

RAY Wow, you're a real star! An autograph, I'm impressed!

FARID Now you understand why she needs a body guard!

Café owner bows in gratitude, mumbles something to Farid.

FARID He's asking if we are making a film here.

Farid mumbles something to café owner. Café owner looks at Ray and nods approvingly, bows, hand on heart, then leaves.

RAY What did you tell him?

FARID I told him you are my cousin visiting this area for the first time. He said you are welcome to stay as long as you wish.

RAY He believes I'm your cousin?

FARID Of course!

YOUNG BELLA None of your cousins are as good looking as Ray. *(Baffled.)* Wait. How come you understand him and I don't?

FARID You forget that I'm just a poor black slave from a village you took under your wing!

YOUNG BELLA And look at you now! *(They laugh.)* Ray, try this.

RAY *(bites the little sandwich Young Bella feeds him.)* Mmm, delectable! What is it?

YOUNG BELLA Tongue.

RAY Oh!

FARID My favourite part is the ear. *(Ray looks alarmed.)* It's actually the muscle behind the ear. Here, try.

YOUNG BELLA I ordered Bana-Goosh for him already.

RAY Bossy, isn't she? *(Beat.)* This meat is very tender.

YOUNG BELLA It's been cooking all night!

RAY *(listens)* What's that music?

FARID What, the radio? It's just old Persian music.

YOUNG BELLA Only in small villages like this people still listen to that stuff. The rest of us listen to American music!

RAY Hum, I like it. It sounds like violin.

FARID Yeah, it's Kamancheh. I have some 45's in the car. I can play them for you later if you like.

YOUNG BELLA Oh no! / Not that weepy stuff!

RAY / I'd love that!

FARID You got it. How's your soup?

RAY (*sipping cautiously*) Surprisingly delicious.

FARID Wait a minute. (*Listens.*) The music is Bayat Isfahan. A good omen!

RAY A song about Isfahan?

FARID No, not about the city. Isfahan is also a musical mode or key. You know how western music has seven modes? Bayat Isfahan is one of the modes – or actually a subset of one – in classical Persian music.

RAY How many modes are there in classical Persian music?

FARID There are twelve. We call them Dastgah.

YOUNG BELLA You have to learn them by ear because nobody ever wrote them down. They call it classical music but really, it's just old and boring.

RAY But this is the argument against Jazz. People learned it by heart and passed it on from generation to generation without writing it down. This is one reason the music establishment dismisses Jazz as formal music. And why Ellington is so adamant about publishing our work.

YOUNG BELLA But Jazz is fun and lively. We use jazz music in all of my films.

RAY What about the Blues?

YOUNG BELLA Ah, I don't like the Blues.

FARID She doesn't listen to Persian Blues or American Blues.

RAY But you can't have Jazz without the Blues. It's the root of everything: Jazz, Rock 'n' Roll, R&B...

YOUNG BELLA I want my music to be uplifting. There is too much sadness in the world.

RAY You misunderstand, sweetheart. The Blues is a dichotomy of tragedy and triumph. When you have nothing but you have everything. Look at this café owner. His surroundings are meagre but he seems very cosmopolitan. It's surprising. This tour has been such an eye-opener for me. I have seen tremendous poverty, and also such richness. Existing side by side. That's the Blues.

YOUNG BELLA That is beautiful, Ray, but we live in a country where people mourn their dead for a full year! The crying never ends and no one ever takes responsibility for anything. We need music that motivates people to move forward.

RAY I think music is a deep reflection of who we are as a people, who we have been. It's rich and complex.

FARID Bella is in denial of our deep-seated issues. She thinks westernization is the solution to every problem.

YOUNG BELLA You don't think we're progressing?

FARID I sometimes feel like we're just covering up our problems. We dress up like Europeans and pretend like we're the same. We're not.

RAY You shouldn't have to assimilate to gain equality.

FARID Exactly!

YOUNG BELLA What if I like dressing up like Europeans? Are you going to force me to cover up in some chador?

FARID Of course not, that's not what I'm saying.

YOUNG BELLA Who are you to preach anyway? You only sing in English!

RAY We can intermingle culturally though, right? You are not advocating insularity. That would be death!

FARID *(picks up his bowl to drink the soup and notices Duke's picture on the newspaper covering the tray)* Hey look! It's Duke Ellington!

RAY   Look Bells! *(To Farid)* What does it say? Is it a review of the concert?

FARID *(translating)* According to *The New York Times*, in an interview with Iranian radio, Ellington condemned racial segregation in the U.S. and hoped for resolving the race issues in favour of Black Americans.

YOUNG BELLA There you go.

RAY   That's surprising. I wonder what instigated that. *(Pondering)* Duke has never criticized America while we've been abroad.

FARID   What do you mean?

RAY   He's too aware of being labelled a communist.

FARID   Labelled a communist? *(Pause)* So, what do we do? Just shut up and let America bulldoze over us?

RAY   That's not what I'm saying but Civil Rights is our cause. Why are you so agitated?

FARID   How can you miss the connection between racial segregation inside America and those same policies abroad? As far as your government is concerned, we are all Negroes!

YOUNG BELLA Calm down. Ray is not a CIA agent.

FARID   Then why does he sound like one?

RAY   You must be joking.

FARID   Am I? We all know the American agenda: send the black musicians abroad so it looks like they are successful and have opportunities. Meanwhile, keep them out of our toilets and our schools.

YOUNG BELLA That's enough!

RAY   Where is this coming from suddenly?

FARID   Am I lying?

RAY *(takes a moment)* No. But you have not earned the right to say those things. I can't escape being American, and I'm quite aware of the hypocrisy of American democracy. But I would appreciate you allowing us to deal with our issues our own way.

FARID Thank you. *(Big smile.)* And that is exactly what we want. We want all foreign powers to – as the saying goes excuse me – pull their dick out of Iran. *(To Young Bella.)* Pardon the expression!

RAY For a moment there I thought you were really attacking me.

FARID This is another local custom!

YOUNG BELLA *(waving her hands in the air passionately)* Oh, my God. You are crazy! *(To Ray)* I apologize for Farid. *(To Farid)* Why can't you be more like Ray? *(To Ray)* Can you teach Farid some manners?

RAY Not sure that I'm up to that challenge. *(Beat.)* I'm sorry – what are those?

YOUNG BELLA Eye balls, my favourite! *(She puts them in her mouth and chews enthusiastically.)*

RAY *(cringing, pushes his bowl away)* Ah, do you think I could have a couple of fried eggs? *(All burst into laughter.)*

Lighting shift to Bella's station. Bella is laughing. Images from the laptop are projected.

RAY *(from the café scene)* I want to know if you ever actually tried pig's feet. *(Bella laughs)* That's what I thought! *(Walking to Bella)* Yet you insisted I try Kaleh-Pacheh. Iranian hospitality! *(Noticing the image on the laptop)* Hey, this looks like the magazine cover you autographed at the Kaleh-Pacheh place. What does it say?

BELLA "Bella returns to cinema."

RAY Beautiful! *(Going through images on the laptop)* Did the students collect these in preparation for your tribute? *(Bella nods)* See? You have not been forgotten. What is this one?

BELLA *"Tomorrow Is Bright."*

RAY You were such a vixen! Look at that platinum blonde hair. This one is from *The Midnight Terror*, I recognize this man.

BELLA That's Fardin! The one I threw up on. Oh, look! This is Vigen, in *Fire and Ashes*.

RAY What is this one called? I hope it's a comedy!

BELLA I think it was called something like *The Spoiled Child*. I don't remember.

RAY *The Spoiled Child?* And there is the infamous kiss! Are they going to show that? It might offend the modesty of the people!

BELLA Exactly! And you want to convince me to face those people again!

RAY I don't want to convince you of anything, Bells. I'm here to help you see your own truth.

Lights down.

SCENE 4 – THE BATTLE OF MURCHEH-KHORT

A desolate desert. Outskirts of the Murcheh-Khort citadel, in ruins. Young Bella/Ray/Farid are on foot, sightseeing.

RAY Why should the colour of my skin determine my taste in music? I started on piano with classical music. My grandma taught me all her favourites: Bach, Beethoven, and Tchaikovsky. But classical music is considered the purview of white society. And I – am expected to pursue Jazz.

FARID You mean you don't love Jazz?

RAY I do. But I also love classical music.

FARID This is the real question: do we wait for society to be ready, or do we force the change?

RAY You know what Khalil Gibran says? Rebellion without truth is like spring in an arid desert.

YOUNG BELLA And what is your truth, Ray?

RAY   My truth? My truth is that I've lost faith in music. I can't bring myself to play, not even on this tour.

FARID   Then why did you come?

RAY   Duke insisted on it. *(Beat)* Frankly, I'm ready to give up music altogether... Where are we?

YOUNG BELLA   The desert! Isn't it beautiful?

RAY   Where is the famous citadel?

YOUNG BELLA   We'll get there

FARID   How can you give up music?

RAY   I haven't felt inspired to compose in almost a year. My music doesn't seem relevant anymore. Not when children are killed mercilessly.

YOUNG BELLA   But it's who you are. No?

RAY   Is it? Is that all I am? What do people see when they watch me play the piano?

YOUNG BELLA   I would like to have the chance to find out.

FARID   You know, language is a funny thing. I actually would love to sing in Persian. *(Young Bella gives him a skeptical look.)* God's honest truth. But I'm afraid. *(Ray/Young Bella stop and wait.)* It feels too honest. Don't get me wrong, I still feel it when I sing in another language but I guess I don't feel naked. That's it. Singing in Persian makes me feel naked.

RAY   Vulnerable.

FARID   Yes. *(Beat.)* Do I feel like I have to protect myself from my own countrymen?

RAY   I know I do. Last year we were at a bar in Chicago and the white bartender refused to serve us. He claimed we were under-age! I didn't have any identification but can't he tell the difference between a 50 year-old man and a teenager?

YOUNG BELLA   You're 50?

FARID   What an asshole!

RAY   I refuse to play for those people anymore!

FARID   As you should!

YOUNG BELLA Shh... listen.

RAY/FARID What?

YOUNG BELLA Silence! Not a soul around.

FARID Don't tell me.

YOUNG BELLA Yes!

RAY What?

YOUNG BELLA *(playfully)* It's time.

Lighting shifts. Bella and Ray at her station. Laptop is open.

BELLA Rayhaneh is going to Isfahan with her new friends. She is so much like I was back then.

RAY Isfahan nesfe-jahan!

BELLA I always wanted twelve daughters. I dreamed of taking them to the film set with me, and they would grow up to be filmmakers: writer, producer, director ... You know, we would have a complete production company!

RAY Bells, you have three beautiful children. That is something to celebrate.

BELLA Something to celebrate. *(Beat.)* I'm sorry I missed your funeral. It was a beautiful concert. I read about it in the newspaper. Duke spoke. They all said very nice things about you and your work. *(Sigh.)* You and my husband both left me too early.

RAY At least I show up when you call.

BELLA Yes you do. Why did you? Why did you show up when I called?

RAY You have to ask? *(Bella waits)* We left something unfinished. I left something unfinished and I would like to – see it through – I suppose. I would like to understand it.

BELLA I left my whole life unfinished in Iran. We had to start from nothing here. I was lucky that I found small parts in television and independent films. But it wasn't so easy for my husband. He was not used to being a small fish in such a big pond.

RAY   You are the resilient one, Bells. You always have been.

BELLA   I did not speak at my husband's funeral. I could not find the words. There was too much emptiness. Some musicians that used to play at Cuccini said a few words. Nobody sang. *(Beat.)* He couldn't take the loneliness. Life in America is very lonely. You have everything and it seems you should be happy but you are not. It's like that Shakespeare quote...

RAY   "The apprehension of the good gives but the greater feeling to the worse!"

BELLA   Yes. You feel worse remembering all that you left behind. I am all alone. The children grew up and left. I see them maybe once a year, if I am lucky, and they can take Nowruz off. Everybody is so busy. They get angry when I call. "Mama-jan, I'm busy now, will call you later." Rayhaneh only emails. When my internet was down, I didn't email her for a whole month and she didn't even notice. She didn't call. When I finally was able to check my emails, there were six emails from her, two lines each. "How are you, BibiBells? I'm fine. Boos, boos!" I think she had scheduled them for automatic sending.

RAY   I'm sure she didn't. She loves you. Bells? *(Bella turns to him.)* Are you worried about how you will be remembered?

BELLA *(sighs)* It's easier when you die young. People don't forget you.

RAY   Thanks! But being alive is much more fun. I can vouch for that!

Lighting shifts. The scene begins at the end of Otis Redding's "These Arms of Mine". Young Bella is dancing dramatically. Farid/Ray watch amused.

YOUNG BELLA Come on, you two, don't be so predictable.

RAY   But you are such a pleasure to watch.

FARID   What was in that Kaleh Pacheh?

RAY   Eye balls!

YOUNG BELLA   My husband used to sing that song to me. *(Softens.)* Extend his arms to me, so handsome, and that voice… I would just melt. *(Shaking her head, to come back to reality.)* I was a fool to listen to his stories, to believe his lies!

RAY   He obviously does not deserve you. It's time to forget about the past and move on.

FARID   You have a great life. What about me? *(Inserts a new 45 – "I Who Have Nothing" by Ben E King, grabs his guitar from the car & strums along. Sings.)* I! doom, doom, doom, doom! I who have nothing! Ba-ba-ba-I!

YOUNG BELLA *(emotional, sings)* I who have no one …

FARID *(sings)*   Believe me, girl when I say …

RAY   Sweetheart …

YOUNG BELLA *(sings)* I'm just a no one with nothing to give you at all! I love you! *(She starts sobbing.)*

Awkward pause. Farid/Ray uncertain how to help Young Bella. Ray begins whistling "My Butterfly" tune and dancing à la Fred Astaire. Farid recognizes the tune, takes out his guitar and accompanies Ray. Ray sings and dances with flair.

RAY *(sings)* Hey fat cats, welcome my baby –
I'm tell-ing you.
Make room for my bu-bu-tterfly.
When she steps in to, to the room –
Va-va-va voom!
You'll see my bu-bu-bu-tterfly.

Young Bella watches appreciatively.

RAY *(sings)* She's no one's fool so don't try foo-oo-ling her –
Haven't you heard?
Bright like the sun that shines up i-in the
air – Her wi-ings are spread.

YOUNG BELLA   That's right! I'm nobody's fool!

RAY *(sings)* Step back and make room for my queen –
Haven't you seen?

Farid and Ray dance: large gestures, trying hard to charm Young Bella out of her tears.

RAY/FARID *(together sing)* She is the beau-ti-e-est.
No doubt, the cu-ti-e-est.
Here comes my bu-bu-bu-tterfly!

Ray/Farid pass out laughing. Young Bella rushes to them and embraces both, they laugh together.

YOUNG BELLA Bravo! That was beautiful! Thank you!

RAY How is my butterfly?

YOUNG BELLA Much better now. *(Wipes away tears, mascara.)*

Ray takes out a bar napkin from his pocket and offers it to Young Bella. He takes another napkin and starts writing on it. He is improvising a new tune, this is Bella's song: "Isfahan Blues."

RAY *(writing)* My heart feels desolate as the desert, but in your eyes – what? In your eyes... *(Looks up at Young Bella)* In your eyes I see stars. *(Smiles.)* Huh, this is interesting. *(Back to writing)* I dream, she holds my hand all night – should this be B-flat or C-sharp? *(Hums)* Soft as a bird in flight, da dee dee dum... *(Puts the napkin in his pocket.)* Bells, dance with me.

Young Bella takes Ray's hand. They dance. Farid accompanies on the guitar.

FARID Is this a new song?

RAY *(sings)* Your eyes... they take me to the stars ...

FARID Hey, are we going to waltz to the citadel?

RAY *(sings)* I dream ...

YOUNG BELLA I dream ...

FARID You're a good dancer.

RAY Shh...

Young Bella and Ray embrace, holding on for dear life. Then Young Bella kisses Ray gently on the cheek and steps away.

RAY *(to the audience)* It was noon. The sun beating on the cracked dusty road. A place more foreign than I had ever experienced before, yet – I felt at home. In her presence, I felt my bones slowly relaxing. *(Pause)* The whole time we were on tour, I had heard no music in my head, only the sounds of four little girls screaming and now, suddenly, the notes flowed through my mind. And I began to breathe again.

BELLA Then you walked away from me.

RAY I didn't mean to...

Ray joins Young Bella and Farid looking at the citadel.

YOUNG BELLA We are here. The Citadel of Murcheh-Khort! My God, isn't it something? This is where Nader Shah defeated the Afghan army. Back in the 17th century, or was it the 18th?

RAY Very mysterious, such desolation. It's reminiscent of a long battle, an entire city sacked, *(breathes it in)* very Shakespearean.

YOUNG BELLA It was a decisive battle. Helped Nader take the throne. This was actually in use for many years, even up until a hundred years ago.

Ray notices Farid pointing to the other direction, gesturing "let's go for a smoke", walks toward him, they go off stage.

YOUNG BELLA Now the city is pretty much abandoned. *(Walks some more.)* Look at this dome – what is the writing underneath? *(Walks closer to the wall, struggles to read.)* Farid, what does it say here? Can you read it? *(Turns around.)* Farid? Ray?

Ray and Farid are not around. Young Bella notices two men, strangers staring at her. They begin walking towards her.

She steps back, alarmed. Looks around her. No sign of Farid and Ray.

YOUNG BELLA Stay away!

MAN 1 Is she the actress in *Tomorrow is Bright*?

MAN 2 I dunno but she sure is making my today bright. *(Enjoys his own wit.)*

MAN 1   Khanoom khoshgeleh [pretty lady], you are too pretty to be unkind.

YOUNG BELLA Don't come any closer or I'll scream.

MAN 2   No need to scream. Just whisper and I'll come to you.

MAN 1   Scream all you want, we're the only ones here.

YOUNG BELLA My friends are back there. They can hear me.

MAN 2   Is that right?

MAN 1   She is that actress on the cover of the magazine. With Vigen. What was the name of the film?

MAN 2   *Fire and Ashes.* They said she used fake tits and ass. Balloons.

MAN 1   No way.

YOUNG BELLA I'm not who you think I am.

MAN 2   What's your name, Jigar [Darling]? We're not going to hurt you.

MAN 1   We just want to have a little bit of fun.

MAN 2   You like having fun. Am I right?

YOUNG BELLA If you take one more step, I'll scream.

MAN 1   She really wants to scream.

MAN 2   Let's give her something to scream about.

The men pounce. Young Bella screams. Farid and Ray appear from the distance, relaxed from their smoke.

RAY   What's going on?

FARID   Nafamidam, Ya'ni Chi! [What the hell is this!]

YOUNG BELLA Komak! Help me!

Farid and Ray run, pull the two men away. Farid holds one and punches him in the face. The other man goes for Ray. Young Bella pushes the man from behind, he falls.

YOUNG BELLA   Get away from me, you animal! *(To Ray)* Are you OK?

RAY   Yes. Are you hurt?

The man on the ground grabs Ray's hands and pulls him to the ground. Ray punches him in the face.

YOUNG BELLA Ray! No!

Farid knocks the first man on the ground and staggers over to Ray. The first man sneaks close behind Young Bella and sticks a needle in her ass.

YOUNG BELLA Ow!

FARID Get the hell away from her, goosaleh [you ass]! (*Kicks the man away.*)

RAY What in the world?!

MAN 2 (*as he runs away, triumphantly*) It's not a balloon!!! It's not a balloon!

FARID Get lost, you stupid ass!

Farid runs after the two men, they get away. Young Bella wipes her dress, her ass, bursts into tears.

RAY What just happened, Bells? Sweetheart ... (*Reaches for Young Bella.*) Ow, my hand...

Sound of police siren approaching from the distance.

FARID (*limping over*) Are you OK? (*Embraces Young Bella, comforts her, wipes away her tears*) All better. (*Straightens out her hair, maybe there is a hair-piece that's come undone that he examines and throws away.*) Good as new, areh [yes]?

YOUNG BELLA I'm OK. But they broke Ray's fingers. How's he going to play?

FARID Let me see.

RAY I don't think it's broken but it hurts like hell.

Spinning red/blue light of police car. A Gendarme walks up to the group as they huddle examining each other's bruises.

GENDARME What's going on here?

He grabs the men's collars and lifts them up.

GENDARME What are you doing?

FARID Let me go! (*Resists*)

RAY *(to Farid)* Stay calm...

YOUNG BELLA No, officer, please.

Farid tries to free himself, but the Gendarme wrangles him down.

YOUNG BELLA These men are my friends. What are you doing?

GENDARME Eh...? Explain it to the Capitaine at the Gendarmerie. *(Frisking Ray)* Where are you from – Kuwait? *(Finds nothing)* Stay right here. *(Frisking Farid, pulls a bag from his side pocket)* What do we have here? Heroin?

RAY Shit!

GENDARME You are coming with me.

YOUNG BELLA But you are arresting the wrong men! *(Steps towards the Gendarme)* Do you understand what I'm saying?

The Gendarme pushes Young Bella back using his club.

YOUNG BELLA *(stumbles/falls)* Ow!

FARID Hey, she's pregnant!

GENDARME Figures. *(Spits at Young Bella.)*

Lighting shifts to Bella's station.

BELLA My so-called protectors abandoned me for a smoke!

RAY Bells!

BELLA Did you and Farid ever...?

RAY Sh... A gentleman never tells. And a lady never asks! *(Beat)*

BELLA How are your hands? *(Ray holds them up, they're OK, smiles)* It's shameful what they did.

RAY Farid took most of the punches. I didn't realize just how desirable you were until I saw the lust in their eyes.

BELLA Why do men always treat women like prostitutes?

RAY All men? All the time? Don't you think you are exaggerating a little?

BELLA My father treated me like a princess.

RAY You are being so unfair... we'll let them decide.

BELLA   Do we have to do this next scene?

RAY   We do. It's my big moment.

Bella sighs.

RAY   Wish me luck!

BELLA   Good luck!

Lighting shifts. Interior of the Gendarmerie. Ray and Farid are nearly passed out on two chairs. The Capitaine is sitting behind a table questioning Young Bella who is sitting across from him.

The Gendarme is standing in the corner grinning.

CAPITAINE   I've had it with these two. *(To Young Bella)* Are you going to tell me anything useful or shall I keep you all here overnight?

YOUNG BELLA If you would just let me make one phone call, sir, I can clear up this whole misunderstanding. I promise you! Please?

CAPITAINE   What do you think this is, Hotel Shah Abbas? *(Gendarme chuckles.)* This is a Gendarmerie! We protect the nation from parasites like you!

YOUNG BELLA Don't you recognize me?

CAPITAINE   Oh, I recognize you. You're the type that sweet talks her way out of every situation. Well, I'm not one of those men! I'm going to keep you here until you talk.

YOUNG BELLA But we need to get out of here. This man is a famous American musician. He has a concert tonight!

CAPITAINE   American? He looks African to me. Hey, Kaka-Syah! *(Gendarme laughs.)* You bring hashish to Iran from Africa? You know the penalty for drug-trafficking? *(To Gendarme)* Did you radio headquarters? Javadi, tell them we don't tolerate smugglers in Iran!

GENDARME   Yes, sir! The General is due back at six.

CAPITAINE *(to Ray)* How do you like to spend the rest of your life in prison, huh?

YOUNG BELLA He is a musician. They're both musicians!

CAPITAINE   Oh yeah? And are you the dancer?

GENDARME   He said she's pregnant.

CAPITAINE *(scoffs)* Which one's the father?

YOUNG BELLA My husband is in Tehran!

CAPITAINE   Eh? It takes three to knock this one up!

YOUNG BELLA You're disgusting!

CAPITAINE   I'll tell you what's disgusting: two smugglers and a whore parading around in the middle of a national monument. That's disgusting!

GENDARME   They were putting on a big show, singing and dancing.

CAPITAINE   And only this imbecile to watch. So sad. *(The Gendarme sulks.)* Now, listen to me! Either you spill your guts right now or I'll lock you up in our top notch basement facility and let the rats suck the information out of you. You get the picture? *(Silence, no answer.)* Good. Where are you coming from?

YOUNG BELLA Tehran.

CAPITAINE   Where are you going to?

YOUNG BELLA Isfahan.

CAPITAINE   Is that your final destination?

YOUNG BELLA ...

CAPITAINE *(louder)* Is that your final destination?

YOUNG BELLA No!

CAPITAINE   Good. Where?

YOUNG BELLA Abadan.

CAPITAINE   What did I tell you? The Abadan ring! *(Gendarme is impressed.)* Picking up or delivering?

YOUNG BELLA What?

CAPITAINE   Who is your contact in Abadan? *(To Gendarme)* I bet they're operating with the Kuwaitis. Not just hashish and heroin either. Those guys move gold, dollars, even cars! Huge enterprise. And we have their gophers right here.*(To Farid)* Hey you! Who're you supposed to meet in Abadan?

FARID *(weakly)* Your wife!

CAPITAINE *(walks up to him)* Didn't have enough, eh? *(Raises his hand.)*

YOUNG BELLA Please don't. I beg you!

CAPITAINE *(calms down)* Punk! *(To Ray)* Are you a loser like your friend here? Or do you know what's good for you, hum? Either you talk here or they'll beat it out of you in Tehran. You think I'm bad news? You haven't seen Sarhang! *(Young Bella and Farid are alarmed.)* He attends to smugglers personally. Is that what you want?

YOUNG BELLA There is no need for that. *(Gently)* Ray? Ray, can you answer him?

RAY *(weakly)* No dogs, keep the dogs away...

CAPITAINE *(grabs Ray by the collar and lifts him off the chair)* Who you calling dog? *(Shakes him.)* Speak!

RAY *(with unexpected energy)* Get your fucking hands off me, you racist pig!

YOUNG BELLA *(surprised)* Ray!

RAY I am an American citizen! You can't touch me! *(The Capitaine lets go.)*

YOUNG BELLA Calm down, Ray! See, Officer? I told you...

RAY *(overlapping)* Calm down? I've been arrested, interrogated, and beaten up and you're telling me to calm down? This is infuriating! My concert is in two hours! I cannot calm down! *(The Capitaine and the Gendarme are in shock.)* Not only is there no proper toilet in this entire country but you are the most inept officers I have ever encountered in my life! *(Not a peep from anyone. They all stare at him. Ray is even more energized.)* You morons are going to be very sorry when the American officials find out about this! I'll teach you capitulation!

YOUNG BELLA Ray...

RAY   I'm not finished! *(Authoritatively.)* Take a look at the side pocket of that suitcase and you will find my American passport. Which you would have found earlier had you properly searched what you confiscated from our car! *(The Capitaine gestures to the Gendarme to search for the passport.)* That's right. Not so loud and feisty now, are you? You big buffoon!

A phone rings. Everyone freezes. Rings again. The Capitaine looks at the Gendarme who wonders if he should answer the phone. The Capitaine picks up the phone.

CAPITAINE   Gendarmerie Murcheh-Khort. *(Stands up)* Yes sir! *(Listens)* Yes, they're right here, sir... *(Listens)* There are three, sir. One is a woman. The car belongs to the culprit. We found one gram of heroin and five grams of hashish in his jacket pocket. However, sir — *(Listens as the Gendarme opens Ray's passport and holds it in front of him.)* Absolutely. We can keep them here as long as you deem necessary. *(Nods)* There is only one detail, sir... Yes, it appears that at least one member of the ring carries an American passport. *(Pause, looks at passport as Gendarme turns the pages.)* Yes, sir. Let me confirm. Just a moment, sir...

(To Gendarme) Turn it to the first page! *(He nervously shuffles through the pages, the Capitaine grabs the passport out of his hand.)* Give it to me! *(In a formal tone)* Yes, sir. The name on the passport is Raymond Wallace Hamilton. He claims to be a musician... *(Listens while being yelled at.)* In Isfahan? *(Looks up at Ray.)* Yes, sir. I will, sir. Right away, sir. I apologize — No, sir. Of course. I understand completely, sir. *(Holding Ray's passport.)* Immediately. Yes, we are only thirty minutes from Isfahan. I will personally escort him, sir. Thank you for clarifying. I appreciate your guidance and will follow your instructions... Yes, sir. Thank you. Please give my best wishes to Mrs...

Looks at the receiver, the other side hangs up. Holds for a moment. Then hangs up thoughtfully. Pause. Everyone is waiting. Hands the passport to Ray.

CAPITAINE   Mr. Hamilton, sorry for mistake. I escort you to Isfahan.

RAY *(grabs passport and walks to his suitcase.)* Let's go.

CAPITAINE *(to Young Bella)* You too.

YOUNG BELLA *(jumps out of her seat)* Thank you! *(Pointing to Farid.)* What about him?

CAPITAINE   He stays. *(Puts hat on.)*

RAY   But –

YOUNG BELLA He is with us.

CAPITAINE *(to Ray)* He is American?

RAY   No.

CAPITAINE   He play music tonight?

RAY *(considers)* No.

CAPITAINE   He stays. *(Heads for the door. To Gendarme)* Keep an eye on him!

YOUNG BELLA Wait—

CAPITAINE   You want to stay too? *(Beat.)*

Ray/Young Bella/Capitaine exit. Light shift. Bella puts on a new LP: James Brown "Please, please, please." Ray walks to Bella's station.

BELLA   We thought we could get away with anything. We thought we were so smart.

RAY   For the first time, the only time in my life, I understood what it's like to create fear in others.

BELLA   It's good to be the American.

RAY   At least back then it was.

BELLA   I'll never forget the look of shame in that gendarme's eyes.

RAY   He should feel shame for what he did.

BELLA   Not for what he did. You made him feel ashamed of being Iranian.

RAY   Are you saying I was wrong to criticize their moronic behaviour?

BELLA   I'm saying you had not earned the right to say those things. *(Beat.)*

RAY   You can be so aware of other people's baggage but not your own. *(Beat.)* You know what I learned that day at the Gendarmerie? I understood how monsters are created. Each of us has a kernel of that potential inside. Anyone under the right circumstances can behave like a monster. Once my Americanness was established, once I saw the fear in their eyes, there was no stopping me. *(Waits)* What are you afraid of, Bells?

BELLA   I stopped acting years before the revolution. The Mullahs didn't stop me. I stopped because of my husband – his jealousy, his accusations – I couldn't take it anymore.

RAY   But all this time you've been saying–

BELLA   Because I was ashamed.

RAY   Why did you give in to him? Why didn't you fight for what was important to you?

BELLA   Could you ever refuse Duke anything? He would wake you up in the middle of the night to rearrange a melody and you would stay up till dawn and do it. Or ask you to fly to wherever he was to help him with a composition problem, and you would run. Isn't that true? It was the same with my husband. I could not refuse him.

RAY   If I was at Duke's beck and call, it's because he was an extraordinary collaborator. He was the best!

BELLA   Duke used you. He stole your career and made you serve his. The same way my husband forced me to stop acting. He loved flaunting me in public, but in private, he criticized me and accused me of flirting with the director or the leading man, and doing all sorts of things behind his back.

RAY   Duke let me live the life I wanted to live. He protected me from the dirty side of the business.

BELLA   He never gave you credit for anything.

RAY　　He did. In the later years, he insisted that I get credit on my compositions. I told you how I left him for a few years and produced my own work. Only to realize it's not what I want to spend my time doing. I didn't want to be the front man. That experience helped me appreciate Duke even more.

BELLA　　I thought my husband was perfect. His ideas, his stories, I could listen to him forever. He could convince anyone to do whatever he wanted. But I could never convince him of anything.

RAY　　Your husband was a visionary, like Duke. He gave you an extraordinary life.

BELLA　　He shut me down. He suffocated me! He made me love him then broke my heart. I should have never returned to him after Isfahan.

RAY　　But you did. *(Beat.)* You chose him.

BELLA　　I chose heartbreak.

RAY　　What is life without heartbreak?

BELLA　　Happy?

RAY　　Boring. *(Beat.)* You will always be disappointed in people if you expect perfection. No person, no country – is perfect. This tribute is your chance to claim your legacy.

BELLA　　But Ray, I am not perfect either. I am not a hero.

RAY　　No one expects that. You are an accomplished artist with a significant body of work. That is what those people want – need to acknowledge and celebrate.

BELLA　　But I am afraid – that if I go back – my heart will break – again. Like it did in Isfahan.

RAY　　Bells, I didn't mean to break your heart.

BELLA　　I know. You were angry.

RAY　　I was angry...

Lighting shifts. Inside the car: Young Bella at the wheel, Ray next to her.

YOUNG BELLA *(agitated, fumbling with the keys)* Oh my god, oh my god, oh my god!

RAY Drive!

YOUNG BELLA *(doesn't start the car)* I can't believe you did that! You sounded horrible. Your eyes – I had never seen so much hatred in somebody's eyes.

RAY I was wrongly accused!

YOUNG BELLA We all were!

RAY And I got us out!

YOUNG BELLA You got yourself out! I was thrown out, and Farid wasn't even that lucky!

RAY Do you realize how much trouble we are in? Now, I'll certainly be fired from the tour!

YOUNG BELLA Don't yell at me!

RAY You're the one yelling!

YOUNG BELLA I can't believe you said those things.

RAY Why didn't you say you're friends with Sarhang when the gendarme mentioned his name? What's the point of knowing important people in high places if you don't play that card?

YOUNG BELLA Sarhang? Are you crazy? He would have put Farid in prison for life! Then he would have lectured me on my choices and sent me home to my father!

RAY I took a beating and nearly died because you don't want to be lectured? You're the selfish one!

YOUNG BELLA I'm selfish? What about you? Leaving Farid behind like that!

RAY What did you expect me to do?

YOUNG BELLA You could have said he is part of the band. That he has to perform tonight. They would have taken your word.

RAY He's charged with smuggling drugs! Do you expect me to put myself in the middle of something like that?

YOUNG BELLA I expected more from you.

RAY Why? *(Beat.)*

YOUNG BELLA You are a musician. Jazz is so free and loving. How can you be so horrible?

RAY You're no better than me. You walked out of that gendarmerie when you had the chance. Stop playing the part of the great humanitarian!

YOUNG BELLA I am not playing a part!

RAY That humble café owner in the middle of nowhere recognized you and even asked for an autograph but this presumably worldlier gendarme had no clue who you are? How is that possible?

YOUNG BELLA Just my bad luck. *(Beat.)*

Silence. Young Bella wipes away her tears. Loud honking noise jolts Ray and Young Bella. Young Bella turns and waves. She starts the engine. Music comes on: James Brown "Please, please, please." They drive on without speaking. After a while.

YOUNG BELLA Let's not tell anybody about this trip.

RAY I don't know how we can keep it a secret, sweetheart. I mean, we have a police escort.

YOUNG BELLA *(tears flowing)* What is going to happen to Farid?

RAY I can't believe Farid had heroin on him. What was he thinking? Did you know? How did I get myself into this mess?

YOUNG BELLA He probably didn't expect to be arrested.

RAY That's all you can say? It seems to me like Farid gets himself into trouble frequently. Which probably means he knows how to get himself out. *(Beat.)* What about you? Will your husband really try to kill you when he finds out about this?

YOUNG BELLA He might be really proud of me.

RAY Proud? Are you being sarcastic?

YOUNG BELLA No. This is exactly the kind of trouble he lives for. He would be sorry that he missed all the fights. *(Ray is stunned.)* Yes, he will be angry that I did not call him but he will also be satisfied that I was jealous.

RAY It sounds like you aren't planning to leave him.

YOUNG BELLA No. I don't know. It seems all men are the same.

RAY Really? You two deserve each other!

YOUNG BELLA You can take a nap. It's about twenty minutes to Isfahan.

Ray swallows his anger. Looks through the 45's on the floor of the car and picks one. Music changes to the Blues. He turns his back to Young Bella and closes his eyes. Slow lighting shift to Bella at her station. She is looking at Ray's album cover.

BELLA Do you regret the trip to Isfahan?

RAY Regret? Never! What doesn't kill you makes you stronger!

BELLA Fortune cookie philosophy.

RAY Doesn't diminish its wisdom. Why? Do you regret that trip?

BELLA No. But I wonder what would have happened – with us. If I had stayed with you after Isfahan.

RAY There was the small detail of your husband.

BELLA And your homosexuality.

RAY Yes, that too. But for a brief moment, I did fantasize about a life with a beautiful Iranian film star.

BELLA You did? My life would have been so different.

RAY Maybe it's the longing that kept us connected.

BELLA And the music. The song you wrote.

RAY I wanted to keep a part of you with me. Our whole journey passes in front of my eyes when I play that song. I remember everything.

BELLA What do you remember next?

RAY Blue ... that beautiful deep blue dusk.

SCENE 5 – ISFAHAN

Music shifts to "Isfahan Blues." Lighting shifts to deep blue then the blue domes of the mosques in the main square. Young Bella/ Ray in the car, it is not moving.

RAY *(opens his eyes)* Why are we stopped?

YOUNG BELLA We are in Isfahan.

RAY *(looks behind the car)* What happened to our gendarme friend?

YOUNG BELLA He drove away as soon as we entered the city limits.

RAY Huh... You would think he would at least escort us to the hotel.

YOUNG BELLA He was probably too scared to face any more Americans.

RAY I, on the other hand, have no other choice.

YOUNG BELLA I am sorry for all this. We should not have forced you to come with us.

RAY You didn't force me to do anything. I wanted to go with you. I wanted to spend time with you – and Farid. *(Silence.)* I'm sorry about what I said before. I didn't mean it. I was angry – at myself – not you.

YOUNG BELLA I know. *(Silence.)* You want to see what all the fuss is about?

RAY What do you mean?

YOUNG BELLA Come, let me show you Isfahan.

They leave the car and look around. Images of the scenery are projected as Young Bella describes them.

YOUNG BELLA This is Meydooneh Naghsheh Jahan, the main square. That's the palace, Ali Qapu. Shah Abbas would sit on that balcony and watch them play polo in this square. You have the Shah Mosque on one side and the Lotfollah Mosque on the other.

RAY   It's breathtaking. I feel so alive, like my heart wants to jump out and run across that field.

YOUNG BELLA This place really comes to life at dusk. The Lotfollah Mosque is my favourite. The tile work is unbelievable. Would you like to see the inside?

RAY   Absolutely. Is it open?

U.S. SECURITY OFFICER *(suddenly appears)* Raymond Hamilton?

RAY   Yes?

U.S. SECURITY OFFICER *(shows ID)* We've been looking all over for you. Where have you been?

RAY   I – I –

U.S. SECURITY OFFICER Come with me.

YOUNG BELLA Is he staying at Hotel Shah Abbas?

U.S. SECURITY OFFICER *(to Young Bella)* Your services will no longer be needed.

RAY   I need to clean up and change before the concert.

U.S. SECURITY OFFICER You will not be going to the concert.

YOUNG BELLA What?

RAY   Says who?

U.S. SECURITY OFFICER You will find out soon enough.

RAY   The concert is in an hour!

U.S. SECURITY OFFICER You should have thought of that before cavorting with the locals.

RAY   Excuse me?

U.S. SECURITY OFFICER Let's go! *(Shoves Ray.)*

RAY   Hey!

YOUNG BELLA Where are you taking him?

U.S. SECURITY OFFICER This is not any of your business. Go back to your whorehouse.

RAY   Watch it!

U.S. SECURITY OFFICER You watch yourself. To the car!

RAY　　　　　　What's going to happen to her?.

U.S. SECURITY OFFICER I suggest you worry about yourself. Let's go!

RAY　　　　　　Bells! Go to the concert hall. I'll see you there!

YOUNG BELLA Are you sure?

RAY　　　　　　Yes, go!

Young Bella watches Ray being led away.

Lighting shifts. Bella is holding up a fresh shirt and jacket for Ray as he walks over to clean up and change.

RAY　　　　　　Did you see how he treated me? Infuriating! In a blink of an eye I went from the all-powerful American to a second class citizen...

BELLA　　　　　Forget him... you are an artist and you need to prepare for an important concert.

RAY　　　　　　They would have fired me from the tour if Duke hadn't intervened.

BELLA　　　　　Thank God for Duke! Here, let me help you. *(Pause)* I like watching you get dressed.

RAY　　　　　　You're all talk and no action.

BELLA　　　　　Oh, really? Look who is talking.

RAY　　　　　　I am known for my romantic nature.

BELLA　　　　　No. You are known as Ray the Robot. And now I understand why.

RAY　　　　　　This is typical. I share a deep wound from my childhood and you throw it back at me. Thanks.

BELLA　　　　　No... did I really hurt you?

RAY　　　　　　You're a handful, you know that? I don't know how much longer I can keep this up.

BELLA　　　　　Oh, stop playing hard to get. This is the best part, the concert.

Ray enthusiastically fixes his tie in an imaginary mirror.

BELLA　　　　　What made you decide to play that night?

RAY   I could say, you. But I think, in reality, it was the Capitaine.

BELLA   What? No...

RAY   Yes. I was offended that he did not believe I was a musician. And I think I decided right then and there to make sure they never forget my music. I told myself, no more missed opportunities.

BELLA   You changed those people's lives that night. The radio DJs had to stock up on Ellington music because they received so many requests after the concert.

RAY   I know. In my heart, I knew that my music mattered to those people. And seeing that young man's website about the tour just reaffirms what I felt that night.

BELLA *(looks up at Ray with a smile.)* How did you convince Duke to let you open the concert?

RAY   It didn't take much convincing. I told him I met a beautiful Iranian film star who inspired me to write a new song that I would like to try out. Duke was elated! Of course, he did have to pretend to be sick so they let me open the concert instead of him.

BELLA   I love you, Ray.

RAY   Now you tell me. *(Beat.)* How do I look?

BELLA   Like a dream ...

Lighting shifts to interior of concert hall. The performance is about to start. Sounds of hustle and bustle of people getting seated, musicians tuning. Young Bella rushes in. She has freshened up. Farid is leaning against the wall.

ANNOUNCER (V.O.)   Khanoomha, Aghayoon, *(In Farsi)* welcome to tonight's program. We are thrilled to introduce Duke Ellington, one of the giants of American music, to Iranian audiences. Warm hellos to our listeners on the national radio! Tonight's concert is being broadcast live. Please take your seats; we will start momentarily. *(Repeats in English)* Ladies and Gentlemen, welcome to tonight's program. We are thrilled to introduce Duke Ellington, one of the giants of American music, to Iranian audiences. Warm hellos to our listeners on the national radio! Tonight's concert is being broadcast live. Please take your seats, we will start momentarily.

YOUNG BELLA How did you get here? Don't talk to me!

FARID Oh, I'm the bad guy? You left me to rot at the Gendarmerie!

YOUNG BELLA *(whispering)* You had heroin on you!

FARID Let it go, Bella-jan.

YOUNG BELLA How did you get out of the gendarmerie so fast, anyway? *(Farid shrugs.)* No – you didn't.

FARID Who else was I going to call?

YOUNG BELLA Where is he?

FARID He took the kids backstage to meet Duke Ellington.

YOUNG BELLA He brought the kids?

FARID There must be thirty or forty musicians back there. It's amazing!

YOUNG BELLA You went backstage? Did you see Ray?

FARID Oh, yeah. He's cool. We got to –

YOUNG BELLA Shh...

Lights go down. Massive applause. Upbeat orchestral opening, is established. Ray walks to the microphone.

RAY Good evening, Ladies and Gentlemen. On behalf of Duke Ellington and the members of the band, I would like to welcome you to this evening's concert. We are truly honoured. *(Applause.)* Unfortunately, Duke is feeling a bit under the weather. I was told he had a little too much Kaleh Pacheh! *(Applause.)* My name is Raymond Hamilton and I have the distinct pleasure to open tonight's program. Duke will join us a little later. *(Applause.)* We have a special treat for you tonight. A new song. And to help me perform it for you, I'd like to invite a talented young Iranian musician to the stage. Farid, won't you join me? *(Applause.)* This cat plays a mean guitar. *(Applause.)* This is a love song called, *"Isfahan Blues." (Applause.)*

Farid walks up to the stage and accompanies Ray on the guitar. Ray begins to sing. It feels essential, pure. It's Bella's song. After the first two lines, Ray sings to Young Bella.

RAY *(sings)* She held – my hand all night.
Soft as the wind – ten-der and light.
Pain-ted my skies so blue
Show-ered in morn-ing dew
Takes me a-way, fills my day.

Music fades into a memory. Ray turns to Bella and invites her to dance.

RAY *(sings)* Dance with me, Bells.

BELLA   Ray... I am sorry that I left the concert that night without saying goodbye. I did not expect it to be the last time I see you.

RAY   No shame and no regrets, remember? We only spent one day together, but you helped me find my music again. And I'm grateful for that.

BELLA   That one day was the only time I felt truly myself. You make me feel like I can accomplish anything.

RAY   I'm gone but you are still here, Bells. You can do anything you want. You can still create beauty. Like we did, together in Isfahan.

BELLA   I can see it now... No more missed opportunities... *(Smiles)* Thank you, Ray.

RAY *(sings)* We walked – in Nesfe Jahan.
Ta-lked of love – in I-is-fa-han.
Then in my heart, she grew
My dreams came true.
Why did you go – without a kiss?
Knowing that I – will re-mi-nisce.
All those love-ly things
That make me sing the Is-fa-han Blues.

During the song, Bella walks to Young Bella and gently kisses her. During Ray's speech, Bella watches Ray and Young Bella for a few moments then returns to her station.

RAY At the end of the concert, I looked for her in the audience. Then I saw him for the first time – the Husband. Tall, handsome, confident. His arm casually resting on her shoulder. Her slender figure leaning against him. She turned and looked at me. A vague smile on her lips, her eyes telling me, goodbye. It didn't matter where she had been, or what he had done. Love is blind. *(Beat.)* She left the concert hall with her family and I left a piece of my heart in Isfahan. Our journey, summarized in one song... Our job is to create beauty. And that's all that will remain.

After all the people are gone, borders are redrawn, rulers have vanished, and buildings have fallen – what will remain of us? What will our legacy be?

A slide show of the Ellington tour, Cuccini, and Bella's film images are projected. Ray, Young Bella and Farid 'disappear' in the projections. Bella closes her laptop.

Lighting fades to black. Music fades.

The End.

Torange Yeghiazarian founded Golden Thread Productions in 1996 where she launched such visionary programs as ReOrient Festival & Forum, Middle East America (in partnership with the Lark and Silkroad Rising), Islam 101 (with Hafiz Karmali), New Threads, and the Fairytale Players.

Torange's plays include *Isfahan Blues, 444 Days, The Fifth String: Ziryab's Passage To Cordoba,* and *Call Me Mehdi.*

Awards include the Gerbode-Hewlett Playwright Commission Award (*Isfahan Blues*) and a commission by the Islamic Cultural Center of Northern California (*The Fifth String*). Her short play *Call Me Mehdi* is published in the anthology "Salaam. Peace: An Anthology of Middle Eastern-American Drama," TCG 2009.

She adapted the poem, *I Sell Souls* by Simin Behbehani to the stage, and directed the premieres of *Our Enemies: Lively Scenes Of Love And Combat* and *Scenic Routes* by Yussef El Guindi, *The Myth Of Creation* by Sadegh Hedayat, *Tamam* by Betty Shamieh, *Stuck* by Amir Al-Azraki and *Voice Room* by Reza Soroor, amongst others.

Her articles on contemporary theatre in Iran have been published in *The Drama Review* (2012), *American Theatre Magazine* (2010), and *Theatre Bay Area Magazine* (2010), and *HowlRound.*

Torange has contributed to the *Encyclopedia of Women and Islamic Cultures* and *Cambridge World Encyclopedia of Stage Actors.*

Born in Iran and of Armenian heritage, Torange holds a Master's degree in Theatre Arts from San Francisco State University. Torange has been recognized by Theatre Bay Area and is one of Theatre Communication Group's Legacy Leaders of Color.

She was honoured by the Cairo International Theatre Festival (2016) and the Symposium on Equity in the Entertainment Industry (2017).

About the Play
Sholeh Wolpé

The greatest number of human rights violations worldwide have historically been committed against women and girls. These violations are too often physically brutal, but in many cases they are overtly, or on the sly, psychological. The trapped bird learns to accept her cage as the world and to impose that worldview to her chicks.

My own mother is such a woman. Growing up in Iran, I was taught that it was paramount to keep what we call abroo, which roughly translates from Persian to "keeping face"— to project to the world that all is well despite dark secrets quietly brushed under the carpet. I rebelled violently against that and everything else that was unjustly imposed upon me because I was a girl. As a result, at age 13, I was sent off to Trinidad to live with my aunt and grandmother. It wasn't until I was well into my 30s that I came to appreciate the selfless kindness of that act.

It was for my mother that I began to write this play. I modelled Simin, the mother character in the play, after her. She is funny, complex, bossy, lovable and a good storyteller. She is also wildly underestimated by her daughters for her capacity to evolve and to forgive. The stories she recounts in the play are based on true events in Iran, Afghanistan and the Czech Republic.

I have structured this play like nesting dolls. There are secrets inside other secrets, stories within stories, each unveiled slowly, revealing the true nature of every character, their fears and strengths, misplaced judgments and love-driven behaviour, but above all, their irrational hold on rigid Eastern and Western cultural values. Ultimately, what thrusts them towards re-evaluation of self and identity is the play's central question: Happiness at what price? That is a question that drives the characters, and by extension, I hope the audience, to a moment of insight that potentially shifts the lens through which we view each other and the world.

SHAME OR
THE SILVER BANGLE
(ALTERNATE TITLE)

Sholeh Wolpé

Characters:

NOOR – Iranian-American woman in her early 30s. She is a physicist and moved to the U.S. in her early teens. She does not have an accent.

SAHAR – Iranian-American. Late 30s/early 40s. Sahar's older sister. She is a stay-home mom and is married to an American man, Luke. Like her younger sister, she moved to the U.S. in her early teens. She does not have an accent.

AHMAD – Iranian man in his late 30s. Mehri's brother. A physicist, he was educated in the U.S. but now lives and works in Iran. He has a slight accent.

SIMIN – Iranian older woman. Noor and Sahar's mother. She lives in Czech Republic with her husband who has a business there. She speaks English with an accent and at times makes errors in grammar, etc.

LUKE – American man in his 40s. Sahar's husband. He is low key and seems like the odd man out but he is keenly aware of everything that is going on. He also has a dry sense of humour.

BABBAK – Iranian man

MEHRI – Noor's lover. Iranian woman in her 30s

PARI – An Iranian woman in her early 20s

AFGHAN STEP BROTHER – Young, horny Afghan man.

AFGHAN GIRL'S MOTHER – Afghan woman in her 30s. Worn by years.

AFGHAN FATHER – Older Afghan man

AFGHAN GIRL – young teenage Afghan girl

239

Actors can double roles. Suggested doubling for 4 actors:
Noor /Pari/ Afghan girl
Sahar/ Afghan girl's mother/ Mehri
Ahmad/ Afghan father/ Babbak
Luke/ Afghan step brother

Time
Summer. Present day
Place
Sahar and Luke's home in Los Angeles.
Setting
Sahar's living room and dining room. The living room is eclectically decorated. There are Persian rugs, a samovar, clear glass teacups on a silver tray, and a large plate of baklava. A large framed picture of Sahar and Luke's children, a boy and a girl aged five and six, is hung on a visible and prominent wall. It exits to kitchen. A hallway leads out of sight to the bedrooms. Upstage area represents the world outside this place and time.

Buried Stories

Mother says bury
your shaming stories
deep in your liver,
take them with you to your grave.

But a burdened liver
explodes in the pressed
quiet of the earth, poisons

the worms, the water,
the soil, the crops that push
toward the sun, that feed our children.

SHAME

ACT I SCENE 1

Noor's *living room. All actors in silhouette.*

Music: "Whisper" by Axiom of Choice, Album: Beyond Denial Vocalist: Mamak Khadem.

In Silhouette, Noor and another figure whose gender is not clear are laughing, and kissing. Slowly the other figure goes down on Noor.

Just as Noor is about to reach a climax, her boyfriend, Babbak, enters quietly, holding a large bouquet of roses, and an open velvet box with a ring. Noor sees him.

The music stops. Silence. He throws down the roses and the ring, and leaves. Noor shouts "Babbak", picks up the ring, looks at it.

She is devastated. But gradually we see her reach a decision as she slowly stands tall and defiant.

SCENE 2

Early evening. The stage is dark. Noor stands in spotlight centre front stage. A long, red scarf covers her head and body.

Lights out.

NOOR *(awkwardly practising a poem)*

> Bathe me in red
> Wrap me in its seductive robe
> And watch me dance
> on the clouds at sunset,
> send me pulsating
> through your veins
> Slithering on your thoughts.
> Bathe me in red
> give me a name, a cause

Lights up in the living room. Noor wraps the scarf around her neck. Her sister, Sahar, enters dressed in pant suit and flat shoes.

SAHAR   Talking to yourself again?

NOOR   I'm rehearsing.

SAHAR   For what?

NOOR   A film.

SAHAR   You're a physicist.

NOOR   So?

SAHAR *(tidying up the apartment)* So you've given up your black holes and particles for the movies.

NOOR *(dismisses her comment with a wave of her hand)*I'm supposed to read this poem standing in front of a house that bursts into flames.

Sahar gives her a look.

NOOR   He's probably gonna blow up his daughter's dolls' house. Can't get this right, though. I mean, at first it sounds really sexy, but then there're these layers I can't get in between. Wanna hear it?

SAHAR   Let's set the table first. She'll be here any minute.

NOOR   Did you check the arrival time?

SAHAR   Luke did. They're probably stuck in traffic. Remember the year we flew back in from Iran?

NOOR   We survived the Islamic Republic and you almost got us arrested in the cradle of democracy.

SAHAR   Just wanted to get home.

NOOR   You opened the windows, turned up Melissa Etheridge singing *"I Wanna Be in Love"* and cut in front of a police car.

SAHAR   Yeah...

Reminiscing, Sahar begins to sing I Wanna Be in Love.

SAHAR "In front of total strangers won't you kiss me, Flowers for no reason but you miss me."

NOOR *(joins in, singing)*

SAHAR/NOOR "O-ho-ho I want to be in love."

SAHAR *(laughs, then wistfully)* That was a long, long time ago. Back then, I was someone else... The food should be here any minute now.

NOOR Not Indian again.

SAHAR Tonight we're having chelo kebab. Ordered it from Mehri's.

NOOR *(distractedly, humming the song)* Mehri's? They deliver?

Noor opens a bottle of sparkling water and begins to water the plants.

SAHAR Aren't we distracted today!

NOOR Are we?

SAHAR Well, for starters we are watering the plants with the sparkling water.

NOOR Oh, pickles! I'm sorry. Is there more?

Sahar fetches another bottle from the kitchen. Noor begins putting ice cubes in the glasses and then in the flower vase.

SAHAR What's on your mind?

NOOR Nothing. Nothing important. Just work.

SAHAR Noor !

NOOR We broke up. Babbak and I... We broke up.

SAHAR What did you just say?

NOOR I said, last week...

SAHAR Last week? And you're telling me this literally minutes before our mother arrives from overseas?

NOOR I've been meaning to tell you. I've been going over and over it in my head, looking for words, some sort of explanation that makes sense. But then you went to San Francisco and when you came back I was too busy at the lab.

SAHAR   You could've picked up the phone. Emailed! Ever heard of text messaging?

NOOR   I was looking for the right time.

SAHAR   And this is the right time?

NOOR   Maman is going to ask about him, isn't she? I know she expects us to get married!

SAHAR   But you love him, Noor. Don't you?

NOOR   I did. I do. I can't... I mean he won't...

SAHAR *(deep breath, guides her to the sofa)* You don't want Maman to see any sign of distress. She always detects it like a radar. I swear she has antennas under that poufy hairdo of hers. Now, tell me. Take your time. *(Checks her watch, impatiently.)*

NOOR   He used to walk into a party full of beautiful women and see only me. He respected what I did. My career. Who I was... am. A man like that is too good to be true. Right?

SAHAR   I don't know. *(Ironically)* All men are the same, eventually.

NOOR   I have a PhD in physics. I know more about the string theory, subatomic particles, hell, even possible alternate universes than I do about myself or what I want. All my life I've been looking for a man, a man like Babbak and when I find him, when I have him right here... *(points to the palm of her hand)* I do like I always do. *(She slam crushes the imaginary man on the palm of her hand.)*

SAHAR   It wasn't a quarrel, was it? He left you. Like the other ones. *(Realizing the cruelty of the statement)* I'm sorry I didn't mean...

NOOR   What's wrong with me? You tell me. It's as if I deliberately sabotage every single relationship that threatens to put me where you are.

SAHAR   Me? What have I do with the mess you create every time?

NOOR   When you married Luke, everything changed. You changed! Became Miss perfect wife. Miss PTA president.

Cookies, soccer and ballet classes. You were sucked out of your skin, lost your style. Became all pant suits and ugly flat shoes! You even lost that deep, guttural laugh you used to have. Remember?

SAHAR   Is this really about me, Noor? But you love him. Don't you?

NOOR   I just...

SAHAR   Ever since we were little girls, you did exactly what you're doing now. You make your reality more appetizing to yourself by kicking mine. For your information, I'm quite happy in my designer pant suits and ballet-style shoes. I chose this life, chose this person I am today, despite that night... *(Stops herself abruptly)* We all make choices; we're responsible for our own actions. I've learned to live with that. If you've got a good man who left you, you've got to deal with the consequences of whatever you did to drive him away.

What the hell did you do to that poor man? He loved you Noor! He called Maman and Daddy asking for your hand. Didn't he propose with that huge diamond ring he had me pick out for you?

NOOR   You picked that ring?

SAHAR   So he did give it to you?

NOOR   No.

Door bell rings.

NOOR   Pickles!

SAHAR   Maman.

Sahar opens the door. An Iranian man (Ahmad) stands in formal suit and tie, balancing several trays of food.

AHMAD   Salaam. *(To Noor)* Salaam. I'm... *(Holds up the trays uncomfortably)* The Chelo Kebab man from Mehri's restaurant.

SAHAR   Oh, yes. Come in. Can you put them in the oven?

AHMAD *(nervously)* Yes, of course.

They exit to the kitchen. The oven door clangs open and shut. They enter with plates and condiments.

AHMAD   Do you want me to put the condiments on the plates for you?

SAHAR   You'd do that?

AHMAD   Yes, I'd be happy to.

Ahmad begins to spoon various condiments onto serving plates.

AHMAD   Mehri, my... my boss, told me to make this a full delivery service.

SAHAR   She did? Do I know your boss, Mehri?

AHMAD   Yes, I mean, no, but she knows your sister.

SAHAR   Noor?

AHMAD *(looks at Noor, smiles)* Yes, I believe they know one another quite well.

NOOR *(uncomfortably)* I can help with the condiments. Sahar, why don't you pay the gentleman and send him on his way?

AHMAD   Oh, no, no. My boss said no charge. And, I'm to offer you my services. *(The women exchange glances.)* I mean, what else can I do for you?

SAHAR   Well that's nice of her, but here's...

AHMAD   No tips. I'm not to take any money from you. She sends her respect and regards, to your sister.

Noor leads Ahmad towards the door. He is reluctant to go.

NOOR   Tell Mehri thank you and that... I'll call her. Later.

The front door opens and Luke, Sahar's American husband, walks in dragging a large, heavy suitcase behind him.

LUKE   Queen mother has arrived.

Simin, their mother, walks in, opens her arms wide.

SIMIN   Dokhtaram! My beautiful girls! *(Hugs and kisses them.)* The light of my eyes. Oh, let me smell you. Breathe you. It's been a year. Too long for old woman like me. Look at you. *(Inspects Sahar and is satisfied. Turns to Noor.)* Noor, you're melting away, skin and bones.

NOOR   Maman, you say that every time you see me.

SIMIN   No, what I always say when I see you is: When am I going to see your children? But I won't ask that now because I happen to know the answer to that question is: very soon. Akh, look at you. You really do look like a stick. I'll fix you with my new lamb recipe.

NOOR   I'm now a vegetarian, remember?

SIMIN   Yes but I'll get, what you call them? The ones that run around and eat grass. *(Calling past her daughters to the rooms beyond.)* Ramin? Suzie? Where are my grandchildren?

LUKE   Summer camp.

SIMIN   It's a joke, no? They are hiding.

SAHAR   They'll be back tomorrow. They're excited to see you.

SIMIN   Where is your husband? There. You see that bag, fatter than a mullah? Stuffed with wonderful things for them.

SAHAR   Maman, you shouldn't have.

LUKE   But they'll be glad you did.

SAHAR   Really, dragging all that. It must weigh a ton.

LUKE *(chuckling as dragging the bag to the bedroom)* I'd say a mullah and a half.

SIMIN   Look, I only have two grandchildren, that is, until this one *(pointing to Noor)* begins to make babies instead of locking herself in a laboratory, playing with what you call them ...party nuns? Partisans?

NOOR   Particles.

SIMIN *(notices Ahmad)* Good God, Ya Ali, you must be Babbak.

She kisses Ahmad forcefully. Ahmad is confused.

NOOR   Maman...!

SIMIN *(ignoring Noor)* I tell you, God has this factory and he makes men like cars. You know? Different models. The low ends, the high ends, the ones that need all-the-time repair but look good, the ones that don't look so good but are reliable, and then there are the top top top models, the ones that not only look ooh-la-la good, but also have mighty good engines.

SAHAR *(laughing)* Maman!

SIMIN Get your mind out of the gutter, Sahar. I mean up here. *(She taps her head, then turns to Ahmad again.)* You, Luke and my husband are the top model. But I think He... *(Pointing up.)* Must have stopped making good models after you were born. No more like you. I thank God on my knees that my daughter has found you.

Ahmad smiles,uncomfortably.

NOOR Maman, actually—

SAHAR *(interrupts)* Yes, Babbak just picked up food from a Persian restaurant around the corner. Maman, are you hungry?

SIMIN You got chelo kebab? *(Sniffs the air.)* Bah-bah. Smells just like Haj Hassan's place in the bazaar.

SAHAR Come on, Babbak-joon. Let's serve up the rice and kebabs. So good of you to pick 'em up.

Sahar takes Ahmad to the kitchen. Noor tries to follow but her mother leads her towards the couch.

SIMIN My darling. Tell me what you've been doing with your super-duper skinny self?

NOOR *(pointing to the kitchen)* Maman...

SIMIN "Super-duper." I just learned that from a teenager on the plane. I'm so happy to meet your Babbak. Finally. The pictures you sent us on the internet, we couldn't open. I was dying to see what he looked like. So good-looking.

NOOR Yes, he is, but...

SIMIN But what, honey? He is also a good man. I know. I've been looking forward to this a long, long time. So, have you set a date? Where's that ring he got you? Your daddy and I aren't getting any younger you know. And neither are you, smart, skinny lady.

Luke enters.

LUKE *(claps his hands, rubs them together)* I hear we're having chelo kebab. Is Babbak here? I didn't see him when I came in.

SIMIN You are getting old Luke-joon, he was standing right in front of your cute American nose. They're in the kitchen.

Luke, puzzled, exists to the kitchen.

SIMIN *(gets up suddenly)* I've got to pee. My bladder's going to pop. It shrinks every year by an inch and three quarters.

NOOR That's good news.

SIMIN Something to look forward to, eh?

NOOR Maman, I have to tell you something.

SIMIN About your bladder?

NOOR No. My bladder's fine.

SIMIN Mine isn't, so you'll have to wait.

Simin exits the stage. Luke enters from the kitchen followed by Sahar and Ahmad.

LUKE Where did she go?

Noor points towards the bathroom.

SAHAR *(to Noor)* Did you know Maman has brought jewelry and grandma's special *Quran* for your engagement party.

NOOR For my *what?*

SAHAR It was supposed to be a surprise. Look, this nice man has offered to help us out. Just for a few hours. Tomorrow we'll figure it all out.

NOOR Sahar, we can't just...

SAHAR Did you see how excited she was when she saw him?

LUKE She does have high blood pressure.

SAHAR Remember Dad?

NOOR Have it your way. You always do anyway.

SAHAR *(defensive)* Hey, that's not fair.

LUKE I'm staying out of this.

AHMAD   Happy to do whatever you ask.

Simin enters. She has put on bright red lipstick.

SIMIN   Mission accomplished! I feel at least a kilo lighter.

Lights out.

SCENE 3

Later the same evening. Everyone at the dining table.

SIMIN   I miss eating chelo kebab like this. Tastes just like the ones we used to get in the bazaars. I used to go shopping with your Aunt Zahra and we'd stop at Ali's Kebab on Champs-Elysées street... *(To Luke)* Not the Champs-Elysées in Paris; we had one of our own. Better, if you ask me.

SAHAR *(laughs)* And she does not lie. *(Bites into a pickle.)*

LUKE   Is that a pickle? Come on Noor! With basmati rice?

SIMIN   We always ordered a couple of Soltani specials: rice with fillet mignon and a skewer of ground beef, roasted tomatoes, peppers and onions. We put mountains of sweet butter in the steaming basmati rice, let it melt. That was before we knew about cholesterol and fat and all the stuff that's suppose to murder you.

NOOR   What about doogh? Which by the way, Sahar forgot to order tonight.

SAHAR *(to Ahmad, slyly)* Babbak-joon, you forgot to order doogh.

SIMIN   Their doogh was made with fresh yogurt and bubbly water from Ab-Ali well. Not like the bottled kind you get here. We'd drink two cold large glasses, then we'd go for more shopping. If I eat like that now, I won't be able to get up for three days, and even then I'd need a crane. One of those big ones with a hook.

AHMAD *(laughs)* We all would.

SIMIN   No, not you. You're a young man still. You can do it. Luke, on the other hand, well, if he wasn't a man I'd say he was pregnant.

LUKE   Blame it on your daughter, khanum. If I had married a Japanese women, I'd be eating sushi and fish and I'd be fit as a fiddle, and probably live longer too.

SIMIN   Fit as a fiddle? Fit as a starving monk! Raw fish? That's a fate I don't wish even for my enemy. Savages eat their meat raw. We are civilized. We slit their throat, let their blood soak into the earth for good luck, then barbecue!

LUKE *(laughs, lifts up his water glass)* Well, here's to Persian civilization.

SIMIN   And good food. There aren't any Persian restaurants in the Czech Republic.

AHMAD   How did you end up there?

SIMIN   It's a long story. Hasn't Noor told you?

AHMAD   Well, she...

NOOR   I didn't want to bore him.

SIMIN   Bore him? If you don't talk about your family, what do you talk about?

AHMAD   Well, we talk about many things. Physics mostly.

SIMIN   Physics? I thought you were a businessman.

AHMAD   I am? I am. *(Realizing he may have blown his cover.)* I'm a physicist too! You know how it is ... you come to this country and you either become a cab driver or a businessman. I used to be a physicist. Now, I'm a businessman.

Noor looks at him in shock.

SIMIN *(to Noor)* You didn't tell me that.

NOOR   Well, yeah Maman-joon. You know how it is. I wanted you to meet him for yourself. Eena-hush! Voila!

SAHAR   OK, everyone up. There's chai and baklava in the living room. It's husband's night, so Luke, being the only husband here, is cleaning up.

LUKE   Here, it's husband's night every night. And I'm always the only husband around.

SIMIN   Not for long.

Luke dons a frilly apron, begins clearing the table. Everyone moves to the living room. Sahar serves tea from the samovar.

AHMAD   So, Maman-joon, how did you end up in the Czech Republic?

SIMIN   I love you calling me that. "Maman" sounds good coming from your perfect lips.

NOOR   Maman, let's not get carried away here.

SIMIN   Well, Babbak-joon, my husband bought a business there. Right after Czech and Slovakia divorced. It was pure luck. The opportunity came, and we took it. You know how it was? After the mullahs took over our beautiful land it was hard for all of us. My husband was a judge, but like you, he became a businessman. Better than cab driver, no?

NOOR *(being contradictory)* I think Persian cabbies are sexy.

SIMIN   Czech's been good for me and Reza, and of course, the best thing of all, I found my calling there.

AHMAD   In the business?

SIMIN   Babbak, what has my daughter been telling you about me? Everyone knows I have no head for business. You give me two dollars, I go in debt four dollars. Everything God has given me, is right here. *(Taps her heart.)*

SIMIN   I love people. So while I was in Czech, something happened that opened my heart and showed me that I, Simin Mustafa, can make a difference even in my old age.

SAHAR   You're not old.

NOOR   Maman, it's a sad story. I'm not sure if... *(hesitantly)* Babbak don't you have to be somewhere tonight?

AHMAD   Oh no, no. I'm up for it.

Noor and Sahar exchange glances.

SIMIN *(to the girls)* He wants to hear, so I tell story.

SAHAR   Your chai's getting cold. Aren't you tired Mom because—

SIMIN *(interrupting Sahar)* So, I was cooking for a party. Ten people coming to dinner. I love cooking, you know. Love giving big dinner parties. I made so many Czech friends there, and they love my cooking. So here I am, in my red apron... *(To Sahar)* The one I won in the Chili contest in Texas... *(To Ahmad)* That's another story, I'll tell you later. Anyway, me in my red apron, my husband chopping onions and crying, not because he was sad, because the onions were mean, I, cutting the eggplant... *(Slowing down to be precise)* You know, eggplants are tricky; you have to peel them, cut them, salt them, then let them sweat. When you see the sweat bead on its flesh, that's when you have to squeeze... all the bitterness out.

AHMAD   Really? I didn't know that. But, I'm not much of a cook. My twin sister's the one... *(Checks himself. Remembers he is supposed to be Noor's fiancée.)*

SIMIN   You have a twin sister?

AHMAD   Yes but please go on. You were saying... eggplants.

SIMIN   Yes, eggplants. They are like people. You must give them kindness and they will sweat out their bitterness. Anyway, I had just salted the eggplants, and was getting ready to sauté the onions and the chicken when — ring! Ring! The telephone. Now, in Czech, life isn't like here. For us when the phone rings, you answer! Always it's an important call, even if it is the neighbour saying "hello", though neighbours never call to say "hello", they just drop by. Anyway, I answer the phone. It's Jana, the woman from the orphanage in Prague. Nice woman. Not so pretty. Buck teeth like this, *(Makes a face imitating buck teeth.)* And between you and me, not sure about her womanhood morality, which makes me very sad because she is very sweet. These days too much perversion. Boys doing it to boys, girls doing it to girls, and how that one goes, I don't know.

Anyway, she said they had brought in two hysterical Afghan kids. No one could understand what they were saying and crying, crying, crying. Jana said, "Simin, come to Prague, now!"

Well, Prague was a two-hour train ride and I had ten dinner guests coming. Ten! But Babbak-joon, something in my heart moved like a bird and told me the dinner would be poison if I didn't go. So I peeled off my red apron from Texas, handed it to my husband, said: "Reza, I'll be back when I can."

At the orphanage, in the corner, cuddled together were a little boy and a young girl, faces like this... *(gestures a big ball)* from too much crying. I walked in, said: "Salaam, Salaam." They looked up, shocked hearing their language. The boy grabbed my skirt, crying like rain, and the girl, fifteen years old, talked like a bullet. The Afghan accent is so hard to understand for us Iranians, but eventually I figured out what she was saying. I cleaned their faces, told them, "Shush, shush, I'm here, I'm not going anywhere."

Music ("Tudra" by Yuval Ron Ensemble, Under the Olive Tree album) gradually rises as the set darkens and light comes up on a room in rural Afghanistan. It is sparsely furnished with cushions on the floor and a low table.

Noor/girl, Luke/step brother, Sahar/mother and Ahmad/father enact the following.

The girl is doing her homework. Her older step brother comes in. Closes the door behind him. She greets him politely.

He sits beside her and pretends to help her with her homework. He casually slips his arms over her shoulder. Soon, he begins to fondle her. She tries to get up, but he pulls down her scarf and caresses her hair. He then, puts his hand on her mouth and whispers in her ear. He pulls up her skirt, slips his hand between her legs. He touches her breasts with one hand as his other hand moves in her underpants. Suddenly the girl's parents walk in. Her mother screams. Her father is furious. The father draws a knife. His son runs out. The mother tries to console her hysterical daughter. Her father points at her with his knife. The mother pushes him away and he accidentally cuts her face. He then takes the blood with his finger and marks an X on the wall and leaves.

Lights dims on the Afghan set and gradually rise on the main set as Simin speaks. The music fades away.

SIMIN   The mother knew their fate was sealed, so she grabbed her shell-shocked daughter and young son and ran. With the little money she'd secretly saved, she hired a smuggler, and they headed for her sister in Germany. You see, if they'd stayed, her daughter would be killed.

AHMAD   It's called honour killing. Honour is sacred, but to kill for it is unforgivable.

NOOR   What about killing a woman's reputation, in the name of honour? Is that forgivable?

SIMIN *(ignoring the exchange)* They make it to Turkey, then, they switch vans, families packed like cattle. The kids are shoved in first. And when there is no more room, the smuggler shuts the door and takes off. The mother runs after the van, screaming. The kids crouch down in a corner. No light. Hardly any air. The van is stopped on Czech soil, the driver runs away, and the families are sent back to Afghanistan. But no one claims the two kids, so they're shipped off to the orphanage in Prague. To Jana. The poor girl thought she was going to be sold in a dirty way... poor thing kept saying, I'm a good girl. We call the embassy, everyone we know, finally track down their aunt in Germany. But the courts wouldn't release the kids to her without – without what do you call it–?

NOOR   Guardianship papers.

SIMIN   Where to get that when the mother is nowhere to be found? The girl kept saying her father had disowned her because she was stained. Because she had brought shame to her family. *(Shaking her head.)* Shame and Stain.

SAHAR   Pain.

SIMIN   What's that?

Sahar looks at Noor.

SAHAR   Pain. Shame, stain, pain.

NOOR   Disdain.

LUKE   Champagne! *(All look at him.)* Maman-jan, you were saying.

SIMIN   We finally found the mother in Turkey. When she arrived at the orphanage she looked like she'd been to a Taliban hell and back. Dark circles around her eyes, breasts sagging down to here, and that awful cut on her cheek. Akh, when the kids saw their mother... If you think we human beings are only this flesh, this blood, this bone? Tah! Think again. This is nothing. What we really are, is invisible until moments like this.

Long silence.

LUKE   "Ah, what an age it is

When to speak of trees is almost a crime

For it is a kind of silence about injustice."

Everyone looks at him, amazed.

LUKE   Bertolt Brecht.

SIMIN   Sahar-joon, give me more chai. The Czech courts wouldn't let her have her kids. No passport, no birth certificates.

AHMAD   Couldn't Jana help?

SIMIN   Jana got permission to let the mother visit the kids in the park. Always, when it was time for her to leave, the little boy buried his head in his mother's skirt and whimpered. *(Wipes away her tears with the hem of her skirt.)*

Noor hands her a tissue.

SIMIN   Thank you, my sweet. *(Blows her nose.)*

SAHAR   Do you want some air? Should I open a window?

SIMIN   By the fourth visit, Jana and I had hatched a plan. I gave the mother money and said, you all take a taxi to this address. At the bus station I bought three tickets to the German border. I kissed the boy. Kissed the sad eyes of the girl, and then took their mother in my arms. I asked Allah to give her all the strength I had in me. Then I said, "Go, go, go and never look back. Take your precious girl to a place where no man can hurt her." Then, she did something that changed my life. She took her only piece of jewelry, a single silver bangle, off her wrist and slipped it on mine.

Touches the bangle on her wrist.

SIMIN   She said, "Take this. It's not much. Just a reminder that my children and I will never forget you. We'll pray for you as long as there is breath in our bodies. May Allah bless you and all your children and grandchildren and great-grandchildren. May you never know hardship, hunger, separation. May you never know shame." Then, she disappeared into the bus. Her bangle was wet with her tears. Here it is.

Holds up her wrist.

AHMAD   Can I – may I see it?

SIMIN   No. I never take it off. Never have, never will. Not until it's ready to leave my wrist for the wrist of the one worthy of its river of tears.

Silence.

NOOR   Sometimes I wish I had these enormous wings that I could spread and rise so high until the world's reduced to what it really is: mechanical toys with mechanical problems, mechanical judgments and denials. And I, high above, safe from it all.

Pause.

LUKE *(breaks the silence, laughing.)* Goodbye physics, hello poetry. It's refreshing really for you, Noor. You've finally moved from the pursuit of the concrete to the chasing of poetic impossibilities.

AHMAD   Impossibilities? If the pursuit of things imposs-ible is poetic... *(looking directly at Noor)* then all scientists are poets. They look at the impossible, and see the possibilities.

SAHAR   Noor has a part in a film.

NOOR   Sahar!

SAHAR   Earlier, she was practising the poem she's supposed to recite while the building behind her falls apart.

NOOR   Blows up.

LUKE *(delighted)* No shit!

AHMAD   Why don't you perform it for us?

NOOR   No. Maman, you must be exhausted.

SIMIN   Is this true? You are in a movie?

NOOR   A no-budget movie. Experimental. Really experimental.

SIMIN   This girl is always surprising me. Tell us your poem.

NOOR   No, I'm not ready.

LUKE   Oh come on, Noor. If you can't recite it in front of us, how could you do it in front of a camera?

NOOR   Sometimes it's easier that way.

LUKE   Bah humbug! Come on, let's hear it.

SIMIN   Yes, just as Luke-joon says, bah honey bug! Do it for me. Please.

NOOR *(hesitantly)* OK, just for you. Because I love you.

LUKE   What are we? Garbanzo beans?

NOOR   Bathe me in red. *(Clears her throat.)* That's what the poem is called: *Bathe in red. (She pulls her scarf over her head.)*

Bathe me in red

Wrap me in its seductive robe

And watch me dance

on the clouds at sunset,

a harem girl before her sultan.

Bathe me in red

Kiss me with parted lips

and send me pulsating

through your veins

slithering on your thoughts.

Bathe me in red,

Give me a name, a cause.

Make of me a revolution...

Come Closer. Here I am.

Take your time.

Pause. Simin gets up, takes Noor's hands, kisses them, looks at her and sighs. Everyone else rises with her.

SIMIN   You are a beautiful girl. I think you almost have it. *(To the others, winding down.)* It was such a long flight and I'm getting old. No, I am old. Twenty hours travelling. That's why your father didn't come this time. He said: "Simin, you go. You're a little younger than me." Can you believe it? Compared to him, I'm a spring chicken. Anyway, he said he'll come for your wedding. Ensh-Allah, God willing. Babbak-joon, good meeting you face to face – finally. You sound different from yourself, on the phone. Warmer, deeper in person. Tomorrow, we will make wedding plans. No more of my sad stories.

AHMAD   Wedding plans? Yes, of course, wedding plans. You have more stories like that?

SIMIN   You kids stay up, chat and whatever. I love that word, "whatever". *(Meaningfully to Noor.)* It covers so much ground. *(To Luke)* Luke dear, could you unzip my bag? It gets stuck.

LUKE   I'll unzip whatever you like.

Follows Simin out of the room.

SIMIN   Watch it. In my culture we cook fresh men.

Simin and Luke exit.

NOOR *(to Ahmad)* Are you really a physicist? Or was what you said just part of the show?

AHMAD   Your mother is an extraordinary woman.

NOOR   Yes, she is.

AHMAD   I see why your sister didn't want to disturb her after her twenty-hour trip.

NOOR   Yes, my sister does whatever it takes to make sure our parents don't suffer. Sometimes at great cost to herself... and me.

SAHAR   Thank you for helping.

NOOR   I'm sure you have to get back to the restaurant.

AHMAD   I have the rest of the night off.

SAHAR   Would you like some more chai?

AHMAD   May I?

SAHAR   Of course, and please have more baklava. I baked them myself.

AHMAD (*picks up a baklava, takes a bite*) They're delicious. My mother bakes baklava like this.

NOOR   Hazardous to one's ass.

SAHAR   Noor!

AHMAD   I wouldn't worry about ...

NOOR   My ass?

AHMAD   I mean there's nothing to worry about.

Noor picks up a baklava and takes a big bite.

AHMAD   Yet.

SAHAR   Does your mother live here in the city?

AHMAD   No. She's back in Iran, with the rest of my family.

NOOR   Then why are you here? A physicist delivering chelo kebab.

AHMAD   I only delivered to you.

NOOR   Sorry?

AHMAD   I'm visiting my twin sister, Mehri. I've been wanting to meet you for a very long time. We are close, Mehri and I. She tells me everything. Well, almost everything.

NOOR   You're Ahmad?

AHMAD   Yes. I asked Mehri to introduce us – properly, and she said, "Oh they've just put in an order for chelo kebab, take it to them and I'll call and tell her you're coming." Then I realized Mehri hadn't called and... well, it was awkward, so I played the delivery man. *(Gets up)* It's time I should introduce myself, properly I mean. Ahmad Lotfi.

SAHAR   Well, nice to meet you Ahmad. Properly.

AHMAD   I really am a physicist, a nuclear physicist. In Iran. *(To Noor)* And I really have been looking forward to meeting you. Not like this, of course. I was hoping Mehri would introduce us. But... *(He touches his coat pocket. Uncomfortably)* May I speak with you in private? *(To Sahar.)* My apologies. I don't mean to be rude.

SAHAR *(confused)* Oh, no of course. Is anything wrong?

AHMAD   From the bottom of my heart, I hope not.

SAHAR   I'll... I'll go see if Mom needs anything. Good night then, Mr. Lotfi.

AHMAD   Please, call me Ahmad. And your baklava is very delicious. Goodnight.

Sahar is about to say something but changes her mind. Exits.

AHMAD   Your sister is a lovely woman. It really is good to meet you, finally. Has Mehri talked to you about me, at all?

NOOR   Are you kidding? She talks about you all the time.

AHMAD   I hope she's painted a charming picture of me.

NOOR   Mehri is very fond of you. Thinks you're the smartest, most handsome man on earth.

AHMAD   And I must be such a disappointment. Forgive me.

NOOR   Not at all. I hope I haven't given you the impression... it's just that I've been very emotional lately and this charade was a little too much for me.

AHMAD   You are not fond of charades then? *(Pauses.)* You and Babbak... I presume, are broken up. But it's none of my business. *(Waits for a response.)* I found something... something I hope is a simple misunderstanding. Has my sister spoken to you about our family at all? Our values? What we stand for?

NOOR   I'm not quite sure what you mean, Ahmad.

AHMAD   As I said, Mehri and I are close. We speak on the phone every week. She talks about you all the time, says you're her best friend. Describes your eyes as "two sunny skies". I know, I know, a bit cheesy but... *(chuckles)* her words, I swear. How you work long hours on your projects. Your obsession with dark matter, the particle collider they've built in Geneva. How you adore saffron ice cream, horror movies, cloudy Sunday mornings so you could stay in bed and read. She said you cried at the opera when Madame Butterfly plunged the knife into her own heart. She's even told me about your obsession with pickles. She says you eat them with just about anything, even bananas; that you even swear "Pickles". Is that true?

NOOR *(laughs)* Drives my sister nuts.

AHMAD   I feel, I felt, I knew you, as in some past life, in another universe ...And for a mad moment I thought if you got to know me, you'd... *(Pause)* It doesn't matter now. I was looking forward to meeting you. I came here with manly intentions.

NOOR *(softly, tenderly)* Manly? I don't understand.

AHMAD   I mean I came here with honourable intentions, only to find dishonour.

NOOR *(hardens as she begins to realize what he may be hinting at)* Forgive me, I cannot reconcile honour with a nuclear physicist working in the Shiraz nuclear laboratories. We are not all fools, you know.

AHMAD   I'm not here to talk about my work. I had an old work visa, and so on an impulse, hopped on a plane and showed up at Mehri's restaurant. Truth is, and I'm not ashamed to admit it... I came here because I wanted to meet you. I had always dreamed of meeting a woman like you. And I wanted to surprise Mehri. It's been two years since I'd seen her. When she saw me, I thought she was going to faint. She was surprised all right. There was a minor disaster in the kitchen and she couldn't leave, so she gave me her key. I went to her house and waited. Bored, I picked up a book from her bedroom shelf. *The Awakening* by Kate Chopin. Have you read it?

NOOR   I gave her that book.

AHMAD   Yes, I believe you did. I read the inscription. Very... passionate. And, there was a picture too. I have it right here. Would you care to see it?

He pulls a picture from his coat pocket, hands it to Noor.

NOOR   You had no right...

AHMAD   A couple's selfie, eh?

NOOR *(more to herself than to Ahmad)* God damn it, I told her to delete it.

AHMAD   Never trust a woman. Maybe she forgot. Or perhaps she couldn't bring herself to delete it. Had to print and keep such a... how shall we put it? A passionate moment between two lovers? No, "lovers" is too good a word for such filth.

NOOR   You had no business going through her things.

AHMAD   How serious is this? Is it a game? A kinky adventure before you each get on with your lives and settle down?

NOOR   Settle down? Like, get married, have kids?

AHMAD *(looks at the framed picture of Sahar's kids)* Yes! To a man. Like your sister. Like any respectable Iranian woman. *(Silence.)* Answer me!

NOOR   Why don't you ask your own sister?

AHMAD   She doesn't know I've seen this. She doesn't know that I know.

NOOR   Know what, Mr. Lotfi? That we are not "respectable" women?

AHMAD   Don't play games with me. If this leaks out, if anyone gets a whiff of this... this filth, my family will disown her. Don't you understand? We are respectable, religious. We'd never be able to hold our heads up in Shiraz again.

NOOR   You speak as if Mehri and I have committed some unspeakable crime.

AHMAD   A crime in my country, yes, but for me, for my family, something worse: an abomination, a sin.

NOOR　　　Look. I think it's your sister you should be having this conversation with, not me. I'm nothing to you.

AHMAD *(more to himself)* You're not nothing to me.

NOOR　　　Sorry?

AHMAD　　　I said, I need to know that I can leave in a few weeks without shame staining my family name.

NOOR　　　You remind me of that Afghan father in my mother's story. *(Points to the door)* Please leave now.

AHMAD　　　Homosexuality carries the death penalty in Iran.

NOOR　　　We don't live in the Islamic Pickles Republic of Iran.

Turns to leave, stops, turns back, points in the direction of the bedrooms.

AHMAD　　　That sweet old woman thinks you're getting married. Married! This will be worse than cancer. How about if I tell her exactly who you are.

NOOR　　　What?!

AHMAD　　　She will die. She'll die from shame.

NOOR　　　Who do you think you are? You don't even know me.

AHMAD　　　I've read all you papers.

NOOR　　　My scientific papers?

AHMAD　　　Every single one of them. You're brilliant. You're beautiful. I came here completely... *(Wants to say "in love".)* Intrigued by you. I had ideas I wanted to... To discuss with you. Not this shame..

NOOR　　　Is that a new word for love?

AHMAD *(takes a deep breath, regains himself)* When I was fourteen, I used to follow our neighbour's daughter every day and watch her buy bread from the baker up the road. That was her chore, four o'clock sharp, right after school. I was in love, and she knew it. But the truth was, I knew nothing about her, except what I was allowed to see – a patch of shiny black hair that fell on her perfect forehead, those long delicate fingers. And her lips! They were like a snapdragon opening and closing as she ordered bread. I was hopelessly in love!

One day, I drew a fat heart with my red marker, put an arrow through it. I crumpled the paper and just before she walked into the bakery I threw it at her shoes. She bent over, picked it up, slid it in her pocket.

That night, her shit brother found the note. He gave it to their dad out of spite, because she had eaten his chocolate or something stupid like that. Her father was a religious, violent man. She got a good beating because she wouldn't tell who gave her the love note.

Loyalty, devotion... measure these and you learn the depth of love. Love is the willingness to sacrifice... at all costs. I never saw her again. That was my sacrifice. I'm sorry. I've got jet lag and it's been a difficult day. Seeing this... *(waving the photograph)* was a shock and... I forgot myself. I'm normally not like this. Really. Please, may I come back tomorrow?

NOOR	You're kidding, right?
AHMAD	We must discuss this – *(loudly)* perhaps more rationally.
NOOR	Not so loud! OK, fine, but not here. At the corner café. Vegan paradise. At ten. Now please, go.
AHMAD	You have a beautiful, magnificent family. Please don't mention this to Mehri. I beg you, not yet.

Ahmad exits. Noor sinks into a chair. Luke enters and picks up a book from the shelf.

LUKE	You OK?
NOOR	I don't know.
LUKE	Attar.
NOOR	What?
LUKE	I've been reading poems of Attar.
NOOR	I'm impressed.

LUKE   Yeah, well... I'm just an apple pie boy from Arkansas, right? Married a pretty Persian and fell into this vortex of kebab, rice, pistachios and baklava, people dancing with their hands like they're changing light bulbs.

NOOR   On your wedding day, I heard your mom tell your dad, your babies were going to come out looking like terrorists.

LUKE   Turns out she was right.

NOOR   Do you talk to them much?

LUKE   I only do that with people I like.

NOOR   Isn't loving one's parents a commandment or something?

LUKE   Love is like a wet soap. It's hard to hold on to it when it gets too wet.

NOOR   Never thought of it that way.

LUKE   Did I ever tell you my granddaddy once helped lynch a black woman because they said she practised voodoo? Charming, no? My dad grew up having to choose between cruelty and remorse. I still haven't figured out which one he chose. Maybe he nibbled on both. He's crazy about Trump.

NOOR   What did you choose?

LUKE   Me? I'm a rebel. I went for forgiveness.

NOOR   Is forgiveness possible without love?

LUKE   That's one of those questions you should ask backwards.

Luke watches Noor with an amused smile as she figures out what that question is backwards.

LUKE   It's late. You should spend the night right here on this very uncomfortable couch. I'll get you a blanket.

Luke exists, comes back with a pillow and blanket.

LUKE   This was your sister's Valentine day present. *(Waves the book)* "The Conference of the Birds". Have you read it?

NOOR   I'm ashamed to say I've been reading only scientific journals for the past I know how long.

LUKE I'm a big fan of Rumi, but this dude, Attar, takes the cake. He's this 12th century Mystic Sufi who must've time-travelled to our crazy century, because what he's written here, is for us. I'm so into it.

NOOR What's it about?

LUKE The birds of the world get together to look for their Creator. To get there they have to cross seven mythical valleys. The first one is the Valley of the Quest. So I say to myself, sure, search, yeah, a logical place to start. Nothing profound about that. But it's like a video game. In order to enter that valley you have to empty yourself of everything you think you know or believe. Everything. It's the only way to get to the next valley.

NOOR Valley of pickles?

LUKE Close. Valley of Love! And if you're lucky enough to get there, you find that:

"Love is fire, mind is smoke.

When love arrives, reason flees." *(Beat)*

Good-night, Beauty.

He turns to leave but stops.

LUKE I know what's going on. I've always known. And maybe I love your sister more than she loves me. But you know what? That's OK. If everything in life was equal, it'd be god-damn boring.

Luke exits. Noor picks up her cell phone.

NOOR Babbak, please pick up. I know you're there. I need to talk to you.

Lights out.

ACT II SCENE 1

Early morning the next day. The sisters are having coffee in their robes. A pot of coffee, milk and sugar sit next to the samovar. Luke walks in from the kitchen in suit and tie, chewing on a piece of toast. He grabs his briefcase.

LUKE   I hope you angels are naked under those robes. Of course I'd stay and investigate but gotta go and make money for the upkeep of my Persian harem.

SAHAR   Yeah yeah. Don't forget to pick up the kids from the Olsons.

LUKE *(pointing to Noor)* Hey, you over there. I know it's hard, but do try to behave.

Luke exits.

NOOR *(calling after Luke)* Bye *Luke. (To Sahar)* When did Maman say God stopped manufacturing Luke's model of men?

SAHAR   Apparently right after the chelo kebab man's blessed birth. *(Laughter)* No, I think my son was the last model. The cute devil. Every day I remind myself how lucky I am.

NOOR   "Remind" yourself. Interesting choice of words. So that you don't forget?

SAHAR   So that I don't wonder.

NOOR   But what if–?

SAHAR   Don't start! No. No what-ifs, Noor. We're much happier with no what-ifs. You can only be happy by feeling grateful for what is.

NOOR   But you would've been some place else. Some place where you might have been even happier.

SAHAR   I'm happy now. I have my children. Can't imagine life without them.

NOOR   You would've had children with Hafez.

SAHAR   Shush! *(Looks in the direction of their mother's room.)* I wouldn't have had these children. And I wouldn't have had a mother sleeping peacefully in that room. She'd either be in her grave or in some hospital bed withering away from grief.

NOOR   You don't know that.

SAHAR   Look, I don't want to talk about this, OK? *(Beat)* What did our mysterious man want with you? Had he come all the way from Shiraz to ask for your hand? Or, maybe he's on a government mission to recruit you for their nuclear research facility.

NOOR   Don't, Sahar. This is my first cup of coffee.

SAHAR   Imagine! You can become Mrs. James Bond, Islamic Republic style. He'd have a beard and hide his gadgets under his turban. And you would wear a thick black veil, except underneath you'd be wearing nothing but Victoria's Secret lingerie rigged with weapons of mass destruction...

NOOR   He's coming back. I'm meeting him at ten.

SAHAR   Here? What the devil should we tell Maman?

NOOR   Not here, silly.

SAHAR   I don't know what I was thinking last night, pretending that guy was Babbak. Why is he coming back?

NOOR   I called him last night.

SAHAR   The kebab guy?

NOOR   Babbak. He won't pick up.

SAHAR   Is it really over, Noor? Or was it just a fight?

NOOR   There's no hope for me.

SAHAR   He loves you.

NOOR   I'm not talking about Babbak, Sahar, I think it's in my blood. This thing with men.

SAHAR   What are you talking about?

NOOR   Don't tell me you've never suspected?

SAHAR   Suspected what?

NOOR   I tried so hard, but there was always something missing, so I drove them all away. Locked myself up in my laboratory. It was only with Babbak that I felt maybe, just maybe, it was possible.

SAHAR   Noor, no.

NOOR   But it wasn't meant to be. And I'm glad it didn't happen. I would've become you!

SAHAR The shame of it will kill our parents.

NOOR No it won't. But it did kill what you had with our cousin. Why did you marry Luke?

SAHAR I loved him. Still do.

NOOR You loved Hafez!

SAHAR That's enough.

NOOR I'm in love.

SAHAR With Babbak?

NOOR No.

SAHAR Who is she? *(Silence. Then a sudden realization.)* Ahmad's sister! The woman who owns the restaurant – Mehri. The tall skinny woman who wears those flowing scarves... How long?

NOOR Don't you see? We, all of us, are like pieces of a puzzle. Some almost fit, just a bit of jabbing and pushing binds us into an uncomfortable fit that'll hold for the rest of our lives. Always together, but uncomfortable, unhappy. Then there are pieces that won't fit at all. Those are the ones who become friends without entanglement. Sit side by side without even touching each other. Yet, in this huge earth-box of pieces, there are a few that are meant for one another.

We had kissed before, cuddled a little, had fallen in love. I didn't know what to do with all that. The night Babbak walked in on us was the first night we let our love take us where it did. It was as if I had unconsciously planned it so he could see it for himself... so I didn't have to tell him, because I couldn't bear to look into his eyes. For days, I couldn't bring myself to touch the roses scattered on my floor. And that ring. That was the last time I saw Babbak.

SAHAR Is she your first... lover?

NOOR *(nods)* Sahar, I love her. That night was the scariest, saddest, most happy night of my life. I could go back to my old life, back to Babbak, if he would still have me. But there's this voice in my head that keeps screaming: "Don't give her up!"

SAHAR You have no other choice.

NOOR It would be like gouging out one of my own eyes. I'd never recover.

SAHAR You've recovered from worse.

NOOR You call this recovered? Don't you see that nothing is ever what could have been because of that single night?

SAHAR Noor, not now. Maman is in the other room.

NOOR Perhaps it's time for her to know what her own brother did to me, to us.

SAHAR That was a long time ago.

NOOR Was it?

SAHAR What good would it do if she knew? I protected you all these years, didn't I?

NOOR You watched him take off my clothes, tell me it was a game, that I was a famous movie star and he was a photographer. When I cried, he told me I was a bad girl and that if Daddy knew he'd sell me to the salt vendor.

SAHAR But he didn't touch you.

NOOR You watched him put me in unspeakable positions, stick his camera so close /to my—

SAHAR I was afraid if I stepped out from behind the curtain, he'd grab me too. But I swear to God, Noor, if he had laid a finger on you, I would've... I was only twelve. *(Pause.)* I saw the scissors on the table. The ones Granny used to cut her fabrics with. *(Pause.)* But he never did ...touch you.

NOOR You're wrong. He did touch me, in the most vile way. With his eyes. The long lens of his camera. *(Pause.)* I was only eight. I looked up to you. You said: "Don't tell Maman, she'd be ashamed of us..." You haven't changed a bit.

SAHAR Don't you think I've suffered enough?

NOOR Even now, when I close my eyes, I see him looking at me with his horny lizard eyes, the thin lips he kept licking.

SAHAR Why do you think I never dated? Huh? All those years in high school, college? You think I forgot his face?

Watching you, from behind that curtain, I kept falling, losing myself piece by piece, year after year, until...

NOOR　　　　　　Until Hafez.

SAHAR　　　　　　Yes, Hafez, our wicked uncle's son... he of all people had to be the one... the man who looked at me and saw me, I mean really saw me, and loved me anyway. I thought I'd graduate from UCLA and we'd run away, even farther than here. But happy secret worlds last only as long as they are secret. I knew that our love affair would destroy our parents. He was married, had three young children... our little cousins. I had to choose, don't you see? And I chose Maman and Daddy. I did what I had to. And recovered from it, as you will too.

NOOR　　　　　　You call this recovered? You live in the shadow of what could have been.

SAHAR　　　　　　Noor, this path you've stepped into is dangerous. I know. There's pain ahead. And pain, pain Noor can suck the pleasure out of just about anything.

NOOR　　　　　　Is that why you left Hafez? Lied to him by telling him you could never be with a man who was our uncle's son? This, to a good, gentle man who saved you?

SAHAR　　　　　　I didn't leave him, you fool. I gave him up, like one gives up sitting in the sun. I knew if I chose to live in daylight, openly, freely, I would've deprived our parents of that same sun I basked in. They would've had to put up with gossip and disgust, their daughter called a whore, a home-wrecker. I made a sacrifice and I don't regret it. Looking at Maman, so full of life and hope, the pleasure she feels looking at her grandchildren, at me, yes that gives me joy and a sense of self respect and honour, and I'll be damned if I let you destroy that.

NOOR　　　　　　Me?

SAHAR　　　　　　If they find out about Mehri, if you choose to live with her, it would mean that the sacrifice I made so many years ago giving up Hafez, and the one we, Noor, made together when we were children, would end up being for nothing. Nothing! Do you understand? I will not let you do that.

NOOR What do you want me to do? Turn my back on happiness? Go back to Babbak and turn my life into a lie? Like the one you forced me into, when I wasn't much older than your little girl? No. I refuse. This time, you can't stop me.

SAHAR From what? From killing our mother in that room?

NOOR Sometimes I don't know who's side you're on.

SAHAR What the hell do you mean by that?

There is a knock on the door.

NOOR *(looks at her watch)* Goddamn pickles!

SAHAR Stop saying that.

NOOR Fucking pickles. Flying pickles. Pickles in hell.

Another knock on the door.

SAHAR It's Ahmad, isn't it? I need a drink. Let Maman sleep for as long as she wants. Don't wake her.

NOOR Why would I do that?

Sahar shrugs angrily. Leaves. Noor opens the door.

AHMAD I waited in the café. What's the world coming to? There was no meat on the menu, no eggs, not even real coffee. They have these soy little things that look like sausages but taste like compacted salted dirt, and what in the world is a glutton-free bread?

Noor smiles despite herself, but does not correct his glutton for gluten.

It tasted like cardboard. And you missed it all. Or did you send me there on purpose? I waited a half hour.

They stare at one another for a beat, then Noor motions him in, turns around and walks in. He follows.

NOOR Coffee?

AHMAD Turkish?

NOOR Starbucks.

AHMAD Five spoons of sugar, with milk please.

Noor goes to the table and slowly pours him a cup of coffee, adds sugar and milk. Ahmad sits down, looking at her intensely. Noor hands him the cup. He takes a sip.

AHMAD May I have more sugar?

Noor goes to the kitchen, brings him a huge container of sugar and a spatula, and plops them in front of him.

NOOR Knock yourself out.

AHMAD A physicist with a sense of humour. I suppose it has to be that way. Or else we'd all go mad. It's a chaotic world, the subatomic world we study.

NOOR No, not chaotic. Unpredictable. What do you want from me?

AHMAD I would have answered that differently a week ago. Different questions, different fantasies, different times. Funny how things change with the click of an iPhone. Now... now, all I want, no, all I'm asking, begging really, is to end this thing you have going with my sister.

NOOR Isn't this something you should ask your sister first?

AHMAD She wasn't this way before she met you.

NOOR What way?

AHMAD Nothing.

NOOR Oh, please Mr. Lotfi. Why hold back now?

AHMAD Do you want me to say it? Name it? OK. Dirty. Twisted.

NOOR I'm sorry this is how you feel about me and your beloved twin sister.

AHMAD No. Not of you, or Mehri. You are so beautiful and talented. Both of you. It doesn't have to be this way. You can change your ways. It isn't too late. We all make mistakes.

NOOR Have you? Made mistakes?

AHMAD Yeah. Plenty. But not of this sort. Noor, nothing is impossible. You, yourself, have said it over and over in your papers: nothing is impossible.

NOOR　　　　In quantum mechanics.

AHMAD　　　　But Noor, how can you talk about anything in this universe without including us in it, figuring us into the equation. The world exists because of actualization of possibilities; we navigate our own path through this eternity of possibilities ... all we need to know is where we want to go. We possess this power, we just have to realize it, admit it, believe in it and practise it. It's like a new religion. A new way of looking at the world. We are each a god and in that sense God is in each of us. How can you turn away from what you, yourself, must believe?

NOOR　　　　Don't tell me what I believe.

AHMAD　　　　Look, our mere observation of events in the subatomic world alters the course of those events, right? That applies in the macrocosm too. I came here for a different reason. I came here thinking I could get to know you, maybe even at least start a friendship with you... *(Chuckles)* Best-laid plans always take one off course, don't they? Listen, I'm here and I've changed the course of events. Nothing will be as it was going to be, had I not come from Iran. Your life, mine, Mehri's and our families are now irreparably intertwined. Perhaps we've always been heading towards one another on a collision course. Let's hope the atom doesn't split... Listen to me, I'm begging you to help me clear a path of happiness for my sister, and for you.

NOOR　　　　For me? For Mehri? You mean for yourself.

AHMAD　　　　This infatuation will pass. You are women. You'll get over it. Once you experience a real man who loves you, gives you children, you'll look back at all this and laugh.

NOOR　　　　You can't even allow us this, can you? ... When a man is gay in Iran, you say he's a pervert, you spit at him, ostracise him, and if you are the Islamic Republic, you either sentence him to death or at best give him money to have a sex change operation to make him "acceptable" in the eyes of Allah, because now the pipe has become an electric socket, ready to receive. Have you ever thought about how there is no gentle word for the act of making love?

AHMAD　　　　Oh please, enlighten me.

NOOR   For men it's Kardan, doing it, pushing it in; for women, it's Da'dan, giving it, presenting it on a platter. We women are always on the receiving end of instructions and pickles. We never know what's good for us. Our desires aren't really our own because half the time we don't even know what we should want. You have to tell us how and what to do and think and desire. Hide our hair because it sends out magic rays that put the devil in you. If you rape us, it's because we're whores, showing our legs or bare arms.

AHMAD   And that's not happening right here, in this so called democracy, cradle of freedom? In colleges? At work places? What's that phrase?... "Sexual harassment"... minted in the good old U.S.A.

NOOR   You know how many times I was pinched in the ass in the bazaars of Tehran? Because I wasn't wearing a chador covering myself? That gave them permission.

AHMAD   Islam respects women, and whether you like the hijab or not, it isn't meant to oppress you. Women have great power in their homes. Take my mother. She rules our family. My father never left his rug store, he worked that hard. Why? So she could stay home and raise us. Is that so bad? During the revolution women were out in the streets too, fighting to oust the Shah and bring Islam back to the land.

NOOR   No, when the revolution came, people fought for their freedom... Christians, Jews, Muslims, the left and the right. In the end, they ended up with a Mullah who executed five thousand people in one fell swoop to obliterate anyone who opposed him. Dumped their poor bodies in a mass grave. Then he got busy with pushing women back under the veil – back into homes. He let loose his second unofficial army, men on motorcycles who roamed the streets in search of women in short sleeve dresses. They'd zoom by and cut them with poison razor blades.

AHMAD   That's a lie.

NOOR   Saket O Samet. "Silent and mute" once again became a high compliment paid to women. Marriage age was lowered to 13. Brilliant. Back to the dark ages.

AHMAD   It isn't as bad as you say. You paint a hellish image. I live there and I tell you, it isn't true.

NOOR   Says the man who tells a gay woman: It's just a phase, get over it. Do you read the news? They arrested six kids who made a video dancing to that song, "Happy". Six months in jail for each of them. Why? Because it was "vulgar" and "obscene"! All they did was dance on the rooftops of Tehran. The girls wore head scarves. It's a dumb thing to say, "all is well".

AHMAD   I am an educated man.

NOOR   Exactly! And educated men like you, Ahmad, should be standing up for us and for yourselves. Instead you have turned into these sad puppets, brainwashed into thinking you get your power by taking it away from us. Wake up Ahmad, and smell the bullshit.

Simin enters.

SIMIN   Oh Babbak-joon, you're here already. I think I slept a little bit too much. But it felt good. I feel one hundred and five percent better and I'm starving. Is there bread and cheese?

NOOR   Yes, Maman. Sit down. We have homemade jam.

SIMIN   What kind?

NOOR   Carrot with pieces of quince and cardamon. Sahar's special recipe.

SIMIN   Oh, so now it's her special recipe? OK. Whatever! *(To Ahmad)* Have you had breakfast, Babbak-joon?

AHMAD   Thank you. This cup of coffee is all I need. But I'll keep you company while you eat.

SIMIN   You're kind, my dear. My heart sings because my daughter has found you. Children. They can make you happy and they can be the end of their parents too. When you and Noor have your own, you'll understand. I tell you, Reza and I thank

God, alham-dulallah a thousand times for our girls. They keep us happy, young and alive.

Noor sets a breakfast tray before Simin. Simin spreads jam on her bread, takes a bite and is impressed with the taste.

SIMIN   Have you set a date? I'm here only for a month you know.

NOOR   Maman, drink your chai. It'll get cold.

SIMIN   Where's the ghand? Ah here they are: nice, big sugar cubes. Can't get used to pouring sugar in my chai, can you?

She notices the big jar of sugar, picks up the spatula, examines it. Noor picks up the sugar container, takes the spatula from her mother and exits to the kitchen.

SIMIN   You and my Noor had a fight, no? My nose is twitching.

AHMAD   No... Well, not exactly a fight. More like a disagreement. Nothing that can't be resolved.

SIMIN   Last night my dreams were like a black pearl necklace: one dark world after another. You know how some people get itches or pains when it's about to rain? Well, I'm that way with my dreams. I dream dark dreams when something terrible is on its way. *(Whispering)* Do you know if something terrible is heading our way, Babbak-joon?

Noor enters from the kitchen.

NOOR   What are you two whispering about?

SIMIN   My nose. *(Beat)* Last night I was thinking about an Iranian Baha'i lady I met in Liberec. I don't know why I started thinking about her. She was sitting in the park, crying because the government had executed her brother. They had even asked his wife to pay for the bullets. They said the Islamic Republic of Iran was not responsible for the cost of killing the infidels. Anyway, she was in the park crying so her children at home wouldn't see her so sad. She had long, shiny black hair.

Last night I dreamt her hair was spread out like a dark lake, and I was on a small boat rowing into it.

NOOR   Eating kebab late at night can give you nightmares, Maman.

AHMAD   My grandmother used to say that the Baha'is worship a cat in a bag.

SIMIN   In a bag? That is very funny.

AHMAD   She was not an educated woman.

SIMIN   They're good people, these Baha'is. They say that so long as we live on earth, God will send guidance through His prophets. That's not so horrible, is it? Sahar's best friend was a Baha'i girl. Her mother once told me if they have to choose between educating a son or a daughter, their religion teaches them to educate their girls. How can anyone persecute a group that believes in something as noble as that? But they are executed, imprisoned and tortured to this day. We blame the mullahs for many things, but we forget that as a people, there is a lot we must change about ourselves. We have to stop looking the other way, and speak up for them.

AHMAD   Well, whatever the government does, they claim it is according to the Islamic laws.

The phone rings. Sahar picks it up in another room.

SIMIN   To carry out injustice, the mullahs have made up new laws. The stronger the laws, the greater the injustice that can be carried out legally.

Sahar enters, phone in hand.

SAHAR   Maman, it's for you.

SIMIN *(into the telephone)* Hello? Yes. This is Mrs. Mustafa. Oh hello Mrs. Sarvar. How is Mr. Sarvar? ... And the children? Alham-Dol-Allah. I can't wait to see you, I just arrived. Good, good. The girls are fine, I just wish Reza was here too. *(Long pause.)* Ya Ali. I knew it. I tossed and turned all night. When?... God bless her soul. She was an angel, and angels suffer in this world... Of course I'll be there. *(Wipes away her* *tears.)* Can you tell my daughter where it is? Thank you for letting me know. *(To Sahar)* She's going to give you directions.

Sahar takes the phone from her mother.

SAHAR   Mrs. Sarvar? Salaam... Thank you.

NOOR   Maman? What's going on?

SAHAR   Hold on, let me get a pen.

NOOR   Is it your Baha'i friend, the one you dreamed about?

SIMIN   No honey, no. I don't know where she is.

SAHAR   This Sunday, 2 pm. All right. Thank you. Yes, yes I'll bring her myself. Merci. Khoda-Hafiz. *(To Simin)* Who died, Maman?

SIMIN   Oh, honey, azizam, someone you don't know. Someone I've never told you girls about. I'm sorry, it's an ugly ugly story.

NOOR   Who Maman? Who're you talking about? What's happened?

AHMAD   Can I get you a glass of water?

SIMIN   Yes, thank you.

Ahmad pours her a glass of water. Simin takes it and has a sip.

SIMIN   She was a childhood friend from my mother's village up north. Had a beautiful daughter, Pari. Born the same year as you, Sahar. Pretty like a full moon smiling. Long hair, dark and wavy all the way to her waist. Eyes like Bambi. When she walked down the street, everybody couldn't help but stare and stare, and say Masha-allah. Then she grew up and fell in love with a boy from a very poor and fanatically religious family. Pari's parents were educated, had money and status, so naturally they were against their only daughter marrying such a boy. But the girl, blinded by love, defied her parents and married the boy. The newly-weds took a little apartment on the second floor of a home and lived there, poor as a doormouse. One day the boy comes home...

As Simin continues to narrate, lights dim on Sahar's living room and rise on a second floor apartment where Pari (Noor) is mending socks.

Music: "Post Traumatic" by Paul Haslinger from Sleeper Cell: American Terror gradually rises.

Pari's husband (Luke) enters.

PARI'S HUSBAND/LUKE   This place stinks. We don't even have a car. Your parents are so rich, and we live like this!

PARI/NOOR   How can I ask them for anything when I defied them? Married you. No, I'm ashamed to crawl back to them. I will not do it.

The husband grabs the hurricane lamp, throws kerosene on Pari, lights a match and flings it at her. She is on fire.

He leaves the apartment and locks the door. Pari runs to the balcony. Sahar, Simin and Ahmad acting as "People" gather beneath her window.

PEOPLE   Jump! Jump! We'll catch you.

Pari looks at herself and sees her dress has burned away and her breasts hang naked. She pulls herself back inside, still on fire. Music ends. Lights shift back to Sahar's living room.

SIMIN   She died because she was ashamed to be seen by her neighbours, naked.

NOOR   She let herself burn? That can't be possible.

SIMIN   But it can. The power of a'broo, dignity and honor. How could she hold her head high in a village when every man had seen her naked breasts, her bared privates? She thought it was better to die than to live with such shame.

SAHAR   I hope they burned the husband limb by limb.

SIMIN   They arrested him but he paid blood money and they let him go. He went on with his life, got married, had children. Every day took his children by the hand, and walked them past his dead wife's family's home to school. My friend told me that watching him and his brats go by her house every single day was like pricking her eyes with needles. Her nerves couldn't take it anymore. They brought her to America for treatment. But how do you cure a mother of such grief? That phone call... my friend died last week. Just laid her head down one night, and never picked it up again.

NOOR   Oh Maman...

SIMIN   Some men do terrible things. And the world lets them. Our crime is pretending it's not happening.

NOOR   Bathe me in red,

Give me a name, a cause.

SIMIN (*dries her tears, smiles*) Look at me. I'm going to pull myself together. Look to the future, not the past. Today we are making wedding plans and nothing else.

AHMAD   Yes, the wedding plans.

SAHAR   Maman, why don't you go and wash up, then maybe we can all go for a stroll? It's beautiful outside.

NOOR   A pickle day in Paradise.

SIMIN   You and your pickles.

SAHAR   We can have lunch at the corner café.

AHMAD   The one with fake meat and glutton free bread?

SAHAR (*remembering the game they are playing*) Gluten... um... Babbak. They make plantains too.

SIMIN   Gluten, Glutton, it's all the same to me and I love plantains with cream. I promise, no more gloomy talk from me.

NOOR   Maman-joon, you can talk about whatever you want.

Simin kisses Noor, exits. Sahar follows her out.

AHMAD   How many of these stories does your mother carry on her back?

NOOR   Too many for her own good. Look, you must leave. I sound like a broken record. What is it you want?

AHMAD   What?

NOOR   What do you want from me?

AHMAD   I've already told you.

NOOR   And if I refuse?

AHMAD   I'm not Babbak and you are not who you say you are. *(Ahmad holds up the photograph.)*

NOOR   This is blackmail.

AHMAD   No. It's an amicable exchange of favours. Shall I leave this with you? I've made copies.

Sahar enters, sees the photo, grabs it and looks at it.

SAHAR   Oh my God! How in the world?

She turns it upside down, then back again, trying to figure out which side is up and who exactly is in the picture.

SAHAR   What are you doing? Is this what he's about? He is here to blackmail us? *(To Ahmad)* Is that what you are doing?

AHMAD   Please...

NOOR   Mehri doesn't know he's doing this. He wants me... He says I must leave her, or...

SAHAR   Or what? Tell Maman? Show our sweet mother this, this picture? *(Sahar sinks into the sofa.)* He's right, you know. I told you, this is going to lead to nothing but heartbreak and pain for everyone.

AHMAD   You've got a wise, sensible sister.

NOOR *(to Sahar)* Sahar, don't you see? Our boogie man is "shame". They know that, and they use it. Be a good girl or the boogie man will get you, will shred you and your parents into pieces. Isn't that so, Mr. Lotfi?

SIMIN *(calling from the other room)* Noor! Come here. I need you to zip me up.

NOOR   Coming.

Noor exits. Sahar looks at Ahmad long enough to make him very uncomfortable. Then she rips the photograph into tiny pieces. Ahmad stands there for a while, not sure what to do next. Then with a sudden determination, leaves.

Lights out.

ACT III SCENE 1

Early afternoon the next day.

Simin enters the apartment, limping almost imperceptibly. She is dressed in black and looks very tired and pale. She puts her old-fashioned black handbag on the couch, goes to the kitchen, comes back with a glass of water and sits down. She drinks the water. She rubs her chest, neck and temples. Sahar walks in dressed in black. Luke walks in from the kitchen.

LUKE   You're back.

SAHAR The place was packed. They had a huge picture of the girl on one pedestal, and one of her mother on another, a mountain of flowers in between. Oh and her poor husband! He looked like he wouldn't live long either. Tragic... Mom cried her eyes out...

Sahar/Luke look in the direction of Simin and notice she is pale.

LUKE   Are you turning anglo on me, or is this a super pale makeup?

SIMIN Is that a multiple choice question? Akh... I'm too old for so much pain. Thank God you're all happy and healthy.

SAHAR I'll make you some chai.

SIMIN No, no I think I'll go lie down.

LUKE   Let me help. Here, take my arm.

SIMIN So I look pale. It's good in Iran to be pale. But here, I will use one of Sahar's tanning sprays.

SAHAR He didn't mean...

SIMIN Yes, yes, I know what he meant. I'm making a joke, like him, but I'm too tired to execute properly. When is Noor coming back?

SAHAR She'll be here soon. You go rest. I'll wake you up in an hour.

Luke helps Simin walk towards the bedrooms. Her limp becomes more pronounced.

LUKE *(mouthing quietly to Sahar)* Is she limping?

SIMIN *(defiantly)* My leg fell asleep. It's snoring like my husband.

LUKE Let's lay it down so it can wake up.

Simin and Luke exit. Sahar begins to tidy up. There is a knock on the door. She opens the door. It is Ahmad.

AHMAD Salaam.

Sahar stares at him.

AHMAD Is Noor here?

SAHAR No.

AHMAD I must speak with you. May I come in?

SAHAR No.

AHMAD Please.

Sahar lets go of the door knob and walks back in. Ahmad follows Sahar to the living room.

AHMAD You don't like me. I don't blame you. I'm only trying... I want to do what is right. For both their sakes.

SAHAR Take it from me Ahmad, sometimes you think you're doing the right thing, but it turns out to be the greatest wrong. Leave them alone.

AHMAD I can't do that.

SAHAR It's hard giving up controlling those we love, isn't it? Yet we all do it, Ahmad, as if it's not enough making decisions just for ourselves. *(Beat.)* Look, we just came back from a funeral. Maman isn't feeling well. I'm tired. Can't you let this go?

AHMAD It's too late. Noor told her. My sister knows and is furious. Asked me to leave. No, she threw me out. Said she didn't want to see me ever again.

SAHAR Can you blame her?

Noor appears in the doorway, a silent and unnoticed witness.

AHMAD She's my twin sister. My flesh and blood. I love her. I want her to be happy. I want what's best for her.

SAHAR   Do you? Or do you want what's best for you?

AHMAD   No.

SAHAR   You simply can't live with this notion of having a lesbian sister in America. This whole honour charade is about you. Not your family or my mother or our ancestors. You. You came here with preconceived notions about Noor—

AHMAD   I don't know what you mean.

SAHAR   Then found out that not only is she not available – which you should have known had you been told about Babbak – but that, my goodness, she is your sister's lover! What a gargantuan blow to your ego. And then you stand there not only bruised and empty-handed, but also have this sudden realization that your own future may be in jeopardy, your marriage prospects suddenly dimmed should a word of this "shame" reach Iran, your family name sullied. Why don't you face it, Ahmad, you don't give a fuck about Noor or your sister.

AHMAD   How dare you!

SAHAR   The only one you care about is yourself!

AHMAD   I've had enough of this.

Ahmad turns to leave but Sahar pulls him back, almost violently, by his arm. He is taken aback and pulls himself free from her.

SAHAR   What is it you call yourself, Ahmad? Progressive? Educated? A physicist? Eh? You're no better than the Taliban, or those puny fellows, the Boko Haram. When it comes down to it, no matter what holy ideology you rub on your hairy chests, you still expect the world to revolve around your golden penises. What's the Persian word for it... dodol tala?

AHMAD   All men are perverts and evil, is that it?

SAHAR   Oh no. No. There are good men in this world like my own husband, many, many of them in the Middle East, but let me break it to you, Ahmad, you are not one of them.

AHMAD   And of course, being a woman, you are faultless, an angel. Clean and unstained.

SAHAR   Unstained. That's a mouthful. Despite what you may think, Ahmad, when two women come together, love one another, it isn't all about sex. Yes, physical attraction is a part of it, but for many it's deeper than anything a man like you could ever know or even begin to understand.

AHMAD *(snickers)* You speak as if you yourself have tasted the rotten apple.

SAHAR   Only after encountering snakes like you. *(Beat.)* Now, please leave my home and never come back. I don't care what you do or who you tell. Noor is my sister. I will protect her with my life. She's grown up to be a beautiful, smart and gracious woman and no matter what she does and who she chooses to be with, we, including my parents, are and will always be proud of her! As for you and your family, that's your business!!! *(Beat.)* Now please, remove yourself from my home.

Ahmad, stunned and very angry turns to leave and sees Noor standing in the doorway. Noor gives him a wry smile, and steps aside to let him pass. He hesitates, reaches out to her, but anger consumes him again. He leaves quickly. The sisters look at one another. (Beat.) The closeness they feel at this moment is palpable.

SAHAR   If I could give back to you the innocent trust our mother's brother stole from you, I'd do it this minute, even if I had to use those scissors on that bastard.

NOOR   I love you too.

Simin emerges from the hallway. She looks pale and sick, dragging her right leg.

NOOR   Maman!?

SAHAR   What's wrong?

SIMIN   I may be old, but I'm not deaf.

Both sisters are stunned. They each try to say something, but Simin holds up her hands.

SIMIN   No need to say anything. In fact, let's not talk about it today. There's always tomorrow, one hopes. *(She sighs.)*

SAHAR   Maman?

NOOR   Are you in pain?

Simin is led to the couch. Her face is droopier. She has suffered two strokes.

SAHAR   Luke, Luke! (*Luke runs in, he has headphones on. He takes them off.*) Something's wrong with Maman.

Luke nods, takes his cell phone out of his pocket, begins to dials as he exits to avoid alarming Simin.

SAHAR   Maman, are you taking your blood pressure medication?

SIMIN *(her speech slurring)* I was feeling so much better. I stopped taking them.

NOOR   Maman-joon, you're not supposed to do that. Didn't they tell you?

SAHAR   Here, drink this. Maman, does anything hurt?

Sahar gives Simin some water, but it runs down her chin.

SIMIN   Only my heart. It is going to burst. Ah, don't worry, I'm all right. Just tired. Too too tired.

NOOR   Maman, I'm sorry. About everything you heard. I want you to be proud of me. I'll do whatever you like. Anything. Just get better. Please.

Simin is unresponsive. Noor takes off her mother's stockings and covers her with a blanket. Luke enters.

LUKE   The paramedics are on their way. Let's lie her down.

SIMIN   Wait– (*Beat*) My beautiful daughter. My smart, wild, good daughter. (*Longer beat as she makes a decision. She takes off her silver bangle and holds it out to Noor.*) Take this... this river of tears. May you never know shame.

Blackout.

SCENE 2

Sahar's apartment. Two days later, early in the morning. Music: English rendition of a Persian song 'Goleh San-gam' ['My Stone Flower'] is playing full blast. Noor is alone in the apartment. She is on the couch, deep in thought, playing with the silver bangle her mother gave her. There is a knock on the door. Noor does not hear. She is too deep in her own thoughts. There is another knock, louder, angrier. Noor turns off the music and opens the door. Ahmad, dressed shabbily, hair in disarray, stands there, holding a large jar of pickles.

AHMAD   I heard about your mother. I called the hospital but they wouldn't tell me anything. Just something about a hippopotamus. They kept saying, hippo, hippo.

NOOR   Hipppo, HIPPA, gluten, glutton –who the pickles cares! *(Beat)* By law, they can't give out patient information to strangers.

AHMAD   To protect old ladies like your mother from goons like me.

NOOR   Guess they're too late for that.

AHMAD   I wasn't even here when she had her stroke.

NOOR   She was standing in that hallway the whole time. She heard you. She heard... everything.

AHMAD   She isn't going to die, is she?

NOOR   Why are you here?

AHMAD *(presenting his jar of pickles)* I thought since you like pickles, you should taste mine. I mean... you know what I mean.

Noor looks at the jar, then at him. She does not want to take it. But he holds it out insistently, determined to give it to her.

AHMAD   Please. It's a peace offering. *(Noor takes the jar, reluctantly.)* She locked me out of her apartment. My beloved twin sister won't even answer my texts.

NOOR   That's between the two of you.

AHMAD I've come with a solution.

NOOR Just because you say there's a problem, it doesn't make it so, Ahmad.

AHMAD Please. Just hear me out. Then I'll go. I promise

Noor lets him in the apartment.

AHMAD We started on the wrong foot. My fault. Jet lag and the shock of... *(makes gestures with his hands)* Well, I think it just set me off, in a most unnatural way. I'm not like that. Normally. I've never... Listen, the reason I really came here, was to... get to see you for myself. And I guess the real anger came after I saw you. Just when everything suddenly made sense, it also fell apart. Do you understand what I'm saying?

NOOR No. I don't.

AHMAD Noor... Will you marry me?

Noor looks at Ahmad as if he's lost his mind.

AHMAD It'll solve everything. You and Mehri get to be sisters, and we, well, you and I can live a respectable life, have children, travel, grow old together. In Shiraz... Or here, if you like.

NOOR Have you gone mad?

AHMAD I've never felt saner in my whole life. Never more sure of what I want.

NOOR What about what we want? Mehri and I?

AHMAD You'll still be together. As sisters. Isn't that even better... than what you have now?

Noor's cell phone rings on the dining room table. She looks over at it but decides not to answer.

NOOR No!

AHMAD You don't want to be sisters with Mehri?

NOOR I don't want to marry you, Ahmad, or have anything to do with you. In fact, I'm repulsed by you. *(She holds out the jar of pickles.)* I don't want this. Take it and go.

Ahmad reaches over, but instead of taking the jar of pickles he grabs Noor's wrist. Noor struggles to get away and lets go of the jar. It shatters on the floor. Ahmad pulls her away from the glass to protect her.

Noor misunderstands his touch and struggles to get away from him. But now, Noor's proximity drives Ahmad crazy. He pulls her in and kisses her forcefully. She struggles to get away, but he has lost himself and is too strong. He pulls her over to the couch and rapes her while Noor's phone rings insistently. At some point Noor gives up fighting and becomes limp. The trauma of her childhood sexual abuse overpowers the independent feisty woman she is today. She reverts back to the scared little girl, abused by her uncle. Once Ahmad finishes, he gets up, wild with the sudden realization of what he has just done. He paces the living room, then comes back and kneels besides Noor, who is limp and in shock.

AHMAD *(emotional, crying, regretful)* I'm sorry, Noor. Forgive me. I don't know what came over me. This is not me. I'm not a monster. I love you.

Noor remains impassive. Ahmad grabs Noor's red shawl from the arm of the couch and covers her with it.

AHMAD   This changes nothing. I still want you to be my wife.

Noor slowly comes back to herself as if waking up from a nightmare. Rage builds up in her eyes. She is about to pounce on Ahmad when the phone rings again. She pulls herself away, picks up the phone and stares at it. She then slowly brings it up to her ear.

NOOR   Sahar?.... Here, at your apartment. No, I.... *(walks to the shards of glass on the floor)* I... I... What?... When?

Noor crumbles onto the floor. She lets go of the phone and sits in the pickle juice, among the pickles and shards of glass. Ahmad watches her not knowing what to do. He eventually goes to her, slowly, and puts his hand on her shoulder. She flinches.

NOOR   She's gone. You said it would kill her to know. It did.

AHMAD   I didn't want her to die. I loved your mother.

Noor grabs a large piece of broken glass and in a quick move pushes Ahmad down, holding the sharp edge against Ahmad's throat.

NOOR   You loved my mother. She is dead. You loved that little girl back in Iran. You let her take the fall for your vanity. You love your sister, you've broken her to pieces. You love me. You just ripped the life out of me.

AHMAD   Is this what you want? Is it? Then, do it. Do it! But it won't relieve you from all this rage, this hatred for men.

NOOR   You're not a real man. You're a nothing from nowhere – a taker, a liar, a fake.

In a quick move, Ahmad grabs the piece of glass from Noor and in that struggle, he accidentally cuts Noor's face, the way the Afghani Father in the earlier story had cut the Afghani Mother's face. Blood gushes out. Ahmad drops the shard of glass and steps back, horrified by what he has just done.

Noor touches the cut on her face, unsure of what has just happened. Ahmad moves to help her, but thinks better of it. He does not know what to do. He is confused and terrified. He hurries to the door, stops, looks back, still torn about what to do. He decides to run. He leaves just as Luke and Sahar rush in.

Their confusion turns to horror as they see the state of the apartment, and Noor on the floor among broken glass and pickles, bleeding from a large gash on her face. Sahar goes to her.

SAHAR   Noor!

Noor looks at her own blood-soaked hands, then realizes the blood is from from the gash on the face. Her shock transforms to a sudden realization and a sense of determined empowerment. She lifts her bloodied hands and shows them to Sahar.

NOOR   Bathe me in red

Give me a name, a cause,
Make of me a revolution.
She then turns to the audience, addressing them directly.
NOOR   Come closer,
Here I am,
Take your time.

Lights out.
The End.

Glossary

Maman – Mom

Salaam – Hello

Chelo kebab – Rice and charbroiled pounded beef

Dokhtaram – My daughters

Mullah – Muslim clergy

Ya Ali – A call invoking Islam's revered Imam Ali

Bah-bah – Expression of culinary delight

Jon / Joon (pronounced like jJhn / June) – Dear

Khanum – Lady (Hence, "khanum-joon" means dear lady)

Eena-hush – Voila. Here it is.

Samovar – Tea brewing urn typical to Persian and Russian households.

Masha-Allah – God bless her/him.

Khoda-hafiz – Goodbye Azizam

My dear *Alham-du-lallah* –Thank God

Kardan – To fuck, done by male

Da'dan – To give, to be fucked

Saket and Samet – Silent and mute

Doogh – Salty yoghurt drink

Dodol Tala – Literally means "golden penis," used casually to refer
   to baby boys

Sholeh Wolpé is an Iranian-born poet and playwright. Her literary work includes five collections of poetry, several plays, three books of translations, and three anthologies. Her most recent book, *Abacus of Loss: A Memoir in Verse* (Univ. of Arkansas Press, March 2022) has been hailed by National Book Award finalist Ilya Kaminsky as a book "that created its own genre, a thrill of lyric combined with the narrative spell."

Sholeh's newest project as a lyricist is a semi-staged oratorio, *The Conference of the Birds,* composed by Fahad Siadat, and choreographed by André Megerdichian. It will premiere at the Broad Stage in Los Angeles in June 2022.

Sholeh's plays have been produced by Oakland Theater Project, Inferno Theater, Northern Illinois University, and The Alternative Theater company, among others, and have been finalists and semi-finalists at Bay Area Playwrights Festival, Eugene O'Neill National Playwrights Conference, Centenary Stage Women Playwrights, Ojai Playwrights Festival, and Ashland New Plays Festival.

She is the recipient of a 2014 PEN Heim, 2013 Midwest Book Award and 2010 Lois Roth Persian Translation prize, as well as artist fellowship and residencies in the U.S., Mexico, Spain, Australia and Switzerland.

She lives in Los Angeles and Barcelona.

About the Play

Nazanin Sahamizadeh

When I first heard the name Manus on the news, it was a place I knew nothing about. I started searching for it out of curiosity and came across a lot of shocking news about an Australian refugee detention centre located on an island in Papua New Guinea. I wondered how I had been unaware of it until that time, even though I had always been following world events and news. I must have heard about it before, but it had probably just passed me by amid all the tragic news from everywhere that causes a kind of desensitisation. This is not just my problem. Most people in the world today are in denial about tragic events. Something must be done about this numbness and forgetfulness. For me, theatre has always been a tool to use to challenge this denial about our surrounding world; it is not just entertainment.

On the contrary, I think that art has the power and duty to save human beings from their desensitisation towards important human issues. That's why I am working in the field of social theatre. The more I read about the detention centre on Manus Island, the more I felt drawn to exposing the injustice there. I could not be indifferent to this unfolding tragedy. I felt that a part of history was hidden in Manus, onto which I had to shine a light.

During recent years, the tragedy of refugees has become one of the most important issues in the world. We have all seen the terrible images of refugees packed into flimsy boats out at sea, but we don't know the reality behind those images. Only asylum seekers themselves can bring us closer to an understanding of the refugee tragedy and they rarely have the means of expressing their experiences.

I decided to bring their voices to the world through theatre and to tell others about the reality of their lives. The first step was to find a way to communicate with one of the refugees who was detained on the island. An Iranian-Kurdish journalist, Behrouz Boochani, was secretly communicating with the outside world from Manus detention centre via his mobile phone. I managed to get in touch with him, and then with other detainees, and that's how the writing of *Manus*, the play, began.

MANUS

A Verbatim Documentary Play

Based on interviews with asylum seekers in Australian detention centres in Manus and Nauro Islands

Research, interviews, commissioned by

Nazanin Sahamizadeh

written by

Leila Hekmatnia & Keyvan Sarreshteh

translated by

Siavash Maghsoudi

With special thanks to Behrouz Boochani for allowing us to accompany him and providing access to the other detainees.

Characters

BEHROUZ BOOCHANI – An Iranian-Kurdish journalist, human-rights activist, and author of *No Friend but the Mountains*, 36 years old

SHAGHAYEGH – An Iranian woman, 27 years old

MEISAM – An Iranian man, 28 years old

AMINEH – An Iranian mother, 53 years old

ALI – An Iranian man, 30 years old

ELI –An Iranian woman, 35 years old

RASOUL – An Iranian man, 32 years old

YOUSEF – An Iranian man, 19 years old

Recorded Voices: OMID and **OMID'S WIFE**, mid-20s.

SCENE 1 – BEHIND THE FENCE

BEHROUZ My prison is the most beautiful prison in the world.

SHAGHAYEGH Here is like a swamp, the more you struggle, the more you go down.

MEISAM You know that the largest trafficking in the world is ... human trafficking.

AMINEH As if death told me to do it, I destroyed my life.

ALI Everything is ready to go crazy here.

ELI Our memory is wounded; we must think hard to remember something.

RASOUL We ruined ourselves, we came here to be ruined.

YOUSEF They tortured us mentally, they insulted us, they disrespected us.

SHAGHAYEGH The first question the psychologists here ask is "Do you want to kill yourself?"

ALI I want to go, I want to run away from you all.

BEHROUZ Escape! I've thought about it a lot.

ELI I've been in limbo for years.

AMINEH Here is Nauru, a small country in the middle of water; it is run by Australia.

RASOUL This is an island surrounded by the ocean it's not connected to anywhere.

MEISAM Here is Manus.

SCENE 2 – IRAN AND THE JOURNEY

Behrouz Boochani enters alone and records a video message on his mobile phone to send to a TV show, which will be interviewing Scott Morrison, an Australian government minister.

BEHROUZ I am talking to you from Manus Prison. The Australian government exiled me here forcefully six years ago.

What is my crime? I am a journalist who has escaped injustice, discrimination, cruelty and persecution after the 2009 unrests. I didn't choose to leave my family. Why I am still here in this illegal prison after six years?

We see a video of the interview with Scott Morrison, in which he claims that he does not know Boochani.

BEHROUZ   I am Behrouz Boochani.

I was a journalist in Iran, and I am a journalist here.

I am Behrouz Boochani

When I got here, I sold my clothes and secretly bought a mobile to send the news out.

I am Behrouz Boochani.

Everybody in the cultural circles of Australia, musicians, journalists, writers and human rights activists, they all know me. All 900 people here know me.

I am Behrouz Boochani.

A free human being. I can't tolerate modern slavery.

I am Behrouz Boochani.

I am still alive and this man is a liar!

AMINEH   My children are in Australia. They came the same way. I was restless, I thought to come and unite with them. I haven't seen them for seven years.

RASOUL   We thought Iran was over for us. Now let's go and live.

ELI   I paid gravely for migration.

SHAGHAYEGH In Iran they took me to a prison for a week, even my family didn't know where I was. Five people came, without a warrant... no uniforms. They only had five radios. They searched everything I had and then took me away. Where they took me...

AMINEH   My daughter used to work. My son studied electrical engineering at the best university. He had 2nd Dan in Taekwondo too. He left university, wanting to be a civil servant, but they wouldn't accept him. He became exasperated. I went everywhere, to the President's office, but it was no use. I went to the Welfare Organisation. They said they'd investigate in the neighbourhood and ask around. I had to think of my reputation. A lone woman does not have much support in Iran and my son had to look after me. He'd seen our miserable life.

RASOUL   I was going to ask a girl's hand; a close relative. She didn't welcome it. I was devastated. Then he said he had a problem too and wanted to leave.

MEISAM   My problem was...

RASOUL   C'mon, say it.

MEISAM   I had a problem in Iran and I shouldn't have stayed... If I did, I might have...

RASOUL   I was a young man who had everything. I'd grown up in the bazaar. I sold all my goods and shop, and got cheques. I ruined myself. Ruined exactly!

ELI   I went to a psychologist and gave him my poems. He threw them at me and said, "What is this nonsense? Here is Iran. Where do you think you're living? Either do something ordinary or leave the country." I was cursing him when I left.

SHAGHAYEGH I tried all the legal ways. I applied anywhere you can think of. This apparently illegal way, was the only way I could leave Iran. I was expelled from university in the first semester of my psychology MA. Their excuse was that I used to work with VOA. They banned me from leaving the country. I came with a forged passport.

When I left Iran, I really knew it. My family didn't but I knew what was ahead. The last piece of news I read about here was that a boatload of Afghans had sunk. I thought I'd either die or arrive.

AMINEH   My son said he wanted to go too because of his sister. I thought it wouldn't really happen and they can't go. I agreed that they go. I just told them to leave me alone. They said, "Mum, we're going. We are leaving." I realised suddenly my two kids had disappeared, like melting ice and they weren't with me anymore. Well, I couldn't bear it. I thought I'd go too; I might get to them.

ELI My problem was 20% the government, 80% people. I always dressed simply, but I always had a problem – stalking and sexual stares. You walk with a stoop when people leer at you. They call me Mr Abbas because my movements are masculine. It forces me subconsciously, so I'll be away from the stares. For example, I wanted to get a loan, but they invited me to dinner. They're all greedy. Every firm I worked in, I had to run after my salary because I was a girl.

AMINEH I divorced my husband... I mean he divorced me. He was the beating type. Rude too. Didn't know how to respect women. What else... That is a lot in itself! He being the beating type is a book in many volumes! It doesn't mean once or twice a year. Ten times a day. Not exactly ten times, but he beat me a few times a day. Why? Was I rude? Never mind all the things I did for him. He left us. I thought he'd return. A few months passed but nothing.

ELI When I looked at my books, I'd see different phases in my life. From Shari'ati to Foroogh, from Foroogh to Camus, from Camus to Sadeq Hedayat. I had five hundred books. I sold them for less than fifteen dollars. I am an architecture graduate, but theatre was my love. It is a disease worse than addiction. I was in Ahvaz Performance Society. I've been in theatre since I was ten. I sang and I was about to have a concert, for women. Of course, it's forbidden for women to sing in Iran, so it didn't happen. They didn't let it happen. I acted in my last play in 2009. Iranzamin was an international theatre festival that was held in Ahvaz. The festival was closed down. We put on black clothes and made halva. We held its funeral. We said theatre was dead.

ALI I want to tell you how I got here. I was studying for my BA when a colleague said his sister had gone to Australia. I wanted to go legally but the law used to change every day. Today, they wanted IELTS score 5. Tomorrow, IELTS 7. He said there was an office in Mir Damad Boulevard. The words "My sister went to Australia" brought something positive into my mind. The next day I got the address and went to that office.

RASOUL *(talking about Meisam)* I said I'd go with you. We bought the tickets and talked to the smugglers.

MEISAM   I thought to myself "What do smugglers look like? Do they have horns?"

AMINEH   There are plenty of them. Lots of smugglers. For example sitting in a park, a friend says, "My daughter left. You ask, "Will you give me the man's number?" And she says, yes.

ALI   A tall, well-built man, wearing a tie, very jovial in a chic and elegant office in Mir Damad explained: "We have different visas. I can get you a visa for Europe. We have this, we have that." In the end, "And there is this. Whichever you like." Although he knew I'd gone there to... I said, "OK, let's talk about the boat and Australia and such things."

AMINEH   From Imam Khomeini Airport to Dubai, from Dubai to Indonesia, from Indonesia by boat.

RASOUL   We'd been told we'd have a house, a job, we'd go on a yacht. Many things.

MEISAM   We'd go by ship. What the fuck! How's that possible?

RASOUL   Completely legal, we started from the country to go to Indonesia.

ALI   He asked, "Ever been to Indonesia? When you are in Indonesia, there is a disco called Stadium. With glasses around it. Ladies spin like this and you choose. Don't stay in the hotel. Go out... Have fun! When you stay in the camp in Australia for a few months, your friends will talk about what they've done but you'll have nothing to say."

RASOUL   We were stuck in Indonesia for three months.

ALI   They call it 'stash'. The place we wait till the time comes. In Indonesia stash, I saw my colleague's sister. She hadn't left yet.

SHAGHAYEGH I was in stash in Indonesia for twenty days. I can't go back... it hurts a lot...

RASOUL The smuggler had told us not to go via Jakarta because it was dangerous. We were stuck in Kendari in a hut.

YOUSEF We were stuck... We were stuck... We were stuck...

MEISAM Has a Gillette ever become a dream for you? Ever thought about it? Ever thought of a little water? About a bathroom to take a shower? We were happy when it rained.

RASOUL We took showers under the downpipe. We didn't have any clothes. We left our clothes wherever we went to travel lightly. We smelled like shit. Everything there was little: little dog, little goat, little donkey, little man, everything little.

MEISAM Everything little. Everything a miniature. Like themselves. As if an atomic bomb had ruined their seed.

RASOUL We knew Jakarta route was a sure death. You had only a shadow of a chance to get to Australia. But as we didn't have a way back, we took that route. We held our lives in our hands.

MEISAM We got on the small boats at the pier. They said we'd get in bigger boats further out; the boat would take us for five hours, and then we'd get on a ship. We changed the boats and got on a fishing boat, what we call a launch. Have you seen a fishing launch?

RASOUL It was like a matchbox in the ocean. A piece of cardboard.

MEISAM What did we do?

RASOUL We went on and on and on and on. It was lost in the ocean for seven days on a 33-hour route.

MEISAM We had food for two days, not seven days. We were lost among the waves. Divide seven days to its number of seconds. We died every second.

RASOUL That's why they told us not to go. It has three whirlpools and the sea is so deep that even big ships do not go there. Very dangerous. And we'd gone in the worst weather. The rain was so heavy the boat was filled with water. The sea and the sky had become one. We couldn't see twenty metres ahead. They had something like a traditional compass. A satellite device too, but they didn't know how to work it.

We had a satellite phone too, but they'd called their families so much it'd run out of battery. Vahid Fatemi and Mehdi Zaghi were in our launch. Middle aged, good family, with technical knowledge. There was Reza Sayyad too. We were four.

MEISAM Without these four, we would've died. Everybody had panicked. Families… Everybody… There was a smuggler too. He said he smuggled crystals. He was crying like a baby. The Arabs held the Quran over their heads and recited it loudly.

RASOUL I told them to be quiet, and not make the mood in the launch worse.

MEISAM Most launches sink because of fights or fright. Everybody was frightened.

RASOUL Nobody had seen such scenes. There were dolphins beside us, whales on the other side, sharks under us. A real mess. The waves lifted the boat up high, twenty metres, eighteen metres, and then we came down, bang! The launch was cracked in three places. Reza Sayyad knew about such things. He said we'd all die… An engine had broken down… One engine…

MEISAM One engine… I'll never forget it. After seven days… on the last day…

RASOUL Let me tell about the last night.

MEISAM You tell it. I was dead.

RASOUL We were so exhausted. There was a storm. The skipper was exhausted too. He was thrown about by the waves. He was sick and weak. We begged the families, "We are dying. The skipper is dying. Give him some food if you have any." They all had something. Honey, tuna fish…

MEISAM Real bastards! You must die.

RASOUL I was in charge of food because they could have killed each other. I made something and gave them each a spoonful of rice.

MEISAM   We cooked rice with ocean water... Bitter... Like bile.

RASOUL   Everybody had fainted from fatigue the previous night. I was dead tired. How many days could I go on? They were all waiting for death. All hopeless... everybody was asleep... they had passed out actually... Nobody had any strength...

MEISAM   To die... Only to die...

RASOUL   Sunlight, flood. Sunlight, flood. The sunlight burnt, the flood destroyed. On the last day, it was me and Vahid Fatemi. His voice was like the singer Daryoosh. Everybody was asleep in the stern. The bow was empty. Even with a little wave, we'd roll ... with Meisam and a few others, we went to the bow in the heavy rain. We held onto the sides so as not to fall off. He started singing... we wept hard *(sings)*.

"I abandoned the world so much
that I was shaped like loneliness.
Watch me, dying inside myself.
This death is worth watching."

MEISAM   Remember? Cyrus the Great had a story. He calmed the ocean with his whip. We were doing the same. We had lost hope.

RASOUL   We did it from the bottom of our hearts with a few others. It was a game at first, but it got serious later. It got serious and we did it. The waves were heavy. We'd say for example, "Quiet, wave!" We hit like this.

RASOUL/MEISAM *(together)* Quiet!

RASOUL   I saw the waves calming down. I swear to the Quran, we felt the energy. We said it from deep down with all our feelings. We'd say something aloud and the wave would really calm down. We passed many waves like that. When the wave came, we'd do this. We were up day and night. When could we sleep? We were worn out. The last moment I slipped into the darkness, Meisam was in the front. He had stretched his feet into the engine room in the cold. Cold water poured on the ropes and only the tip of his toes were near the heater. I went down to Meisam. I felt awful when I saw Meisam. I thought, I have a brother but he is the only son. My aunt had left him in my care. I went to Meisam. He was lying down. I laid down beside him. He said beautiful things. We talked and I felt bad. There was a light in my heart. Everybody was asleep... There was nobody. I said, "God! Is it possible? Is it done?" No, it isn't. It mustn't be. I started right there. He saw it. I got up, tired, exhausted. In the front of the launch, a tricky place where a person this height... You had to jump and go up... And I was tired... I got up. I saw the skipper. We were really dying. It was very dangerous. Terrifying! I said, "Vahid, wake up. We are dying." I looked for Reza Sayyad. I said, "Reza, get up. We are dying. Wake Mehdi up." He woke up Mehdi. I told Mehdi to go to the engine room. "Reza, sit by the skipper. Be careful." I woke Mehdi up. His English was good. He was known as Mehdi the Chubby, from Qazvin. I told him, "Hold this. Whenever..." We didn't have a bell. They texted us and asked where we were. Where are we? We didn't know.

MEISAM   When you enter their orbit, the satellite finds you. They texted us and asked where we were so they could arrest us. We couldn't answer. Out of battery. And they were looking for us everywhere. Australia... They were doing the right thing. We were in free waters. We'd gone somewhere but we didn't know where. Our smuggler had called Australia from Iran. They'd called from Indonesia, but there was no reception.

RASOUL   We tried to manage it. I held the mobile like this. (*Arm stretched up, awkwardly*) A head up every second. "Vahid, please stay awake for a few seconds, so I can sleep for five minutes. Only five minutes!" I gave it to him and stood up, but he was already asleep. I asked myself who I could give it to. I gave it to him and he slept. I got up in the end. I slapped, pinched myself, many other things. Dead tired! I hadn't slept for four or five nights. At first we slept on and off. We didn't know we were dying. We were a bit relaxed. We thought maybe it was the way it had to be. Then we saw lots of broken boats, worn slippers...

MEISAM   Slippers, hair clips...

RASOUL   How many had drowned! Everything...

MEISAM   What scenes we saw! We thought, "Will we end up like them?"

RASOUL   There was SMS after SMS. It was daybreak. At last we had passed the night. It was morning. At last Australia called. I told Mehdi to talk as I didn't know any English then. He talked to them. But they couldn't find us. They kept calling when they couldn't find us.

MEISAM   They couldn't find us. We were hopeless. It was over. Is it possible? In a hay stack? A hay stack as big as Iran with a needle in it.

RASOUL   No, bigger. The ocean. Much bigger. It didn't end. They didn't find us. We went on and on. In the storm.

MEISAM   GPS. We lost it as we went. No reception. Nothing!

RASOUL   Even God had no reception there.

MEISAM   Really didn't.

RASOUL   We went on and at last in the distance... At last the awful scenes ended. We saw something in the distance. The guys said something was there.

MEISAM   A mountain in the ocean. We saw something black was coming towards us. We told the skipper to turn on the engine so we could run away. It was a British warship.

RASOUL   Very big.

MEISAM   From here to where? It was a town! Nobody was on deck. Nobody saw us. They saw us after two hours.

RASOUL   They came on deck. Blonde guys. "Help us" and such stuff. Everyone took their clothes off. "We are coming European style!" He said, "Free shores here." Where do you want to go?

MEISAM   We could've said anywhere you can think of.

RASOUL   We said, "Well, Australia, of course." They said "OK."

MEISAM If we'd sunk our boat, they'd have to pull us up. Then we would be on British territory.

SHAGHAYEGH The last Indonesian border before free waters, our launch hit a rock. It was 2.am. Our launch sank. It was dark. We couldn't see the shore. There weren't enough life vests. I jumped into the ocean.

BEHROUZ I opened my eyes. I was underwater. I swam for about twenty metres till I found a piece of wood from our boat. I grabbed it. One of us lost his life. His name was Sa'eed. His body was never found. I was on the wood for almost an hour till a boat came. Exactly at the Australia Indonesia border. They called the Australian warship and it came.

RASOUL The Australian warship came seven hours later.

BEHROUZ The Australian warship took us to Christmas Island. I got there on 23rd July. We'd been dying the night before, and the next day was my birthday. When I reached Christmas Island and looked at my card, I realised I'd got there on my birthday.

ALI We were to be sacrificed and they'd make a documentary, films, news about us.

AMINEH I was on Christmas Island on 19th July.

ALI They kept us outside that night. They arrested us on 20th not 19th. It was over.

AMINEH They changed our clothes, gave us food, they treated us well, injected vaccines, and took us to the camp.

RASOUL They handed us over to the camp on Christmas Island. They took our stuff. Everything was confiscated. We were quarantined.

We were in quarantine in the camp for a week. Our families thought we were dead. We called them when they were mourning for us. All of us, women and kids were in the same place in quarantine. When they separated us in the quarantine, they weighed us, ran tests, and sent us to special camps.

MEISAM When I saw it, I said, "Rasool, this is not a camp. It's a jail." Everything was electric.

General Campbell, Australian Commander Operation Sovereign Borders announces the new immigration law on a video.

RASOUL   The law had passed on 19th July. We had set out on 17th. If we hadn't been lost at sea, the law wouldn't have included us.

MEISAM   They say according to the 19th July Law, we had no way to go to Australia and all men had to go to Manus Island. Everybody froze.

RASOUL   They read it out a month later. You must change your camp and go to Manus Island. I do everything to be taken with him. They took us to Melbourne on a plane. We went to Melbourne. I said, "Wow! It was a lie. We reached Melbourne!" But they only changed the crew. Took off again and took us to the Cannibals' Island.

MEISAM   Manus.

RASOUL   The end of the world. The last place in the world.

BEHROUZ   Often I think to myself, when I left Iran, I was 28. I've been in jail for about six years. I'd have been 34 years old, but I don't really know how old I am now...

SCENE 3 – MANUS

We see videos of refugee boats, sinking in the ocean.

BEHROUZ   Here is Manus. There are four prisons here; Oscar, Delta, Mike, Fox. Here is Manus. Outside this prison and on this island, there are seven languages and thirty-six tribes. Here is Manus. Here people have to stand in line for their basic needs. Here is Manus. Here the identity of every refugee has been belittled to a prisoner in a mug shot. Here is Manus. My name is MEG45.

ALI   My name is TIB59. Five hundred people, thirty toilets, fifteen of which are always out of order. We must queue to go to the toilet. We must queue for food for many hours in the sunlight. We must queue to get medicine; nerve tablets, malaria tablets. When they took us on the plane to bring us to Manus, they said it was for malaria. We had crazy hallucinations on the way, thinking, where are they taking us? Manus is loaded with malaria bugs.

RASOUL   My name is MEG42. When they got us off the plane, the camera men are there. There are lots of officers around us; they hold our hands like this and take us away. Like criminals. We were ruined. We were shown on the media. They took us to Fox, the oldest camp in Manus which is like a garden. Its rooms were older. While they were taking us, they were building camps hurriedly. Collective camps and solitary camps. It was just the beginning. They made fences. A traditional island. A warehouse. For cigarettes, the locals... They haven't seen cigarettes much. They have a grass they call Bruce. They wrap it in newspaper and smoke it. Their mouth and teeth become red. I took a puff and I was dying. It was so heavy. We give cigarettes and get marijuana. They do anything for a cigarette. Everything...

MEISAM   My name is MEG49. Want me to tell you the end? You give them a cigarette and did anything you wanted with them. You get me? Green hell! Really green hell! Christmas Island was Alcatraz, Manus Island was Guantanamo. Humidity 52%, temperature 48°C. When we got up in the morning, water was dripping from our sheets. We had a fan which sounded like a jet engine. Four of the rooms made the hospital. Then we'd told our families we were living in a nice, chic place with swimming pool, sauna, Jacuzzi, ladies... But we saw everything there – a tank, a crashed airplane. Even some radioactive material that killed many. You'll die if you cut your hand this much. It gets infected and the infection goes to your heart. Bye.

Yousef tries to tell his codename but he can't. He faints.

BEHROUZ   Here it is very small; eighty metres by eighty metres with nine hundred people in it. Everyone talks together. People have nothing to do here except talking. Out of the nine hundred, three hundred are Iranian. Iranian, Sudanese,

Nepalese, Kurd, Vietnamese, Burmese, Pakistani, Afghan. There are Afghans who have run away from Iran. They hate Iranians. They were hurt in Iran and had a hard time. Iraqi, Palestinian, Somalian, Syrian. The Syrians have run away from war. Their families are still at war. The Immigration Office won't let them return. They say, "Give us the visa to go to Australia." They say, "No, you must go to Guinea." All nine hundred people know me. I must always be alone. I can't write if I'm not alone. I can't create...

MEISAM   I had to use the toilet, it was 4am... I don't give up my sleep for anything but it was like someone was telling me to get up. The toilets were in rows in corridors. I heard someone hitting the door. There was a rustling sound too. I went up and saw two legs hanging. He had stuffed nylon in his throat and hanged himself to die. I kicked the door open. I shouted, "Rasool! Rasool! Mehdi! Help! Help!" They took him to Medical.

We hear a loud alarm noise. All except for Behrouz scatter.

BEHROUZ   Many tried to kill themselves in the camps. One day a boy cut his wrist with a razor. I found out later his girlfriend was raped on Nauru. They had sent women and families to Nauru.

SCENE 4 – NAURU

SHAGHAYEGH Those days, they had just opened the Nauru camp's doors after two and half years. We could go out three or four days a week from morning till 5.pm, and then return. One day Nazanin went out but didn't return. Then we heard her brother's shouts. They said the next day they'd found her, naked ...somewhere. She had been waiting on the street to return to the camp. A van had arrived with four or five people in it and...

ELI   There's been refugees raping refugees before. Single boys. There were families with boys of 20, 25 and 19 years of age. They were not in Manus camp, they were here with their families with us in Nauru camp. Families took sleeping pills to be able to sleep. The kid got up at night to go to the toilet. Among the children, an 18-year-old and a younger child...

SHAGHAYEGH It might have been a refugee, or an Australian, or probably a local from Nauru. You know, people here still live in tribes... These things happen a lot among them. And facilities here are so poor... the end of the world that people talk about is here... so imagine we all came here for a better life. I'll never forget what I saw when I first got here. The island is twenty-one km. It has nothing. They say it's smaller than Melbourne airport! Only one street. When the airplane was landing, there was no space. It was going into the ocean. They closed the road. Everything stopped so the plane could land.

AMINEH It's a very small island, you can see everything in four or five minutes. It is very hot. No winter, no spring, just hot all the time. We sweat constantly under the sunlight. There isn't water in the tents, even at 47°C. We couldn't drink cool water. Small ice cubes in the thermos for so many people. There were lots of brawls. Women miscarried in the fights. Very hard conditions. Many killed themselves with detergent or a razor or with cigarette butts. Can you believe it? They ate cigarette butts.

SHAGHAYEGH Those who were on the launch with me are all in Australia now. My friends told me to do something to get out. When we got here, they told us the water we'd come from is our case. But later...

ELI Some started having babies to help their cases and so they could go to Australia. Hatching! Eventually the government changed the law. Many kids have been born here in Nauru prison.

AMINEH I came only for my kids. This is my daughter, this is my son. Haven't seen them for seven years. They can't come to see me. It's like a jail here, the only difference between here and prison is that we can't have visitors. They give us points. I collect my points to get telephone credit and talk to my children. I rarely talk to my son. Because he says someone who wants to be successful after migration must get disconnected from his family, so that they don't tell him if his grandfather has got Alzheimer's or his grandmother fell down, and such things. He says these things make him stressed. I used to talk to my brother a lot. But then I called him and... his phone was off... off!

ELI   They used to bring a telephone once a week only for ten minutes, and they'd disconnect it right after ten minutes. You were talking ... receiving news of the death of someone ... they'd just disconnect it. I called 7th October to talk to my father. It was his birthday and I hadn't spoken to him for a long time because he cried whenever I talked to him. He also cried when I was coming. He begged me not to go. I told him, "You want me to go and get my residency and you come join me, or do you want me to stay and kill myself and you can come visit my grave?" We used to go to the doctors in Iran a lot. He had Parkinson's. I couldn't stand watching him drop the spoon. Couldn't stand to see him slowly die. I preferred leaving and letting him grieve himself to death than to stay and see his destruction.

AMINEH   I went to my social worker. She found out my brother had passed. She started sobbing. I asked if I upset her. She said no. "Then what? Why did you cry?" She showed me a 3-D tattoo of her dog on her arm. She said, "I was on a trip and my dog died." They compare a human to their dog. Really!

ELI   I told my mother to give the phone to him. She said he couldn't talk and that he'd be upset and cry. I said, "I haven't talked to him for six months. He cries, I'll cry too." I called from 9.am–9.pm and they told me he was asleep. I was worried they might've taken him to a sanatorium. I told them to wake him up and I wanted to talk to him. My mother said, "What do you want to know? Your father hasn't woken up from 4th of April." He'd been dead for six months but I didn't know. My dad was dead. There is a playground in the camp. I go there at night. One night I took my father's photos and a speaker there. My brother called. He played from Iran and I sang in the camp. *(sings)*

My night, a window to no tomorrow

My day, a story of loneliness and sorrow;

Left on the ground, trapped on the beach

I am a fish from the sea, but far from which;

No mate, no compeer

For this wanderer heart I bear;

To me, a gadabout

Cities opened their gates, not;

A gipsy, a worn-out gadabout

A full of rain, yet sad, cloud;

Tired of leaving, are my feet,

Abandonment has become the story;

To anyone, I gave my heart

Our paths, alas, were apart;

The rain cannot destroy the cliff

Crying cannot treat this grief;

My soul, after me,

Will wander, will be in motion

Like a gipsy, ocean to ocean;

What is at the end of the way,

It is not known

Always and always, will be alone.

A gipsy, a worn-out gadabout

A full of rain, yet sad, cloud;

Suddenly the shouting of a man is heard. Omid's voice is heard on a recording.

OMID'S VOICE "It's enough... we are tired. We have had enough..." "What? You wanna see our misery? Yes ... we are miserable..." "It's been three years... you've skinned us ...you've screwed us..."

SHAGHAYEGH Omid only wanted to scare them.

ELI He didn't really want to kill himself.

SHAGHAYEGH My roommate had told me to pour petrol on ourselves to scare them. It happened two days later.

ELI When they came here from the UN, there was a rumour that the UN had said we were going to stay here for ten years.

SHAGHAYEGH I was passing by. I saw Omid and his wife going to the petrol station and buying a gallon of petrol. It happened an hour later.

ELI When the UN people came, his wife took the petrol and said, "I'll kill myself." Omid said, "Why you? I'll do it." They were to pour petrol only on their feet, but Omid had poured it on his body. He wanted to light the lighter to threaten them but the flames came up suddenly and covered all his body. He panicked and started running. Someone found a plastic cloth and covers him but the plastic sticks to him. He ran and screamed in front of the people, in front of his wife.

We hear a recording of Omid's self-immolation

OMID'S WIFE'S VOICE "Omid!... God ... What have you done? ... God ..."

OMID'S VOICE "Uhh... I am tired ... I am tired"

SHAGHAYEGH Someone called and said Omid was in hospital and he'd set himself on fire.

ELI When he was in the hospital, he'd asked the guys, "My face isn't ruined, Is it?"

SHAGHAYEGH Omid didn't die of the burns. They took him to Australia twenty-five hours later. It was so late. He was very weak in the last moments. I had one nightmare for a week. Omid was burning before me and calling my name.

AMINEH Omid was only 23.

Video of detainees on Nauro, protesting after death of Omid. Detainees chanting:

Omid! Omid!

Happy freedom...

Omid! Omid!

Rest in peace ...

Dictator... Dictator

After three years...

Where is freedom?

ELI I thank the Australian government because I always thought in first world countries everything happens on the basis of human rights and freedom of speech, but the Australian government woke me up from my dream.

SHAGHAYEGH Politics is dirty everywhere. Makes no difference. People who have power step on you and pass on. Politics is stronger than you everywhere. The dirty politics of my country couldn't force us to set ourselves on fire for a better life or make kids younger than me to sew their lips, but the dirty politics here could do it. It forced kids of 14 or 15 to sew their lips together. I talked to these kids to open their lips because they hadn't eaten anything for days. I saw the kids without anything and joined them, we secretly kept threads and needles, without any anaesthetic. One of us was sewing the lips. I'll never forget. I had gel in my lips and it poured out. It started bleeding.

SCENE 5 – BLOODY NIGHT OF MANUS

Videos of refugees' riot and being attacked in Manus camp

Voice of a refugee from Manus:

They'd shoot and break into the rooms

Asking where are you from?

If you were Iranian, they'd hit you more

MEISAM They had read the law again in the morning that we would never go to Australia. They had aggravated the guys.

ALI Two big countries announced their readiness to take us: Canada and New Zealand. They said they would accept the refugees. Mr Scott Morrison and Mr Tony Abbott said, "We will not hand over refugees to any country. They must either stay in Papua New Guinea or return to their countries."

MEISAM   We started insulting Papua New Guineans. We couldn't do anything else. We thought if we insulted and fought them, they'd throw us out or take us somewhere else.

RASOUL   We were good friends with Guineans. Simple people.

MEISAM   We'd give them cigarettes and got marijuana.

RASOUL   We started insulting Guinea.

MEISAM   There was a real war. They cut the power and water. Internet and telephone too. We didn't have anything. Only our slippers. They were our only weapons in the big camp.

RASOUL   Our camp – Fox – started it on the first night. We alone started the war.

MEISAM   Locals were only standing and watching us. They didn't come forward.

RASOUL   The second night, man. The second night guys from Mike came and they joined the fight. They said, "You go and we'll follow you." "OK", we said. They started it. Man, there were locals with swords coming from one side, and Special Forces from the other side.

MEISAM   We demolished the walls, us.

RASOUL   You know what I was called there? "Rasoul, the way-opener!" I was heavily built, strong. Ten people couldn't open the camp doors. One by one I broke the doors open. I broke three doors and we went on. I did that on the first night.

ALI   The doors between Fox and Mike Camps were broken and the guys came and went between them.

RASOUL   They tied wire rope the second night. It wasn't easy to do anything.

MEISAM   Our officers had served with NATO in Afghanistan and Iraq. They'd seen war. The condition of the camp was in a way that ordinary people couldn't manage it. You had to make a balance between cannibals and refugees. Their job was hard too. They feared we'd get the island. We were more than a thousand. We could take over the island.

RASOUL   We were taking it man. They told them to take back control even by killing us. The locals used guns.

MEISAM   Bursting bullets...

RASOUL   The guys said they were blanks...

MEISAM   It was a massacre...

ALI   The second night was the carnage. They gave the locals police riot gear. They attacked the camps and for every refugee, there were two or three fully-armed security guards attacking us. The locals had 1.5-metre-long sticks and when the guards beat the guys and they fell on the ground, the locals started to beat him to a pulp.

RASOUL   They raided the rooms and beat to kill. They shot, eyes popped out, arms were severed, many were thrashed. They beat three hundred or more people to near death.

MEISAM   They finished the other camp and came to ours. Our corridor was the first. Locals, security, from one side and Special Forces with shields and stuff from the other side.

RASOUL   They were coming room after room. Didn't care if you were guilty or not. I was in the last room. Meisam was in the one before that. Meisam had hidden behind the bed pillows. So he wasn't beaten much.

MEISAM   No not me, not much.

RASOUL   Your room-mates were thrashed.

MEISAM   I put four pillows and sat behind them like this. They beat and I watched. It wasn't a joke. He's got a gun, what can you do? Even if you were a superhero!

ALI   I told the guys to say "Jesus". "Say Jesus and leave the rest to me." I told him, "Papa, we are Christians." Papa means brother. He was touched. He shook hands with us and said we were safe.

RASOUL   I had a room-mate, Mehdi the Kurd, about 30 or 40. Moustache, scars, tough guy with tattoos all over. "We are Kurds, we are this and that." He was done for. Then another one, Mas'ood Armineh, a singer. My friend Mehdi was going to hide under the bed. He said, "Come, Rasool. They are killing." I said, "They don't look. They'll beat you worse if you hide." Something told me I had to do something, something special. I took my trainers quickly. Mehdi asked what I was doing. I said, "I'm ready. They are killing. We must kill!"

MEISAM   Who is there to fight beside you? What are you going to fight with? He'd put on his trainers to fight.

RASOUL   When they reached us, I kicked and broke down the door. They were shocked. Nobody had gone on the offense till then. I kicked. Nobody was there. I thought I must go. They were taken aback. The locals' eyes widened. I went and Mas'ood, the skinny one, came after me and didn't leave me alone. He went crazy later.

ALI   The third one came in and looked at the hands. Nobody had sweated. He realised we hadn't been in the fight or thrown rocks. He told us to sit. We almost knew him. He was wearing anti-riot gear. The so-called cockroach gear. One of the guys hugged him and burst into tears. He was really scared.

YOUSEF   I was hiding under the bed. They didn't see me. I saw their daggers, covered in blood. There was blood everywhere. If they'd found me, they'd have chopped me to pieces. I was afraid to sleep at night. I'd sleep during the day. I'd wake up a few times and scream.

MEISAM   It got out of hand. The police started shooting directly. Yahya was shot in our camp. A rock hit someone's eye and blinded him.

ALI   Whoever was big, they'd beat him more.

RASOUL   They beat the big ones a lot.

ALI   That night in Mike, Reza Barati...

MEISAM   Reza Barati was hefty.

BEHROUZ   We were from the same town.

RASOUL   He was my friend and roommate. Born in '89. A quiet guy, not a fighting type.

ALI Reza was the giant child in our camp; the kindest one. When we greeted him, he was too shy to say hello. He always told us not to face them. "We are their captives till the end."

BEHROUZ Reza was in the internet room.

MEISAM A few guys in the internet room informed others we were being attacked. They had recorded what had happened the previous day and were sending the footage.

ALI Someone tells him they are beating your friends and he comes out.

BEHROUZ Their camp got dark. There was still light in ours.

ALI Because of his build, he was almost two metres tall, the guards thought he was a riot leader. They followed him when he came out and went up the stairs. They were beating him while he was going up.

BEHROUZ We could hear moaning. Shouts, screams.

RASOUL A local had tied a rock to rope. He'd hit him on the head on the stairs.

MEISAM He falls down. They slit his throat.

ALI Suddenly a hundred people screamed.

BEHROUZ Someone said something in Kurdish. Only one word. He called his mother. It was Reza's voice. His father had sold their plot in the village to pay for Reza's journey. Reza grew up close to the place where I grew up. River Samireh with a mountain between us. I think my mother will climb the mountain one day to soothe Reza's mother.

I hear River Samireh and the mountain and the wild mountain flowers crying with our mothers. We are born with songs in Kurdistan. We live with songs. We fight with songs and we die with songs. My mother sings Moor, a song mothers sing for their sons to be brave, to be able to fight. Reza had fought the darkness of the ocean, the darkness of the nights of Manus.

SCENE 6 – RETURN

We see a video of asylum seekers with their lips sewn together.

BEHROUZ   After the night of the attack, they gave us only one meal a day for a week. They used the meat of animals which weren't edible. They rationed water. They purified seawater as drinking water. They threw the food at us. We had to eat the bits of disposable bowls besides the rice. The previous protest had failed. We were looking for something more peaceful. The hunger strike started with nine hundred people in January 2015. It lasted five days.

ALI   We were seven or eight who ate food, but the others didn't. True I got food, but I couldn't swallow it. It would get stuck in my throat. And the stares... Everything was a mess. All my friends with sewn lips... Those I chatted and laughed with, now I'd become their enemy.

BEHROUZ   During the hunger strike, they took me and many others from the camp to a jail on the island. We were with the criminals there. They took me to solitary. I was there for almost a month. They tortured me. Mentally, I mean.

YOUSEF   The guards attacked and started beating nonstop. Several guards beat one prisoner together. Six of them were beating me. Head, nose, teeth, they'd break everything. I couldn't believe I was being beaten that much. I couldn't believe someone could be beaten that much. They picked up the smashed bodies of the beaten people and took them inside. We were about a hundred. There were two jails there. A police detention centre and a prison. Reza Barati's killer was detained there too. I was cold. I was shivering. A very small hall without anything. We had to sleep on the hard cement floor. They didn't give us food the first day. Not much on the other days either. Someone said they gave us expired food. It was like a cage. They'd left those who were bleeding in the yard and didn't see to their wounds. They insulted and disrespected us. We begged to go to the toilet. They insulted us, laughed at us, and said: "Do it in your clothes. That's what you deserve."

One day they brought three guys from Manus and started beating them in front of our cage with rocks and sticks. They kept beating them. One passed out, but they kept beating. They hadn't done anything. They were just drunk. They beat him so much he came to. After beating, they brought them to our cage and left them to bleed. We were about forty people in the cage. All men above 20. Everybody just watched. Nobody cried. Nobody... My illness started there. I had nightmares, bad dreams. I talked to nobody. My friends told me I talk and scream in my sleep. Doctors said it's schizophrenia.

BEHROUZ   Torture is a systematic and complicated issue here. After the strike, the water in the toilets was cut almost every day. They cut the power in the middle of the night, everybody would wake up with worry and exasperation, and they would walk in the yard till morning. We told them to hand us over to the United Nations and we didn't want the country they had chosen for us. They told us constantly we had to live in Guinea, and if anybody wanted to live on that island, he had to both present a case and win it.

ALI   I said, "By God I want to go out! I don't want to stay in a cage. You want to stay? Be my guest! Go to Australia! I don't want to go to Australia. There was a dog behind the fence. I told myself, "How miserable you are! You can't even pat this dog." I went out to the island. I made it public. I wrote in my Facebook, "Living in Papua New Guinea". It was 23rd January 2015.

RASOUL   We fought with all our might. One died and many were wounded. Nothing happened. I told him it wasn't a place to stay.

MEISAM   Australia, land of dreams.

SHAGHAYEGH I may be the only person who will come this way again if I return. I have nightmares. I still have nightmares I have returned to Iran and they have arrested me in the airport. When I open my eyes, when I see the moulded ceiling here, I feel very happy I am here. In this twenty-one km island where I am.

AMINEH   Australian government said refugees should stay here and build Nauru. I wanted to get to my children. It's been seven years and I hadn't seen them ... Living alone in Nauru is meaningless for me. At least in Iran, if I am sad, I can go out, sit in a park, and talk to someone and feel better. But not here.

ELI   I'd come to die in the ocean or live somewhere better. Instead I've been in limbo for years.

BEHROUZ   People look at the wall and metal fence all day long here. They'd told them they could go out and see the ocean and forest from behind the fences. Out of nine hundred people in Manus around eight hundred and sixty have requested asylum from Guinea. The only one who never gave a case and got a positive answer was me. They sent me a letter: Mr Boochani, you are accepted, you are a refugee, and you must go and live in Guinea. You must do this at 8am tomorrow and if you don't, we'll give you ten minutes before we come with the police and take you. They'd brought the police beforehand and the refugees had been scared and had moved. Without any problem. I wrote on my Facebook page I wanted to resist and that I didn't want to go to Guinea. Because it is modern slavery. There is a tree in the middle of the prison. It is very hard to climb it. But I am a village boy. I climbed it easily. I reached the top and threatened I'd jump down.

 I'd written an announcement the night before. I had two articles too. Political articles about here. I'd done everything before going up. I went up the tree as a poet. As a... I had a theatrical feeling. As an actor, a theatre actor. I was up there for almost ten hours and talked to the people three times. All the Australian officers came. All people, all refugees came. I talked to them poetically like a real anarchist, a crazy poet. I really thought I was a lecturer or philosopher from ancient Greece, on a tree in a square and having a philosophical argument.

They brought a psychologist for me. Everybody came. They brought the police. Thirty, forty officers but I sent them away. I told them I'd jump down each time. The psychologist said, "You must come down and talk to me." I said, "You are not in a position to tell me to come down and talk. My power is that I am up here." The psychologist lowered his head to leave when I did something dangerous. I almost jumped down and I really wanted to do it. I told him, you must apologise to me. There are many people in the world who are ready to die for their political beliefs. They apologised to me. After one hour, I requested music and said, I want music, I want to listen to Mozart, to Vivaldi's *Four Seasons*, to Beethoven on this tree on this faraway island. They told them not to give me anything. I hanged myself again. Then I said, be sure when a poet on a very faraway island goes up a tree in a prison and wants music as his first request, he has the power and he is crazy enough to jump down. I am a free human. I can ask you anything I want and you must answer my need. They found the music for me.

We hear the sound of the Moonlight Sonata by Beethoven.

I felt I was on the theatre stage. From here, I hear the punches of a crazy man on a decayed heavy bag. I see the coconut trees that look at the forgotten prisoners like the sad prostitutes. I see the toilet queue, the cold bathrooms.

I see men who still ask each other the time and try to talk to each other for hours so they might be able to defeat time.

I can even see Nauru from here. The women who walk on the hot sand, the children whose game is to make paper boats and to sink the boats in the rainwater beside the tents.

I can see a mother who begs her 14-year-old kid to open the stitches on the lips...

I can see a girl who has wanted to talk on the phone for three months but she has lost her voice because she has had detergent and her larynx has been destroyed. In her mind, she is calling Mother ... Mother ... Mother ... but she doesn't have a voice.

We see a video of children on Nauro Island, playing with paper boats:

Children playing:
    Then they came and rescued us
    These are many boats
    They rescued us... help... help...
    They rescued us... help... help...
    We are drowning... help...

Lights down

The End

Endnotes

1 A kind of Iranian stew with minced meat, peas and tomato paste, usually served with rice.

2 The shrine of a Muslim saint in uptown Tehran, sacred to Shia Muslims, where people go to pray and make donations.

3 The Iranian grading system is based on a scale of 0 – 20, with 10 being the passing grade. Here, 15 is equivalent to a C+ or B

4 It refers to a superstition that if two people say exactly the same thing at the same time, the wishes of the one who pulls the other one's hair first will be fulfilled.

5 You can change the name of the animal based on the look of the actress.

MANUS

Nazanin Sahamizadeh is a director, author and actress who was born in 1985 in Tehran. She graduated with an M.A in Polymer Engineering in 2011 but because of her strong passion for art and theatre, she began training with veteran directors like Hamid Samandarian and Ali Rafei. Since then, she has acted in many theatre, TV and cinema productions.

She established the Verbatim Theater Group in 2013 to make documentary theatre about social and political problems, especially about women. Her first play, *An Eye for an Eye*, is about a woman who was acid attacked. She researched and interviewed many victims and authorities to produce it. She also made a short film on this subject in 2015. Her second verbatim play, *Manus,* is about asylum seekers in Australian detention centres. It was performed in Iran, Bangladesh, India and at the Adelaide Festival, Australia. She received international acclaim for the play and an award for Social Responsibility. Her most recent project is about child labour, postponed due to the pandemic. She is now working on a new project about Middle Eastern women.

Leila Hekmatnia is a playwright, poet and reasercher. She was born in 1991 in Yazd and received the youth award of the Kharazmi festival in 2009 for her essay on contemporary Persian neo-poetry. In the same year, she entered the University of Tehran with the exceptional talents scholarship and wrote her dissertation on New Historicism. She received a scholarship to pursue her master's degree in 2018 in which she addressed the issue of human evil in modern tragedy from Hannah Arendt's point of view.

She co-wrote the verbatim play *Manus* based on the testimonies of asylum seekers held in Australia's off-shore processing centre on Manus Island. Her book of poetry titled *One of Them* was nominated for the Journalists' Poetry Award and the Iranian Women's Award (Khorshid). As a poet, playwright, scriptwriter and researcher she received the Fadjr International Festival's award, 2009, as a member of the National Elites Foundation of Iran. Some of her works include: *Drunkenness of the Depths* (play about war performed for first time in September 2021 at Charleville Puppet International Festival, France) and also two short scenarios which have been written by her and they are in development in Canada and Iran. She has also assisted famous theatre directors such as Dr. Ali Rafiee.

Keyvan Sarreshteh is an author, performer and theatre maker, born in 1987 in Tehran. In 2013 he received his BA in Puppet Theatre from the University of Tehran, has translated several books and numerous articles on documentary theatre and is currently based in Tehran. His own experiences, both interpersonal and political, inspire his artistic creation.

Apart-ment, his first work has been performed in many different venues in Iran and was invited to Wiener Festwochen 2019 for its international premiere. *Stage Direction,* his second work, was completed in the same year before the pandemic cancelled its premiere. He has collaborated on a wide range of projects, each of them with their own distinct historical, political or personal thread that drew him to them. *I was King Richard* is an adaptation of Shakespeare's *The Life and Death of Richard the Second* that focused on his deposition as king and the reversal of power; *Pink Cloud* is based on a short story about an Iranian soldier who is killed in enemy lands and follows his remains as they are misplaced and misattributed.

He co-wrote *Manus,* a verbatim play about Australian detention centres for asylum seekers and most recently, he created *Fore(named),* an experimental documentary piece about a famous Iranian director whose project gets cancelled in a Russian festival which was selected for kunstenfestivaldesarts in 2020 (postponed). His last collaboration was with Amir Reza Koohestani on an adaptation from the novel *Transit* by Anna Seghers, for Thalia Theatre Hamburg. He is currently working on two new projects for post-pandemic theatre.

Siavash Maghsoudi is a humanitarian worker, born in 1976 in Mashhad, Iran. He is an architect by background but before graduating from architecture school, he found his passion in social photography. He worked as a photojournalist from 2000 to 2005 when he got to know Médecins Sans Frontières (MSF/Doctors Without Borders) and joined them. He worked with MSF for eight years and in 2013 he joined UNHCR, where he currently works, serving refugees, asylum seekers and other persons of concern, mostly Afghan refugees residing in Iran. Feeling passionate about theatre, from 2012 he worked also as Performance Manager on different plays such as *Blue Feeling of Death, Mother Courage, Outside the Door* and *Manus* in national and international performances. He has also written a few movie scripts, poems, short stories and playscripts throughout the past few years.

Manus production photo by Mohammad Sadegh Zarjooyan 2017